FREEDOM AND ADAPTIVE PREFERENCES

Traditional welfare economics works with the assumption of the fully rational economic agent (homo economicus) whose preferences are fixed: that is, they are not influenced by their economic environment. To the contrary, this book presents a theory of welfare economics that maintains the principles of normative individualism while allowing for adaptive or changeable preferences.

Why do economists talk of preferences? In this book, Carl Christian von Weizsäcker shows that the concept is intimately related to freedom of action. The concept of preferences is the mode by which normative economics introduces the idea of freedom or liberty into its theory of human interaction. Moreover, the economic research of recent decades has provided a large amount of experimental and other empirical findings – e.g. the work on bounded rationality – which contradicts the assumption of fixed preferences. This book argues that this large body of findings is consistent with the hypothesis of adaptive preferences. This, together with the proposition that adaptive preferences allow a generalization of traditional welfare economics, has implications for policy applications of behavioral economics based on "normative individualism". Normative individualism is an approach which intrinsically connects with the value of liberty or freedom. It is argued that normative individualism is indispensable for a society of free citizens, thus providing the foundations of civil liberty.

This book will be of great interest to readers of welfare economics, behavioral economics and economic theory.

Carl Christian von Weizsäcker, former Chairman of the German Monopoly Commission, is a Fellow of the Econometric Society and is a member of the American Academy of Arts and Sciences, the North Rhine-Westphalian Academy of Sciences and Germany's National Academy of Science and Engineering.

The Graz Schumpeter Lectures

Freedom and Adaptive Preferences
Carl Christian von Weizsäcker

Ricardo's Theory of Growth and Accumulation
A Modern View
Neri Salvadori

The Economics of the Good, the Bad and the Ugly
Secrets, Desires, and Second-Mover Advantages
Manfred J. Holler

Public Economics in an Age of Austerity
Tony Atkinson

Growth, Distribution and Innovations
Understanding their Interrelations
Amit Bhaduri

Dynamics of Industrial Capitalism
Schumpeter, Chandler, and the New Economy
Richard N. Langlois

For more information about this series, please visit: www.routledge.com/The-Graz-Schumpeter-Lectures/book-series/SE0392

FREEDOM AND ADAPTIVE PREFERENCES

Carl Christian von Weizsäcker

Routledge
Taylor & Francis Group
LONDON AND NEW YORK

Designed cover image: Joseph A. Schumpeter, 1935, courtesy of the Harvard University Archives; photograph by Bachrach

First published 2024
by Routledge
4 Park Square, Milton Park, Abingdon, Oxon OX14 4RN

and by Routledge
605 Third Avenue, New York, NY 10158

Routledge is an imprint of the Taylor & Francis Group, an informa business

British Library Cataloguing-in-Publication Data
A catalogue record for this book is available from the British Library

ISBN: 9781032726298 (hbk)
ISBN: 9781032726601 (pbk)
ISBN: 9781032726410 (ebk)

DOI: 10.4324/9781032726410

Typeset in Times New Roman
by Apex CoVantage, LLC

To Elisabeth

CONTENTS

About the Author *x*
List of Figures *xi*
Preface *xii*

BOOK I
Introduction: The Concept of "Preferences" **1**

1 Normative Individualism 3

2 "Preferences" in Positive and in "Normative" Economics 5

3 "Compossibility" of Freedom Rights 9

4 Preference Systems: The Comparability Problem 11

5 Overview of the Following Books II to VI 15

BOOK II
The Classroom Model of Adaptive Preferences **19**

6 Introduction and Definitions 21

7 Improvement Sequences 25

8 Theorem 1 for the Classroom Model 29

9 Prices and Quantities: A Simple Example 32

10 The "Meaning" of the Long-Run Demand Function: Theorem 2A 35

11 Kaldor–Hicks–Scitovsky With Adaptive Preferences 40

12 Social Welfare Function With Adaptive Preferences 43

BOOK III
The Real-World Model (Continuous Time Model) 47

13 Introduction, Theorem 1B for $n \geq 2$ 49

14 Theorem 2B for $n > 2$ 53

15 Equivalence Theorem 1 (Theorem 1C) 58

16 Theorem 2 for the Continuous Time Model (Real-World Model) 60

17 Theorem 1 for the Real-World Model 64

BOOK IV
Freedom and the Phenomenology of Adaptive Preferences 69

18 Freedom and Compossibility 71

19 Phenomenology of Adaptive Preferences and Pragmatic Compossibility 79

20 Phenomenology of Adaptive Preferences: Intertemporal Complementarity 84

21 Digging Deeper Into Adaptive Preferences 93

BOOK V
Interpersonal Influences on Preferences 113

22 Adaptive Preferences as a Result of Evolution 115

23 Non-Convexity of Preferences: Phishing for Phools 118

24 Freedom Mode and Causal Mode of Government Action 122

25 Imitation of Others: A Case of Adaptive Preferences; Advertising 125

26 Complexity, Private Property, Democracy, Public Goods 132

27 Two Generalized Media of Exchange: Karl Popper vs Erich Fromm 140

28 Three Levels of Economic Activity: Externalities 150

29 Social Market Economy 157

BOOK VI
Partial Equlibrium Welfare Economics for a Free Society With Adaptive Preferences 171

30 Introduction 173

31 Cost-Benefit Analysis With Adaptive Preferences, Part 1 175

32 Cost-Benefit-Analysis With Adaptive Preferences, Part 2 186

33 Pragmatics of Incomplete Compossibility 190

34 Private Anticipation of Preference Change: Innovation 193

35 Concluding Remarks 196

References *200*
Annex for Book II *207*
Mathematical Annex to Book III *210*
Definitions, Axioms, Theorems *213*
Index *219*

ABOUT THE AUTHOR

Carl Christian von Weizsäcker received his PhD in 1961 from the University of Basel for a dissertation in which he showed that the optimal rate of interest is equal to the growth rate. Edmund Phelps published the same result, also in 1961, and called it the "Golden Rule of Accumulation." Following research visits at MIT and the University of Cambridge, he became full professor of economics in Heidelberg at the age of 27. From 1968 to 1970, he taught as a full professor at the Economics Department of MIT. His students included Robert Merton, Robert Shiller and Stanley Fischer. During these years, he co-authored papers with Paul Samuelson and Robert Solow in the field of capital theory and macroeconomics. Later, Carl Christian von Weizsäcker turned to topics in industrial economics, with special emphasis on Schumpeterian economics, the economics of telecommunications and energy economics. He developed a theory of adaptive preferences that can serve as a basis for welfare economics beyond the homo economicus. He also co-authored a book on macroeconomics. He taught at the universities of Bielefeld, Bonn, Bern and Cologne. Since his retirement from teaching, he has been working at the Max Planck Institute for Research on Collective Goods, Bonn (Germany).

In 1977, he was elected to the Board of Academic Advisors of the German Minister for Economic Affairs, of which he is still a member today. From 1986 to 1998, he was a member of Germany's Monopolies Commission, and from 1989 to 1998, he was its chair.

Carl Christian von Weizsäcker, former Chairman of the German Monopoly Commission, is a Fellow of the Econometric Society and is a member of the American Academy of Arts and Sciences, the North Rhine-Westphalian Academy of Sciences and Germany's National Academy of Science and Engineering.

FIGURES

4.1	Preference System	12
6.1	Preference System and Budget Constraint	23
7.1	Two Different Sets of Indifference Curves for Two Different Baskets of Past Consumption	26
8.1	Indiff. Curves	30
10.1	Income (ΔY) and Substitution (S) Effect Due to a Price Change Δp_1 and Corresponding $\Delta p_2 = -\Delta p_1 (x_1 / x_2)$	37
11.1	KHS Theory With Adaptive Preferences	42
14.1	Short-Run Preferences, Long-Run Quasi-Preferences and Improving Paths	56
17.1	Smoothly Adaptive Preferences	67
19.1	Gross Benefit of Rights Depending on Rights Extension	81
19.2	Disturbance Depending on Rights-Extension	81
19.3	Net Benefit of Rights Depending on Rights Extension	82
19.4	Net Benefit of Rights: Range of Pragmatic Compossibility	82
21.1	Indifference Curve and Quasi-Indifference Curve Under AP	109
22.1	Survival Value of the Degree of Adaptiveness	116
22.2	Short Run and Long Run Elasticity of Substitution: Adaptive Preferences	117
23.1	Path Dependence of Long-Run Demand	120
25.1	Imitation Is a Case of Adaptive Preferences	127
26.1	Near-Decomposability	133
27.1	Path Dependence of Long-Run Demand	147
29.1	Cumulative Income Distribution in Two Regimes	164
29.2	Optimal Redistributive Income Tax	168
31.1	Dupuit's Bridge With Adaptive Preferences	176

PREFACE

It's a long story. In the time of the Vietnam War, around 1968, I was a young professor of economics at the University of Heidelberg. Many of my best students were Marxists. They ridiculed my adherence to economic models with agents who had fixed preferences. They were unimpressed by Milton Friedman's remark in his textbook *Price Theory*, where he suggests that it was not the economist's, but the psychologist's task to explain tastes – whereas the economist's program was to concentrate on the consequences of given preferences. Educated by Marx on topics like "false consciousness" and "bourgeois ideology", they rejected neoclassical theory, which for me was the backbone of economics. I thought it would be productive to pursue a theoretical research program with the aim to develop some welfare economics with endogenously determined preferences.

My first product was a model, published in the *Journal of Economic Theory* (Von Weizsäcker 1971) with the title "Notes on Endogenous Change of Tastes". In the meantime, I continued to pursue applied work, which took a substantial part of my time. My paper did not strongly resonate among the economics profession. And, after a while, general interest in Marxism receded. After all, the Vietnam War was over, and the Oil Crisis and ensuing stagflation absorbed the attention of the economics profession. I myself began to work on industrial organization, a fascinating field for economists. I became a member of the advisory council of the German Minister of Economic Affairs. I started a project on telecommunication; in the 80s I became an energy economist, doing advisory work on the introduction of competition in the telecommunication sector and in the energy industry. I became a member and then Chairman of the German Monopolies Commission.

Occasionally, between applied work, I returned to my topic of endogenous preferences, as can be seen in Von Weizsäcker 1984b or in my Thünen-Lecture

Von Weizsäcker 2002. In the meantime, academic interest in behavioral economics and related topics had become quite active. After my retirement from the chair in economic theory at the University of Cologne in 2003, I started to spend more time on endogenous preferences, but I still was quite active in different applied industrial organization projects. It was in 2010 that I left that field. I was invited to deliver the Graz-Schumpeter Lectures 2011 at the University of Graz: on this occasion, I wrote down a larger manuscript on endogenous preferences. In these years I was invited to a number of lectures at different universities and academies, where I could present my ideas on endogenous preferences. One example is my Hayek Lecture Von Weizsäcker 2014.

But then, my much earlier involvement in capital theory made me think that I could contribute ideas to the macro-economic issues of the Financial Crisis, which started in 2008. Therefore, I again interrupted my research on endogenous preferences. Hagen Krämer and I wrote a book, which came out in 2019 in German and in 2021 in English Von Weizsäcker and Krämer 2021.

After this detour, I started to work on the present book. Late in the year 2022 I sent a draft around to fellow economists – and I received very useful comments, criticism and encouragement. I want to thank Michael Adams, Philippe Aghion, Thomas Apolte, Douglas Bernheim, Felix Bierbrauer, Reinhard Blomert, Friedrich Breyer, Daniela Broenstrup, Michael Burda, Billy Christmas, Giacomo Corneo, Malte Dold, Jürgen Eichberger, Christoph Engel, Armin Falk, Lars Feld, Klaus Gärditz, Hans Martin von Gaudecker, Thomas Gehrig, Hans Gersbach, Nils Goldschmidt, Thomas Gräber, Michael Grubb, James Heckman, Helena Helfer, Martin Hellwig, Bodo Herzog, Martin Höpner, Karen Horn, Otmar Issing, Martin Kessler, Rainer Klump, Günter Knieps, Ekkehard Köhler, Stefan Kolev, Matthias Kräkel, Dorothea Kübler, Wolfgang Kuhle, Heinz Dieter Kurz, Marco Lehmann-Waffenschmidt, Erik Maskin, Dorothee Mischkowski, Rolf Nagel, Klaus Nehring, Ulrike Neyer, Hans Nutzinger, Axel Ockenfels, Ingo Pies, Christian Proaño, Martin Raiser, Michael Dan Richter, Wolfram Richter, Albrecht Ritschl, Johannes Rottmann, Bertram Schefold, Ekkehart Schlicht, Klaus Schmidt, Dieter Schmidtchen, Friedrich Schneider, Jan Schnellenbach, Antoinette Schoar, Wolfgang Schön, Christian Schubert, Willi Semmler, Leon Sieverding, Urs Schweizer, Hans-Werner Sinn, Peter Spahn, Richard Sturn, Andreas Suchanek, Uwe Sunde, Viktor Vanberg, Roland Vaubel, Björn Vollan, Gerhard Wächter, Adolf Wagner, Achim Wambach, Jakob von Weizsäcker, Heinz Welsch, Bernhard Wieland, Ulrich Witt and Elmar Wolfstetter.

References

Von Weizsäcker, Carl Christian, 1971, Notes on Endogenous Change of Tastes, Journal of Economic Theory, 3 (4), 345–372.

Von Weizsäcker, Carl Christian, 1984, The Influence of Property Rights on Tastes, Journal of Institutional and Theoretical Economics, 90–95.

Von Weizsäcker, Carl Christian, 2002, Welfare Economics Bei Endogenen Präferenzen – Thünen-Vorlesung 2001, Perspektiven der Wirtschaftspolitik, 3 (4), 425–446.
Von Weizsäcker, Carl Christian, 2014, Die normative Ko-Evolution von Marktwirtschaft und Demokratie, ORDO, 65, 13–43 (Hayek-Lecture at University of Freiburg).
Von Weizsäcker, Carl Christian and Krämer, Hagen, 2021, Saving and Investment in the 21st Century – The Great Divergence, Cham, Springer, XXII + 344 pages.

BOOK 1

Introduction

The Concept of "Preferences"

> Truth is ever to be found in simplicity, and not in the multiplicity and confusion of things. As the world, which to the naked eye exhibits the greatest variety of objects, appears very simple in its internal constitution when surveyed by a philosophical understanding, and so much simpler by how much the better it is understood.
>
> – Isaac Newton

DOI: 10.4324/9781032726410-1

1

NORMATIVE INDIVIDUALISM

A society of free people needs a measuring rod for economic policy performance. This measuring rod is the collection of citizens' preferences.

Traditional welfare economics works with the assumption of the fully rational economic agent, that is, with the assumption of "homo economicus". It includes the hypothesis that preferences of homo economicus are fixed, once and for all. Thereby economists were able to develop normative economics, which was fully individualistic. *Normative individualism* (Vanberg 2000) was thereby possible. The measuring rod for the performance of an economic system is fullyanchored in the preferences of individuals. There is no "collectivist" value judgment about the worth of particular goods involved. On "normative individualism", see also Schubert 2005. (Of course, distributional justice considerations always require some "collectivist" value judgment – even in traditional welfare economics.)

If you admit that the economic environment can influence preferences, normative individualism faces a fundamental difficulty: the measuring rod of economic system performance no longer is independent of the object that it is supposed to measure. It is like a measuring rod that changes its length as a function of the length of the table it is supposed to measure. Such a measuring rod no longer allows a straightforward measurement of the length of objects.

I believe that this difficulty is the reason for the tenacity with which economists have stuck to the assumption that preferences are fixed, are exogenously given. They did not see a way to maintain normative individualism if they gave up the assumption of fixed preferences. One form this tenacity took was the Stigler and Becker 1977 paper: "De gustibus non est disputandum". There the authors present the hypothesis that every person has the same preferences – and, as a corollary, preferences are fixed, exogenously given. They reject the traditional method of economists who explain observed differences in behavior by differences in

DOI: 10.4324/9781032726410-2

preferences. They say that this "explanation" really is no explanation at all but a tautology. Stigler and Becker cling to the assumption of fully rational behavior.

We should clarify one point at the very beginning. Many critics of the homo economicus assumption depict homo economicus as a complete egoist. However, this has never been the opinion of mainstream economists who have used the homo economicus model. Indeed, many papers that assume preferences to be fixed do include altruistic or "social" preferences. The important logical point has been that preferences are exogenously given so that one can use them as a measuring rod of economic performance. Thus, in the following, I use the term homo economicus for the model in which people maximize their utility in a fully rational way and in which the utility function is exogenously given, be it fully egoistic or partly altruistic.

In this book, I want to present a theory that allows us to maintain normative individualism and yet to get rid of the assumption of fixed preferences. It builds on an observation about the "laws of motion" of preferences, which I call *adaptive preferences*. To come back to the measuring rod analogy: if you know the way in which the measuring rod changes its size as a function of the object to be measured, it might still be a useful tool for indirectly measuring the length of objects.

Economic research of recent decades has provided a large amount of experimental and other empirical findings, which contradict the assumption of fixed preferences. Bounded rationality is just one example (Simon 1956; Selten 1998; Gigerenzer and Selten 2001; Artinger et al. 2022). In this book, I suggest that this large body of findings is consistent with the hypothesis of adaptive preferences. This, together with the proposition that adaptive preferences allow a generalization of traditional welfare economics, should be useful for everybody interested in policy applications of behavioral economics – based on "normative individualism".

Normative individualism is an approach which intrinsically connects with the value of "liberty" or "freedom". In a sense, normative individualism is indispensable for a society of free citizens. My book is about the foundations of civil liberty.

References

Artinger, Florian M., Gigerenzer, Gerd and Jakobs, Perke, 2022, Satisficing: Integrating Two Traditions, Journal of Economic Literature, 60 (2), 598–635.

Gigerenzer, Gerd and Selten, Reinhard (eds), 2001, Bounded Rationality – The Adaptive Toolbox, Cambridge, MA, MIT Press, XV + 377 pages.

Schubert, Christian, 2005, A Note on the Principle of Normative Individualism, Papers on Economics and Evolution, 0517, Jena, Max-Planck-Institute on Economics, 24 pages.

Selten, Reinhard, 1998, Aspiration Adaptation Theory, Journal of Mathematical Psychology, 42, 192–214.

Simon, Herbert, 1956, Rational Choice and the Structure of the Environment, Psychological Review, 63, 129–138.

Stigler, George J. and Becker, Gary S., 1977, De Gustibus non est Disputandum, American Economic Review, 67 (2), 76–90.

Vanberg, Viktor J., 2000, Der konsensorientierte Ansatz der konstitutionellen Ökonomik, in Leipold, Hellmut und Pies, Ingo (ed.), Ordnungstheorie und Ordnungspolitik – Konzeptionen und Entwicklungsperspektiven, Stuttgart, Lucius und Lucius, pp.252–276.

2

"PREFERENCES" IN POSITIVE AND IN "NORMATIVE" ECONOMICS

Adaptive preferences are a "law of motion" of preferences. Before we can understand the concept of adaptive preferences, we need to understand the concept of preferences. Why do economists talk of preferences? In my view, this concept is intimately related to the idea of freedom of action. The concept of preferences is the mode by which normative economics introduces the idea of freedom or liberty into its theory of human interaction.

Positive economics does not really need the concept of preferences. Take the Stigler-Becker view of 1977: "de gustibus non est disputandum". Here the authors essentially argue that preferences are an empty concept. Concerning human behavior, preferences do not explain anything. They are used only as a kind of stand-in explanation, as a joker, where the researcher has not been able to explain observed human behavior. A "true" explanation of the causes of some observed behavior does not refer to the person's preferences. To say that person A prefers chocolate ice cream over vanilla ice cream does not add anything to the observation that, if given the choice between chocolate ice cream and vanilla ice cream, person A will choose chocolate ice cream. Thus, referring to the preferences as the cause for an observed behavior is not a causal explanation of such behavior, and if positive economics hence aims at explaining human behavior, it can dispose of the concept of preferences.

Preferences are an important concept in another research program, one that asks the following questions: how does a society of free individuals work? In addition: how can we improve it? It is the research program of normative economics, in particular: of normative individualism. This research program is important – and one can do this kind of research even without having finished the research program of positive economics. Indeed, it is the research program of traditional welfare economics. Obviously, there exist interdependencies between the research program of positive economics and the research program of normative economics.

DOI: 10.4324/9781032726410-3

To understand the importance of the concept of preferences in normative economics, we have to discuss the concept of freedom or liberty as it is implicitly used in normative economics. There we understand liberty to be a situation in which an agent has the choice between different alternatives; moreover, her/his choice is justified and legitimate in society simply due the fact that it is her/his choice. The degree to which the agent has a freedom of choice, that is, the degree to which the agent is free, rises as her/his choice alternatives rise. Greater freedom, intuitively speaking, is greater choice.

An important example of freedom of choice is an election for public office in which the voter has the choice among different candidates. No matter what his or her reasons are for his or her voting decision, the ballot is valid and it counts. Freedom of choice exists if the reasons and causes for the particular choice decision are irrelevant for the legitimacy of that decision. Thus, in a sense, it is the very emancipation from the causal chain leading up to the decision which characterizes the concept of liberty.

The set-up of free elections in a democracy is a model for the general institutional set-up of a society of free people. Ballots are cast in a voting box to provide secrecy of voting. The secrecy of voting is the device by which it is guaranteed that the vote can be cast without any pressure from other citizens. Thereby modern democracies come close to the ideal that individual voting decisions are legitimate, irrespective of the causal chain that leads to the individual's decision. In a similar way – in a free society and within the available choice set of the individual – other decisions by individuals ought to be shielded against legitimizing or de-legitimizing pressures from others and from the government, irrespective of the causal chain that leads to the particular decision. We then need a kind of imaginary "voting box" or "decision box" for the citizens, allowing them to do what they want without interference by others.

No doubt, this "decision box" is a close relative of the privacy rules that are part of the institutional set-up of a free society. However, there is a conceptual difference. The set of privacy rules is one of several instruments that enable society to implement that "decision box". "Due process" in the legal system is another such instrument. A specific "bill of rights" of citizens is a further such instrument. Property protected by law, as John Locke and other social philosophers taught us long ago, is important to build up and enlarge that "decision box".

Seen from the point of view of the social philosopher interested in a theory of a free society, the "decision box" is a kind of filter concerning the facts and causal links he or she is allowed to use in this normative theory. This filter has taken a particular form in economics. It is the distinction between constraints and preferences that explains to him or her the behavior of the citizens of a free society.

The way the economist incorporates free decisions into his/her models is by means of the concept of preferences. For the purposes of modeling, the economist treats the agents as determined in their decisions, almost like automata or machines whose behavior can be predicted. This determinism is technically useful for the economist's goal of predicting the outcome of any given institutional set-up. Thus, the economist transforms the actual freedom of choice into a seemingly deterministic outcome by means of the concept of preferences. The behavior of the agent is determined by two classes of factors: 1) the constraints (for example, the budget constraint), determining his/her choice set and 2) his/her preferences, which determine the choice within his/her choice set. The first class of factors is the *constraints* of his/her freedom; the second class of factors is the *expression* of his/her freedom. Thus, given the preferences, the person is free and at the same time predictable for the onlooking researcher.

Normative individualism as an approach for economic theory, then, is the expression of the researcher's goal to understand the workings of a society of free persons and to recommend changes in the institutional set-up that increase the wealth and freedom of choice of the members of that society. Normative individualism thus tries to avoid impositions of values by the collective of individuals on each individual. It works observing the citizen only partially and hiding the rest of the causal explanation of their behavior behind a "veil of ignorance", to borrow a phrase introduced by social philosophers with a somewhat different meaning (Rawls 1971).

However, if the general norm behind normative individualism is to enhance individual freedom, we see that, in an ideal society, preferences of individuals play a quantitatively important role for the results of this human interaction. This is the opposite of the treatment of preferences in positive economics. There, the degree to which one refers to preferences as an explanation of behavior and thus of human interaction is a measure of our ignorance of the true causes of behavior. The goal is to minimize the degree to which one relies on preferences as an explanation.

Is there a logical contradiction between the two research programs? I do not think so. Two different concepts of the term "preferences" are involved. Preferences in positive economics are the unexplained remnant of a science that tries to explain as much as possible about human behavior. Preferences in the research program of normative individualism represent the realm of legitimate decisions of the individual, irrespective of their causes. It should then be perfectly possible to develop a theory that tries to explain the voting behavior of citizens alongside a normative theory of democracy that works with the assumption that ballots count – irrespective of the causes for any particular voting behavior.

However, the freer citizens are, the more is determined in a society by the choices taken by citizens (rather than the constraints) and the more we need to acknowledge the fact that choices or preferences are influenced by the social environment of the citizens. It is, then, a strong desideratum for normative individualism to have a welfare economics that does not have to rely on the assumption of fixed preferences, that is, a welfare economics that works even with endogenously determined, that is, induced preferences.

References

Rawls, John, 1971, A Theory of Justice, Cambridge, MA, Belknap Press of Harvard University Press, 521 pages.

Stigler, George J. and Becker, Gary S., 1977, De Gustibus non est Disputandum, American Economic Review, 67 (2), 76–90.

3

"COMPOSSIBILITY" OF FREEDOM RIGHTS

Every society of free people has to limit the freedom of each citizen in order to protect the freedom of other citizens. The rights of the citizens must be compatible with each other. These rights must be "compossible" (Steiner 1977).

Before entering our approach towards "endogenous preferences", it is useful to understand the concept of "constraints" in such a normative theory. As we use this term in everyday life, we have a conception that there are possibilities of choosing freely among alternatives. The constraints then determine the choice set of alternatives among which the agent chooses. In the positive theory, the "constraints" ideally fully determine the "choice". The "constraints", then, are the "causes" of any given action. To the extent that the causes are not yet fully known, explaining choice by "preferences" is not explaining them at all. "Constraints" in the normative approach are not necessarily the constraints that the agent subjectively would consider to limit his or her choice. They also are not the "constraints" which positive economics would call "causes". Rather, "constraints" in normative theory determine the realm of legitimate and thus free choice of the individual.

If we want to be quite radical concerning the distinction between the positive and the normative approach, we could say: in normative theory, constraints are *exclusively* determined by the limits of the rights, which are set by law in the interest of "compossibility". Physical constraints within each private household can be accounted for by the (ordinal) utility function of the agent. If the agent is unable to jump two yards high, we simply designate a "utility" of minus infinity ($-\infty$) to any consumption basket containing a two-yard jump of the agent.

I postpone a more detailed discussion of this concept of compossibility to Book IV. It is a difficult concept. Here I follow this radical approach of defining the "constraints" in terms of the compossibility criterion. It means that for any given rights of the agent, any changes in the agent's condition change the agent's preferences

DOI: 10.4324/9781032726410-4

and do not change the agent's constraints. Thus, for example, if, for a given budget constraint, the agent catches a cold, the agent may change his/her consumption basket, reflecting a change in "preferences". For the outside observer it is then not possible to distinguish between a change in demand behavior due to subjectively felt changes in constraints and a change in demand due to a subjectively felt change in preferences.

Does this procedure involve a loss of information? The answer is: yes, it does. However, this is the very idea of civil liberty: for the social legitimization of the agent's actions, it is not relevant to make this distinction between changes due to subjectively felt changes in constraints and subjectively felt changes in preferences – as long as the agent obeys the observable constraints due to the principle of compossibility.

As I shall discuss in some detail in Books IV and V, a society of free people can only sustain order and stability if a certain degree of rationality of human behavior persists. Moreover, such rationality does not simply fall from heaven; people have to learn it. The central idea of this book, "adaptive preferences", seems to me to be a close relative of the concept of "learning rationality".

Reference

Steiner, Hillel, 1977, The Structure of a Set of Compossible Rights, Journal of Philosophy, 74, 767–775.

4

PREFERENCE SYSTEMS

The Comparability Problem

I introduce the concept of "induced preferences". It is part of a structure, which I call a "preferences system". The following graph indicates the meaning of a preference system. It is applicable to any given agent. Together with constraints (here symbolized by the price vector p), preferences (here symbolized by some vector q) generate a certain choice of a consumption basket (symbolized by the consumption vector x). So, this is a mapping from the set of possible preferences $\mathbb{Q}$ to the set of consumption baskets $\mathfrak{X}$. Then, there is a feedback. The chosen consumption basket x induces particular preferences q. This, then, is a mapping $q = \rho(x)$ from the set of consumption baskets $\mathfrak{X}$ to the set of possible preferences $\mathbb{Q}$.

An equilibrium exists if x and q induce each other: q (together with p) generates x, and x again induces q. If the process of preference induction takes time, the preference system is a dynamic system, which we may describe by means of difference equations (in models with discrete time periods) or by means of differential equations (in models with continuous time).

If preferences are endogenous, we may face a comparability problem: Assume the set of possible consumption baskets consists of two elements A and B. Now, case 1, it could be that A induces preferences q under which A is preferred over B, and B induces preferences r under which B is preferred over A. We then have two equilibria A and B. It seems difficult to say which basket is "better": A or B.

Or, case 2, A induces preferences q under which B is preferred over A, and B induces preferences r under which A is preferred over B. In this case, no equilibrium exists, and again, we are at a loss to say which basket is "better": A or B.

However, possibly there is a way out of this dilemma. For a positive answer, we need more than two baskets. If the goods in the basket are "infinitely" divisible, the set of possible baskets may have infinitely many elements even if we only distinguish two different consumption goods. Let us take case 1 first. Even though, seen

DOI: 10.4324/9781032726410-5

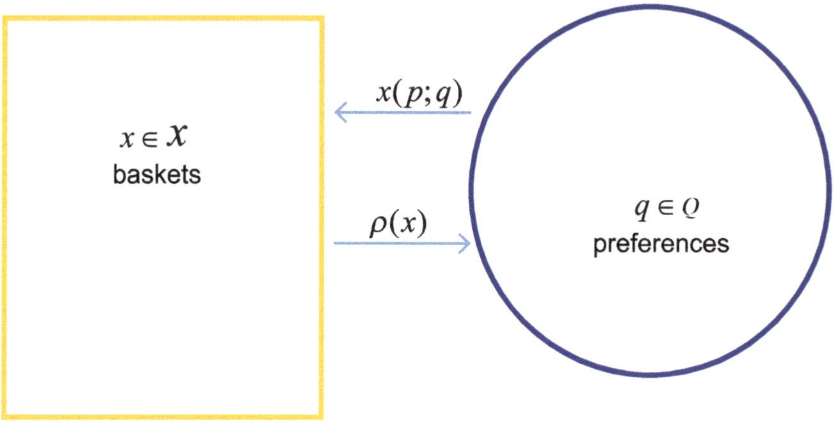

FIGURE 4.1 Preference System

without further choice possibilities, we cannot decide whether A or B is "better" in some sense, seen in a larger array of choice possibilities, we might find a sequence of choices with $x(0);x(1);x(2);\ldots..x(T)$ with $x(0)=A$ and $x(T)=B$, such that for each integer i from $i=0$ up to $i=T-1$ we find that $x(i+1)$ is preferred over $x(i)$ with preferences induced by $x(i)$. Let us call such a sequence $x(0)=A;x(1);x(2);\ldots..x(T)=B$ an *improvement sequence*. Moreover, we may find that there exists no improvement sequence starting at B and ending at A. In that case, we may designate B to be somehow "better" than A. A series of small steps, each of them being an improvement under preferences induced by the preceding one, intuitively should lead us to something better than the beginning.

It is this intuition which led me to think about the possibility of a welfare economics of normative individualism. In a first publication, Von Weizsäcker 1971, I presented a more precise positive answer to the comparability dilemma under variable preferences. The present book provides a comprehensive theory of civil liberty, which no longer needs the assumption of fixed preferences.

The concept of "progress" is central for any kind of value-oriented social science; for the economist, for any kind of normative approach. But "progress" is only a consistent concept if it is never the case that (due to changing induced preferences) an improvement sequence of the kind just described ends up at the beginning. It is therefore important to understand sufficient conditions so that any improvement sequence is *acyclic*. A large part of the present book is devoted to this acyclicity issue – in theory and empirically.

Just to show that acyclicity conditions are not a trivial thing, I observe that in case 2 of our A and B thought experiment, we obtain cyclic improvement sequences: starting with basket A and preferences q induced by A, the movement from A to B is an improvement; continuing with B and preferences r induced by B, the movement from B to A is improvement. Thus, we have an improvement sequence starting at A and returning to A. Case 2, then, is not compatible with a consistent concept of progress.

Dos moi pou sto! ($\delta o\varsigma\ \mu o\iota\, \pi o \upsilon\, \varsigma\tau\omega$). Archimedes said, "give me a (fixed) point, where I can stand – and I shall move the globe". This is also the logic of freedom: Human behavior, as legitimized by society and its agent, the State, eventually derives from a starting point, which is exogenous from any societal influences on behavior. The traditional assumption of fixed preferences was a way for the social philosopher, or the economist, to generate such an exogenous starting point for modelling a free society. In this book, I replace the unrealistic assumption of fixed preferences by the idea of an exogenously given "preference system".

However, this is not enough: in the world of fixed preferences, you need the Samuelson (1938)–Houthakker (1950) axioms of revealed preference. Only then is human behavior internally consistent to "reveal" preferences, which can be used as a measuring rod for the performance of society on the basis of "normative individualism". What is the axiom corresponding to the Samuelson–Houthakker axiom if preferences are variable but preference systems are exogenous? It is the axiom of adaptive preferences. This is the central message of my book.

Most of Book II and all of Book III show this central role of adaptive preferences on the level of internal consistency of individual behavior. In Book IV, and in particular in Book V, I take up interpersonal influences on preferences. Book VI then shows the specific welfare logic of decentralized decision-making. This logic again presupposes the axiom of adaptive preferences.

Another observation is worthwhile to put at the beginning of this book. Traditional fixed preference welfare economics is a quasi-static general equilibrium theory. The welfare economics of preference systems and adaptive preferences is evolutionary. At any given moment, there is a status quo of the economy. However, there are breakouts from the status quo underway, and new ones are in a planning stage. Using an analogy from biology, we may say: the traditional neoclassical paradigm is pre-Darwinian. The theory of a given preference system allowing for endogenously changing preferences and the axiom of adaptive preferences are post-Darwinian. Explaining any complex object involves the reduction of its phenomena to a set of exogenously given causes. In pre-Darwinian fixed preferences theory, the exogenous causes are the available technology and the given preferences. In pre-Darwinian biology, the different species were given (given by God?). In post-Darwinian biology, the laws of mutation and selection are given – and the surviving species are explained by their adaptation to their environment ("survival of the fittest"). In post-Darwinian welfare economics, preference systems are given – and the actual preferences are explained by the working of the preference system and in particular by the adaptation of preferences to their social (and in particular economic) environment.

At the end of this chapter, I want to refer to James Buchanan's important work. In the collected works of James Buchanan (1999–2002), you find an impressive critique of neoclassical welfare economics. Using Vanberg's 2019 description,

Buchanan posits neoclassic "utility individualism" against his own "choice individualism". Here I do not discuss Buchanan's (and Vanberg's) position in detail. I only want to remark that my own approach in the present book belongs to the "utility individualism" camp. I am motivated to take this choice, because we can analyze the competition between a freedom-based democratic constitution and an authoritarian/totalitarian system only if we look at their relative performance in terms of the wants and needs of the citizens. For this performance competition, we need to look at the monetary equivalents of the citizen's "utilities".

References

Buchanan, James M., 1999–2002, The Collected Works of James Buchanan, 20 volumes, Indianapolis, IN, Liberty Fund.

Houthakker, Hendrick, 1950, Revealed Preference and the Utility Function, Economica, 17 (66), 159–174.

Samuelson, Paul A., 1938, A Note on the Pure Theory of Consumer's Behavior, Economica, 5, 61–71.

Vanberg, Viktor J., 2019, Introduction: Individual Choice and Social Welfare – Theoretical Foundations of Political Economy, in: Vanberg, Viktor J. (ed.), Choice and Economic Welfare, Cheltenham, Edward Elgar, CIX + 725 pages, XIII–CIX.

Von Weizsäcker, Carl Christian, 1971, Notes on Endogenous Change of Tastes, Journal of Economic Theory, 3 (4), 345–372.

5

OVERVIEW OF THE FOLLOWING BOOKS II TO VI

Book II is devoted to the *classroom model*. It is a drastically simplified two-commodity discrete time model. In it, I can show with modest mathematical effort Theorem 1 and Theorem 2. These two theorems together show that the assumptions of adaptive preferences and of acyclicity of every improvement sequence are equivalent. Adaptive preferences are a special case of a preference system. In words, the definition of adaptive preferences is this: if, with preferences q induced by basket x, the basket y is preferred over x, then, a fortiori, y is preferred over x with preferences r induced by basket y. I then show that due to Theorems 1 and 2, welfare economics in the spirit of normative individualism remains possible, even if preferences are endogenously formed – as long as they correspond to the assumption of adaptive preferences.

Book III generalizes the results of Book II, using a model which I call the "real-world model". In it, there are n consumption goods, with n any natural number. Time is modeled as continuous time. The mathematical effort for this generalization is substantially higher. It is partly contained in a mathematical annex.

Book IV has two main purposes. The first one is a precise definition of "compossibility" of rights owned by the citizens. For the rest of the book I use a particular form of compossibility, which I call "pragmatic compossibility". It is defined and discussed in Chapter 18. In Chapter 19 I argue that compossibility of freedom rights can only work if preferences are adaptive. Chapter 20 derives some well-known "phenomenology of adaptive preferences" from the assumption of adaptive preferences. I argue that the assumption of adaptive preferences corresponds to the actual human behavior. In Chapter 21 I discuss well-known facts of behavioral economics, and I show that they imply that preferences are adaptive. For example, I take loss aversion as a robust result from behavioral economics to show its consistency with the assumption of adaptive preferences. Other topics are "decision

DOI: 10.4324/9781032726410-6

costs", "rational inattention", "habit formation", "uncertainty aversion" "ambiguity aversion", "religion", "traditionalism", "complexity of intertemporal choice", "theory of chosen preferences", "nudging" and "long-run price elasticities larger than short-run price elasticities". I believe thereby to have shown that normative individualism remains compatible with the results of behavioral economics.

Book V is devoted to interpersonal influences on preference formation. Its length is almost twice the average length of the other Books. It is here in particular that my approach of combining the idea of freedom (in the form of pragmatic compossibility) with the idea of adaptive preferences bears fruit in explaining the working of a free democratic society combined with an economy of competitive markets. Here I do not report the details of Book V. I start out arguing that adaptive preferences are the likely result of evolution (in the Darwinian sense) of the human species. Then, by reference to the important book *Phishing for Phools* by Akerlof and Shiller 2015, I show that there are cases in which State intervention in competitive markets is justified. Using my adaptive preference theory, I show that such government intervention is connected with the path dependence of improving sequences. This leads me to a classification of State action into two "modes": the "freedom mode" and the "causal mode". In the "freedom mode", the government lets market results happen, because these results (if markets are competitive) come about due to free action of the citizens. The "causal mode" means that the government acts due to a causal analysis of the situation. For example, the decisions about the provision of public goods are made in the causal mode. But also protection of people with a limited degree of autonomy may cause government intervention, for example, protection of small children. I have a chapter on externalities.

I also discuss imitation of others as an important case of interpersonal influences on preferences. I show that imitation corresponds to the assumption of adaptive preferences. A discussion of advertising follows. By pointing to the "double helix" of advertising and imitation, it is very likely that they together enhance the price elasticity of demand. Apart from a few special cases, the conclusion is that from a welfare point of view, advertising is okay.

Then there is a chapter on philosophical conceptions of a free society, where I use adaptive preferences as the backbone of society's debate about capitalism. Here I refer to Karl Poppers idea of the "Open Society" and to Erich Fromm's critique of capitalism as a system which may destroy humanity. I connect this opposition of these two great thinkers with two co-existing generalized media of exchange: "Money" and "Time". I show that the Popper-Fromm opposition corresponds to a long historical tradition of two opposing threads of social thinking, which we may label "pro-market" and "anti-market". At the end, I do not remain neutral but join the "pro-market" party.

Book V ends with a chapter on the "Social Market Economy". Here the important point is that free competitive markets under pragmatic compossibility tend to raise average living standards more than other economic regimes. Distributional concerns get an answer by means of progressive taxation – and not by direct government intervention into competitive markets. Whereas these results are no news for most market economists, the novel result is their consistency with the observation that preferences are not fixed but are adaptive.

Book VI is about cost-benefit analysis. The critical point is this: for any project breaking away from the status quo and implemented by justifying it in terms of ex-ante preferences, can we be sure that such a project is also justifiable with the ex-post preferences induced by the project itself? If this, on a regular basis, would not be the case, it would turn out to be highly difficult to convince people to undertake such projects. Society would then end up in stagnation. I derive Theorem 3, which basically says: provided that collective preferences satisfy the freedom mode of State action, and provided that individual preferences are adaptive, then an ex-ante justification of a project leads to an ex-post justification – thereby generating sufficient "project optimism" to avoid social stagnation. Moreover, a market economy allows entrepreneurs (call them "Schumpeterian entrepreneurs") to undertake projects against the majority preferences – in the expectation that the project ex-post swerves preferences in favor of the project. We may call these entrepreneurs "preference entrepreneurs".

Reference

Akerlof, George A. and Shiller, Robert J., 2015, Phishing for Phools: The Economics of Manipulation and Deception, Princeton, NJ, Princeton University Press, 288 pages.

BOOK II

The Classroom Model of Adaptive Preferences

6

INTRODUCTION AND DEFINITIONS

It is useful for an understanding of my approach, when I first present it in a very simple model, which does not claim realism. I call it the "classroom model". It may serve well for teaching purposes. So this Book II is mainly devoted to the classroom model. Beyond that, I work with a "discrete time model" and a "continuous time model". The latter I also call the "real-world model". In Book III, I develop the mathematical skeleton of the discrete time model and the real-world model. However, here in Chapters 6 and 7 I also introduce general concepts that are applicable in all three, the "classroom model", the "discrete time model" and the "real-world model".

The classroom model is a special case of the discrete time model. The latter deals with n distinct commodities (with n any positive integer greater than 1). In the classroom model I look at a world with just two distinct commodities ($n = 2$). This allows me to draw indifference curves. These figures may help in understanding the economic meaning of the mathematical apparatus employed to obtain precise concepts and results. It also turns out that proof of my Theorem 1 is particularly easy to read for the two-commodity world.

The second major simplification in the classroom model concerns the feedback from the actual consumption basket to the preferences. I explain this in this chapter.

Conceptually the most difficult part of the theory is the link-up between the citizens' preferences and the ensuing social welfare function, taking account of the idea of civil liberty. The classroom model has a structure which makes this link-up particularly straightforward. It also provides an easy route to take account of distributional concerns. As we shall see in Books III, IV and V, the classroom model then helps to appreciate the quite different approach, which we take in the general case.

We need to formalize the meaning of the terms "induced preferences" and "adaptive preferences". In the following, I proceed by first providing the definitions for

DOI: 10.4324/9781032726410-8

the general case, which includes the three models: the classroom model, the discrete time model and the real-world model. Alongside this, I describe the classroom model in detail.

The intuitive meaning of "adaptive preferences" is this: individuals have a tendency to value their present position P1 higher relative to alternatives than they would value P1 if their present position were a different one, say, P2. We may call this "preference conservatism": a tendency of agents to stick where they are. I shall discuss the realism of the assumption of adaptive preferences in Books IV and V. Here it may suffice to mention the concept of the "default option" in behavioral economics. The empirical/experimental research shows quite clearly how strongly the default option influences actual choices: people quite often "opt for not opting", that is, for opting for the "default option", that is, for their present status.

Causation runs through time: first, there is a cause, and then there is an effect. However, as every economist is aware, the cause may consist of expectations concerning future events. In the context of the theory presented here, we should not be disturbed by the formation of expectations. The reader may think of adaptive expectations, a concept frequently used in economic model building. Following the approach in general equilibrium theory, á la Arrow and Debreu, we can subsume subjective probabilities under the heading of "preferences". It then is also possible to subsume "adaptive expectations" under "adaptive preferences".

In order to endogenize the formation of preferences, I use the concept of a "preference system". I define this first. I denote any choice object by x or y or z or A or B or C. For concreteness the reader may interpret any such object as an n-dimensional commodity basket, where each component is non-negative. Preferences then are denoted by q or r or s. For concreteness, the reader may interpret q as a point in some N-dimensional Euclidean space of preference characteristics. We do not impose any restrictions on N, except that it is a natural number. In fact, the theory is more general. However, the preference space needs a well-defined metric and a well-defined topology so that concepts like "continuity" and "convergence" make sense.

Definition 1: A *preference system* $\{x;q;\dot{q}\}$ is a system consisting of a commodity space $\mathcal{X}$ containing commodity baskets x, consisting of a preference space $\mathcal{Q}$ containing preferences q and consisting of a rule $\dot{q}(x;q)$, describing the change through time of preferences as a function of the currently prevailing commodity basket x and the currently prevailing preferences q.

Any particular person is characterized by a preference system. I assume that the preference system is exogenously given.

Definition 2: Induced Preferences. For any given preference system $\{x;q;\dot{q}\}$ preferences $\rho(x)$ are induced by basket x if, for x constant through time, preferences converge towards $\rho(x)$.

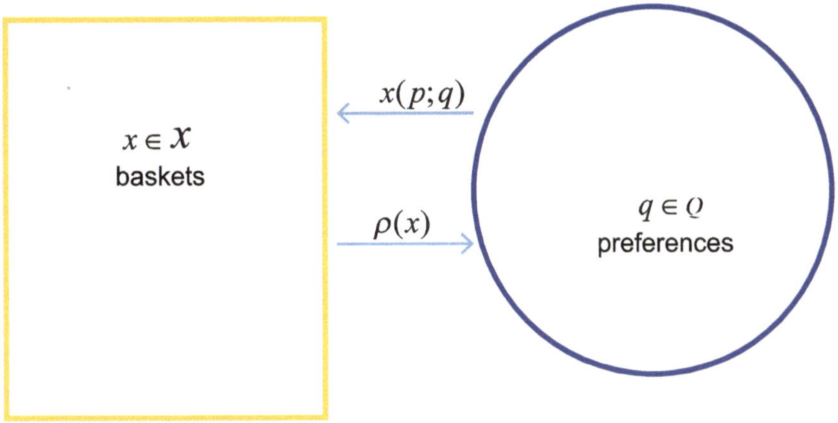

FIGURE 6.1 Preference System and Budget Constraint

The function $\rho()$ is a mapping from commodity space into preference space, indicating the inducement of preferences by actual consumption.

For the special case that the commodity basket is determined by a price vector under a budget constraint (p) and by the preferences, the picture above depicts a preference system

The preference system is a dynamic system because the impact of the commodity basket on preferences works with a time delay. In the real-world model, we work with continuous time, and hence we express the dynamics of the system by means of a differential equation. In the classroom model and in the discrete time model, I work with discrete time periods. Here I assume (unrealistically) that actual preferences are induced by the consumption basket of the preceding period. Thus $q(t) = \rho(x(t-1))$. Concerning notation, I use the expression $\{x;q;\dot{q}\}$ for the general case and for the real-world model. When I write $[x;q;\dot{q}]$, I always work in the classroom model or in the discrete time model.

For a stationary price vector and a stationary budget constraint, the preference system is in a stationary equilibrium $\bar{x};\bar{q}$ if simultaneously we have $\bar{x} = x(p;\bar{q})$ and $\bar{q} = \rho(\bar{x})$.

As a special case of the real-world model, assume that the mapping ρ can be inverted so that we can write $x = \rho^{-1}(q)$. We may then look at a "law of motion" of preferences, such that for q represented by $z = \rho^{-1}(q)$ and for the actual consumption basket x we have a linear vector differential equation. It reads: $\frac{dz}{dt} \equiv \dot{z} = \alpha(x-z)$, which by integration leads to the equation $z(t) = e^{-\alpha t}\left(z(0) + \alpha\int_0^t e^{\alpha\tau}x(\tau)d\tau\right)$, with α and n times n positive definite matrix. In this case, for x constant through time, z converges toward x. This means that q converges toward $\rho(x)$.

In a system where a stationary budget constraint influences the consumption vector, we distinguish between a short-run demand function $x = h(p;q)$ and a long-run demand function $x = H(p) = h(p;\rho(x))$. Later I come back to the welfare economic significance of the long-run demand function, which obviously does not express demand with any given preferences q. What does it reveal, if it does not reveal preferences?

Notation of preferences: If with preferences q, basket y is preferred over basket x, we write $y(>;q)x$. If with preferences q, basket y is preferred over basket x or indifferent to x, we write $y(\geq;q)x$. If with preferences q, basket y is indifferent to basket x, we write $y(=;q)x$.

Definition 3: Adaptive Preferences. Assume that a preference system is characterized by a well-defined mapping $\rho()$ of induced preferences. The preference system $\{x;q;\dot{q}\}$ exhibits adaptive preferences if the following holds: For any two baskets x and y, if $y(>;\rho(x))x$, then $y(>;\rho(y))x$. For any two baskets x and y, if $y(=;\rho(x))x$, then $y(\geq;\rho(y))x$. In words: Preferences are adaptive if a basket y, which is preferred over x with preferences induced by x, is, a fortiori, preferred over x with preferences induced by y.

Note that the traditional homo economicus with fixed preferences is a special case of adaptive preferences. Thus, the latter are a true generalization of fixed preferences.

To see the connection between this definition of adaptive preferences and the intuitive meaning of preference conservatism, think of $\rho(x)$ as the initial preferences inherited from the past. Consider now some change in the consumption from x to y which by preferences $\rho(x)$ is considered an improvement. Now, keep y constant for a while. The preferences converge to $\rho(y)$. Preference conservatism thus would indicate that y would still be considered superior to x.

7

IMPROVEMENT SEQUENCES

I start this chapter with the comparability problem. It was this problem, which led to my thinking on variable preferences, and thus led to my paper Von Weizsäcker 1971. If, in a two-commodity world, preferences depend on past consumption we may see a picture like this:

As I have drawn the two sets of indifference curves, they indicate the property of adaptive preferences. Given the choice between A and B, the person chooses A, provided past consumption has been A. Given the choice between A and B, the person chooses B, provided past consumption has been B. Is it then appropriate to say: "stay put, where you are"? This, surely, would not correspond to the tradition of normative economics. It has always been reform minded. After all, economics is a child of the age of enlightenment. Economists always considered improvement a possibility. As we shall see, it is the concept of adaptive preferences which is closely linked to the concept of progress or improvement.

In this particular case of the two baskets A and B we can ask the following two questions. First: Although a jump from A to B – given the blue indifference curves – is not an improvement, is it perhaps possible to move gradually from A to B by means of a number of smaller intermediate improvement steps to B, exploiting the fact that preferences change alongside during this longer journey? Second: and if that is a possibility, could it be that a reverse improvement journey from B to A is not available? Could we then – in a certain sense – consider basket B superior to basket A? In addition, could it be that this "superiority" can be "revealed" by the long-run demand function, which I introduced earlier, the function $x = H(p)$?

As we shall see, we obtain positive answers to these questions if and only if preferences are adaptive.

For further analysis, we need an axiom about the way agents cope with their awareness that their preferences may change. I call it the "improvement axiom".

DOI: 10.4324/9781032726410-9

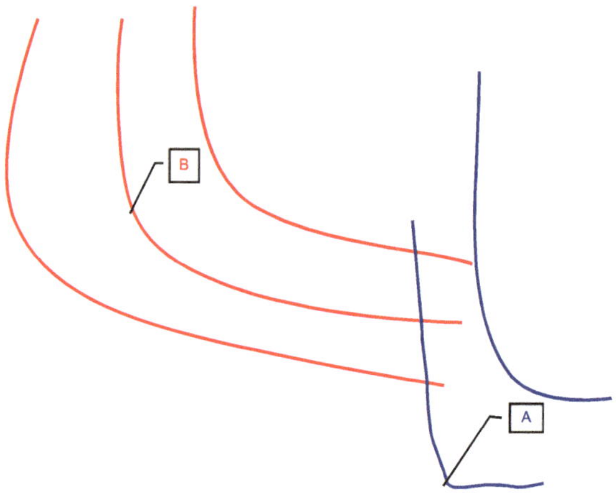

FIGURE 7.1 Two Different Sets of Indifference Curves for Two Different Baskets of Past Consumption. Past consumption A: blue indiff. curves. Past consumption B: red indiff. curves

Definition 4: Let A, B, C, . . . K be a finite set of consumption baskets, which have the following properties. For preferences induced by A, the basket B is preferred over A; for preferences induced by B, the basket C is preferred over B; and so on. Each basket is preferred over the preceding one with preferences induced by the preceding one. Such a sequence I call an *improvement sequence.* If, in addition, each basket is different from all other baskets in the sequence, we then speak of an *improvement path.*

I now introduce the "Improvement Axiom".

Improvement Axiom: Given the choice between a stationary consumption path and an improvement sequence, both starting with the same basket and the same preferences induced by that basket, people prefer the improvement sequence, provided they expect that any improvement sequence is an improvement path.

Although generally people do not know precisely how their preferences will change under new consumption circumstances, they do accept an improvement if it is offered to them. And they do assume that they will do the same in the future after further improvement is offered to them and after their preferences then have changed due to the first improvement. However, they would be reluctant to accept the first improvement if they feared that an improvement sequence were "cyclic", that is, would lead back to the starting point. They explicitly or implicitly have to expect the improvement sequence to be a-cyclic before they accept the first step of the improvement.

I consider the Improvement Axiom a convincing assumption. Everyday life tells us that people behave in accordance with this Improvement Axiom. People want improvement even if they are aware that their wants will change with this improvement. Most of the time people don't know in advance how their preferences will change after they have changed their consumption basket.

The Improvement Axiom is the single point where I introduce something like an evaluative comparison of different preferences, albeit quite a local one. This is in contrast to approaches by other economists like Becker 1996 or Sen 1977, who talk about meta-preferences, that is, about preferences over different preferences. In a sense, what this meta-preference approach does is to return the theory back to the paradigm of fixed preferences. Indeed, the assumption of the meta-preference approach is that meta-preferences are fixed, are exogenously given. This then again leads to decisions of the individual, which one can predict as if preferences themselves were exogenously given.

What about erroneous decisions? The agent, equipped with preferences $\rho(x)$ induced by basket x, may decide to switch to basket y, considering this an improvement. In a formula: $y(>;\rho(x))x$. However, once arrived at y, he/she may find out that this movement was a mistake. This then would mean that we now have $x(>;\rho(y))y$. In other words: erroneous moves contradict adaptiveness of preferences. Real life is full of erroneous decisions. Is it then worth pursuing a welfare economics of adaptive preferences? From the point of view of scientific investigation the answer is clear: erroneous decisions come from an incomplete ex-ante view of the new basket y. The "real" y is different from the imagined y. Therefore erroneous decisions do not falsify the hypothesis of adaptive preferences. From the liberty-induced "veil of ignorance" point of view, the "imagined" y and the "real" y may not be distinguishable. The hypothesis of adaptive preferences from the veil of ignorance point of view then is an hypothesis about the preponderance of adaptive preferences in real life: "Most of the time, decisions to improve one's own position are not erroneous."

As this book is about adaptive preferences (in the context of a society of free people), it is convenient to describe the calculus of induced and of adaptive preferences without all the time repeating that we exclude erroneous decisions from the analysis.

To get through our research program it is not enough to rely on the assumption of adaptive preferences. Indeed, here is a very simple example, which shows that improvement sequences can be cyclic, that is, return to their origin despite adaptiveness of preferences. Let the space of commodity baskets consist of three baskets, A, B and C. The following table defines the induced preferences.

As we compare the entries within a given row (each row representing one of the three different induced preferences), we see that given preferences are "rational", that is, consistent or transitive. Thus, for example, with preferences induced by A (top row), B is preferred over A, and A is preferred over C and also B is preferred over C. This shows transitivity and thus consistency. Also, as we compare the first column with the second column, we see that preferences are adaptive. Yet we can construct an improvement sequence A,B,C,A, which is not an improvement path; that is, it is cyclic.

TABLE 7.1 Cyclic Improvement Sequences

$B(>;\rho(A))A$	$A(>;\rho(A))C$	$B(>;\rho(A))C$
$C(>;\rho(B))B$	$B(>;\rho(B))A$	$C(>;\rho(B))A$
$A(>;\rho(C))C$	$C(>;\rho(C))B$	$A(>;\rho(C))B$

References

Becker, Gary S., 1996, Accounting for Tastes, Cambridge, MA, Harvard University Press, 292 pages.

Sen, Amartya, 1977, Rational Fools: A Critique of the Behavioral Foundations of Economic Theory, Philosophy and Public Affairs, 6, 317–344.

8

THEOREM 1 FOR THE CLASSROOM MODEL

As already mentioned, the classroom model is a model with just two distinct commodities. Beyond that, we introduce three assumptions, which are the following

Assumption 1: Continuity: The space $\mathfrak{X}$ of commodity baskets consists of all strictly positive baskets $x > 0$, that is, $x = (x_1, x_2)$ with real numbers $x_1 > 0$ and $x_2 > 0$. $\mathfrak{X}$ has the Euclidean metric and the usual topology. The space $\mathcal{Q}$ of preferences has a topology, so that open sets can be defined. Preferences are continuous: if $y(>;q)x$, then there exist neighborhoods $N_1(x)$, $N_2(y)$, $N_3(q)$ such that for $w \in N_1$, $z \in N_2$, $r \in N_3$ we have $z(>;r)w$.

Assumption 2: Non-satiation: Let x and y be two baskets in $\mathfrak{X}$. Let $y_1 > x_1$ and let $y_2 > x_2$. Then for all $q \in \mathcal{Q}$, we have $y(>;q)x$.

For the third assumption I introduce the concept of indifference curves:

Definition 5: Indifference curve: Let $I(x;q) = \{y : y(=;q)x\}$. It is the indifference curve going through x with preferences q. Because of continuity and non-satiation we know the set $I(x;q)$ is a curve through the two-dimensional space $\mathfrak{X}$.

Assumption 3: Single crossing: If the indifference curve $I(y;\rho(y))$ is not identical to the indifference curve $I(x;\rho(x))$, but $y(=;\rho(x))x$, then $I(x;\rho(x)) \cap I(y;\rho(y)) = \{y\}$.

Concerning Assumption 2, non-satiation, I should remark that it is not inconsistent with a "no-growth-philosophy". One simply has to define a good called "leisure", which in the relevant range provides positive marginal utility. In a two-commodity world, we may then have the two goods "material consumption" and "leisure". The person then may have a utility function with a marginal utility of zero for

DOI: 10.4324/9781032726410-10

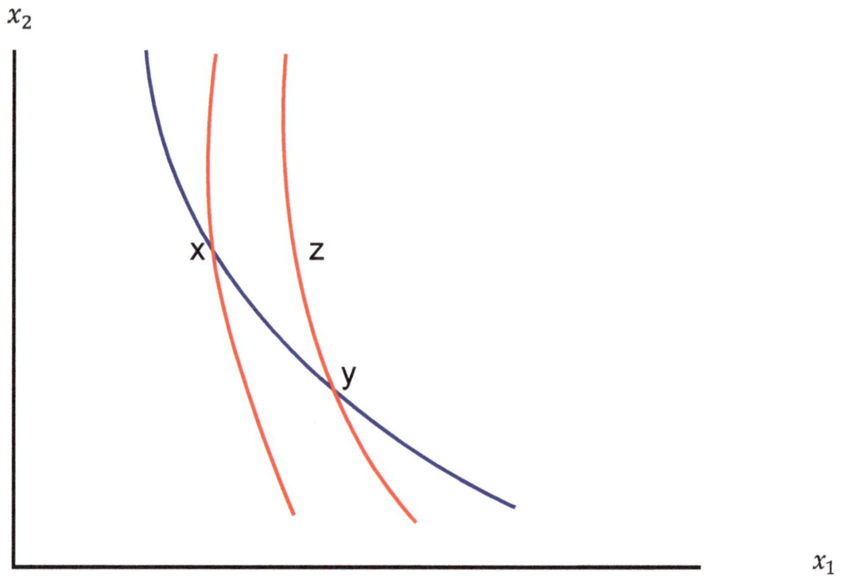

FIGURE 8.1 Indiff. Curves: Blue Induced by x. Red Induced by y

material consumption above a certain threshold value and positive marginal utility for "leisure".

One consequence of the further assumption of adaptive preferences can be easily seen. We look at the figure above. Basket y is indifferent to basket x with preferences induced by x. But, by adaptive preferences, basket y is preferred over x with preferences induced by y. As we have drawn the curves, basket y is to the "south-east" of x. Let us then look at basket z, which is on the indifference curve going through y with preferences induced by y. We give basket z a position to the "north-west" of y. It is clear from the picture that z is preferred over x with preferences induced by x and hence by adaptive preferences also preferred over x with preferences induced by z. Due to the single crossing assumption, we know that this result is correct irrespective of the precise location of z as long as it is in the red indifference curve passing through y and to the "north-west" of y.

We may consider this observation to be

Lemma II.3: Under Assumptions 1, 2 and 3 and under adaptive preferences, let $y \in I(x;\rho(x))$ be to the "south-east" of x. Let $z \in I(y;\rho(y))$ be to the "north-west" of y. Assume $I(y;\rho(y))$ to be not identical to $I(x;\rho(x))$. Then $z(>;\rho(x))x$ and $z(>;\rho(z))x$. Let $y \in I(x;\rho(x))$ be to the "north-west" of x. Let $z \in I(y;\rho(y))$ be to the "south-east" of y. Then $z(>;\rho(x))x$ and $z(>;\rho(z))x$.

(Lemma II.1 and Lemma II.2 can be found in the Annex to Book II.)

Theorem 1A: Within the classroom model, Assumptions 1, 2, 3 plus adaptive preferences imply that every improvement sequence is acyclic – and hence is an improvement path.

Sketch of Proof (the mathematical proof is in the Annex to Book II): It is a proof by induction on the length T of the improvement sequence. Due to adaptive preferences, we know that the sequence $\{x, y, x\}$ cannot be an improvement sequence. Thus, if $\{x, y, z\}$ is an improvement sequence, then $z \neq x$. Thus, we know that for $T = 2$ the theorem is true. Let us now assume that the theorem is true for improvement sequences of length $T \geq 2$. (Induction assumption.)

Now, we look at an improvement sequence $\{x^0, x^1, x^2, ..., x^{T+1},\}$ of length $T+1$. If there is some integer $k \leq T$ such that $x^k < x^{k+1}$, then, due to non-satiation, $x^{k+1}\left(>; \rho\left(x^{k-1}\right)\right)x^k$. But, by the definition of an improvement sequence, $x^k (>; \rho\left(x^{k-1}\right))x^{k-1}$, and, by transitivity, $x^{k+1}\left(>; \rho\left(x^{k-1}\right)\right)x^{k-1}$. But then we can construct the improvement sequence, which leaves out x^k. It is $\{x^0, x^1, x^2, \ldots x^{k-1}, x^{k+1}.., x^{T+1}\}$ and thus is of length T. Therefore, by the induction assumption, it is acyclic.

Therefore, if an improvement sequence of length $T+1$ were cyclic, for every x^k (with $k \leq T$), it must be the case that x^{k+1} is to the "south-east" or to the "north-west" of x^k. For each such k, first assume x^{k+1} is to the "south-east" of x^k. Then, obviously, x^{T+1} is to the "south-east" of x^0, and so the improvement sequence is acyclic. The analogous result applies to "north-west".

We then are left with improvement sequences, for which there exists $k \leq T$ where x^k is, say, to the south-east of x^{k-1}, and x^{k+1} is to the north-west of x^k. This corresponds to the situation of Lemma II.3. We then know that $x^{k+1}\left(>; \rho\left(x^{k-1}\right)\right)x^{k-1}$ and also $x^{k+1}\left(>; \rho\left(x^{k+1}\right)\right)x^{k-1}$. Again, as before, we can construct an improvement sequence of length T, which is: $\{x^0, x^1, x^2, \ldots x^{k-1}, x^{k+1}.., x^{T+1}\}$. By induction assumption, it is acyclic, and therefore $x^{T+1} \neq x^0$. Alternatively, we find x^k so that it is to the north-west of x^{k-1} and that x^{k+1} is to the south-east of x^k. By the analogous procedure we show that $x^{T+1} \neq x^0$. QED.

9

PRICES AND QUANTITIES

A Simple Example

Here I provide a simple example for the price–quantity interaction with adaptive preferences. Assume the ordinal utility function of a person to be $U = \frac{1}{1-\gamma} g x_1^{1-\gamma} + \frac{1}{1-\gamma}(1-g) x_2^{1-\gamma}$. Here, x_1 and x_2 are the quantities of the two goods consumed, $g \in (0,1)$ is a weight parameter of the two goods and $\gamma > 1$ is a substitution parameter of the two goods. $1/\gamma$ is the elasticity of substitution. The latter, then, is smaller than unity. Given the prices of the two goods, the ratio $\chi = \frac{x_1}{x_2}$ in which the goods are consumed can be computed to be $\chi = \frac{g}{1-g} \pi^{-\frac{1}{\gamma}}$ with $\pi = \frac{p_1}{p_2}$ the price ratio of the two goods. Now, I introduce the influence of past consumption on present tastes. In this simple classroom model, I can assume that the weight factor $\frac{g}{1-g}$ is influenced by ω, which is the value of χ in the preceding period. We may write $\frac{g}{1-g} = b\omega^{\mu}$, where $b > 0$ is a constant weight parameter of the two goods and μ is a parameter, which indicates the strength of the influence of past consumption on today's preferences. We assume $0 \le \mu < 1$. The case $\mu = 0$ is the case of fixed preferences. The assumption $\mu < 1$ corresponds to the property of adaptiveness of preferences. So the demand function now reads $\chi = b\omega^{\mu} \pi^{-\frac{1}{\gamma}}$.

DOI: 10.4324/9781032726410-11

There is a long-run demand function if prices remain constant. We can compute it by solving for χ under the assumption that $\omega = \chi$. From $\chi = b\omega^{\mu}\pi^{-\frac{1}{\gamma}}$ we obtain

$$\chi = \left(b^{\frac{1}{1-\mu}})(\pi^{\frac{-1}{\gamma(1-\mu)}} \right)$$

The long-run demand function is of the same type as the short-run demand function. Only the elasticity of substitution $\frac{1}{\gamma(1-\mu)}$ is larger than the short-run elasticity of substitution $\frac{1}{\gamma}$. Thus, for example, if the short-run elasticity of substitution is one half (corresponding to $\gamma = 2$) and the influence parameter μ of past consumption is equal to one half, then the long-run elasticity of substitution is equal to 1.

As is known from traditional utility theory, the long-run demand function of this specific form has the property that there exists a utility function, which would generate the long-run demand function. For $\gamma(1-\mu) \neq 1$ we can write

$$V(x) = \frac{1}{1-\gamma(1-\mu)} \left[\beta x_1^{1-\gamma(1-\mu)} + (1-\beta) x_2^{1-\gamma(1-\mu)} \right]$$

where $\beta = \dfrac{b^{\frac{1}{1-\mu}}}{1 + b^{\frac{1}{1-\mu}}}$

For $\gamma(1-\mu) = 1$ we can write $V(x) = x_1^{\beta} x_1^{1-\beta}$.

Here, I give a numerical example of an improvement sequence – generated by an initial reduction of price p_2. Throughout the improvement sequence, I assume a nominal consumption budget of 10,000 €. Initially, both prices equal 2 €. I assume $\gamma(1-\mu) = 1$, with $\gamma = 2$ and $\mu = \frac{1}{2}$. Further, I assume $b = 1$ and therefore $\beta = \frac{1}{2}$.

The short-run demand function then reads $\chi = b\omega^{\mu}\pi^{-\frac{1}{\gamma}} = \omega^{\frac{1}{2}}\pi^{-\frac{1}{2}}$. For the long-run demand function we have

$$\chi = \left(b^{\frac{1}{1-\mu}})(\pi^{\frac{-1}{\gamma(1-\mu)}} \right) = \pi^{-1} = \frac{1}{\pi}$$

The following table shows the improvement sequence generated by the reduction of price p_2 from $p_2 = 2$ to $p_2 = 1$.

TABLE 9.2 Improvement Sequence Due to Price Reduction

Period	p_1	p_2	π	χ	ω	x_1	x_2
$T=0$	2	2	1	1	1	2500	2500
$T=1$	2	1	2	0,70710678	1	2929	4142
$T=2$	2	1	2	0,59460356	0,70710678	2716	4568
$T=3$	2	1	2	0,54525387	0,59460356	2608	4784
$T=4$	2	1	2	0,52213689	0,54525387	2554	4892
$T=5$	2	1	2	0,51094857	0,52213689	2527	4946
$T=6$	2	1	2	0,50544464	0,51094857	2514	4973
$T=7$	2	1	2	0,50271495	0,50544464	2507	4987
$T=8$	2	1	2	0,50135564	0,50271495	2503	4993
$T=9$	2	1	2	0,50067736	0,50135564	2502	4997
"$T=\infty$"	2	1	2	0,5	0,5	2500	5000

A single but permanent price reduction generates an extended sequence of improvements, because preferences adapt with delay to the growing consumption of good 2 and the declining consumption of good 1. At the beginning demand for good 1 increases, because the income effect on x_1 of the reduction of p_2 is stronger than the substitution effect. But, due to the gradual adaptation of preferences to the declining proportion of good 1 consumption relative to good 2 consumption, the substitution effect gets stronger, thereby gradually reducing the demand for good 1. Due to the long-run elasticity of substitution of unity, in the end the substitution effect and the income effect of the lower price for good 2 cancel each other for good 1, whereas, of course, the income and substitution effects work in the same direction for good 2. In the long run its consumption doubles due to the halved price.

Depending on the choice of parameters μ and γ we can, of course, develop numerical examples of long-run demand with income effect stronger or weaker than the substitution effect. However, it is always the case that adaptive preferences make the long-run substitution effect larger than the short-run effect.

Why is the consumption sequence an improvement sequence? The price reduction at the beginning obviously implies an improved budget with given preferences. Thus, the consumption basket in period $T=1$ is better than the consumption basket in period $T=0$. The fact that in every period, the consumption basket changes "reveals" improvement (in the sense of revealed preference theory), because the budget situation did not change and therefore the person could have consumed the preceding basket.

10

THE "MEANING" OF THE LONG-RUN DEMAND FUNCTION

Theorem 2A

The simple example of the preceding chapter may suggest an intuition for the following observation, which provides an economic "meaning" of the long-run demand function. Here we walk in the footsteps of revealed preference theory, as developed by Samuelson 1938 and Houthakker 1950. Under the weak (for the two goods case) and the strong (for the case with more than two goods) axioms of revealed preference theory, an economist can obtain the preferences of the consumer from her/his demand behavior. However, if in a preference system there is two-sided interaction between preferences and actual consumption, what does the long-run demand function reveal? It cannot be the actual preferences, even if the long-run demand function satisfies the pertinent axioms of revealed preference.

The answer comes from improvement sequences generated by an "improving" price change and by a series of consecutive "improving" price changes. Assume that the long-run demand function $H(p)$ conforms to the weak axiom of revealed preference. We then have an ordinal utility function $V(x)$, which corresponds to that demand function.

First, we observe that due to the assumptions of Theorem 1A, every improvement sequence is acyclic. For any given initial consumption basket x, let $A(x)$ be the set of baskets y such that y can be reached by a finite improvement sequence from x with initial preferences induced by x. I call the set $A(x)$ the "improvement set" of x. Because of Theorem 1A we know that x is not contained in $A(x)$. However, due to non-satiation and continuity of preferences, any neighborhood $N(x)$ of x contains elements of $A(x)$. Due to continuity and non-satiation, $A(x)$ is an open set: for any $y \in A(x)$ there exists $N(y)$ such that $N(y) \complement A(x)$. We may then define $B(x)$ as the "south-western" border of $A(x)$. Let $N(y)$ be any neighborhood of basket y. In a formula we then write

$$B(x) = \{y : B(x) \cap A(x) = \emptyset; \textit{for any}\, N(y) \exists z \in N(y) s.t. z \in A(x)\}$$

DOI: 10.4324/9781032726410-12

We then know that $x \in B(x)$.

$B(x)$ is a curve in the two-dimensional commodity space $\mathcal{X}$: for, due to non-satiation, $B(x)$ does not have an interior in the usual topology of the space.

We now look at the long-run demand function $H(p)$. For any given x we look at the indifference curve of $H(p)$ containing x. We denote it by $\hat{I}(x)$. I show that $\hat{I}(x)$ is the same as $B(x)$.

Let $p^0 = H^{-1}(x)$, that is, it is the price vector, which generates long-run demand x. Let us remember that it also is the price vector, which generates $x = h\left(p^0; \rho(x)\right)$, that is, demand under the price vector p^0 and the preferences induced by x itself.

Next I replace p^0 by p^1. The new price vector fulfills the condition

$$p^1 x = p^0 x$$

We write $\Delta p_1 = p_1^1 - p_1^0$ and $\Delta p_2 = p_2^1 - p_2^0$. The equation above then reads

$$x_1 \Delta p_1 + x_2 \Delta p_2 = 0$$

or

$$\Delta p_2 = -\frac{x_1}{x_2} \Delta p_1$$

In words: the price vector p^1 generates a new budget constraint which has the same value at the consumption basket x. If p^1 is different from p^0, it is an improvement, because x could still be implemented. There is an income effect and a substitution effect of this price change. We can specify them in the following way.

Income effect: Let Δx_1 and Δx_2 be the change in consumption of the two goods upon the price change Δp_1 and Δp_2. Let $\Delta Y = p_1^0 \Delta x_1 + p_2^0 \Delta x_2$ be the income effect. In terms of the preferences $\rho(x)$ induced by the original consumption basket x, it is positive if the new consumption basket is different from the original one, because otherwise the consumption basket would not have changed. (This corresponds to the weak axiom of revealed preference, because it is equivalent to the condition $\Delta p_1 \Delta x_1 + \Delta p_2 \Delta x_2 < 0$.)

I then define the substitution effect S as

$$S = -p_1^0 \Delta x_1 + p_2^0 \Delta x_2$$

Given this definition, S is positive if Δp_1 is positive, and thus $\Delta p_2 = -\frac{x_1}{x_2} \Delta p_1$ is negative. S is negative if Δp_1 is negative, and thus $\Delta p_2 = -\frac{x_1}{x_2} \Delta p_1$ is positive. We note that ΔY is positive whenever Δp_1 is different from zero. ΔY being a differentiable function of Δp_1 and being zero at $\Delta p_1 = 0$, we conclude that its derivative at $\Delta p_1 = 0$ also must be zero. On the other hand, S is a rising function of Δp_1, and thus, its derivative at $\Delta p_1 = 0$ also must be positive.

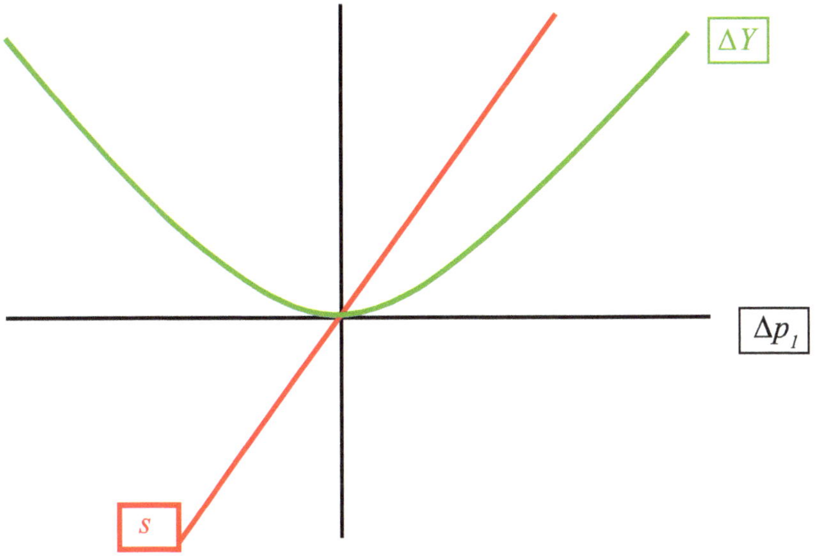

FIGURE 10.1 Income (ΔY) and Substitution (S) Effect Due to a Price Change Δp_1 and Corresponding $\Delta p_2 = -\Delta p_1 (x_1 / x_2)$

Figure 10.1 gives a schematic picture about this analysis. We note in particular that the ratio between the income effect and the substitution effect approaches zero as the price change approaches zero. For "small" values of Δp_1 we may approximate the two functions by means of their first derivatives at the value $\Delta p_1 = 0$. We get

$$\Delta Y \approx 0 \Delta p_1 = 0$$

$$S \approx \frac{dS}{dp_1} \Delta p_1$$

where $\frac{dS}{dp_1} > 0$ is evaluated at $\Delta p_1 = 0$. For any $\varepsilon > 0$ we then can find some $\Delta p_1 > 0$ such that $\frac{\Delta Y}{S} < \varepsilon$ and some $\Delta p_1 < 0$ such that $\frac{\Delta Y}{-S} < \varepsilon$.

Consider now some basket y with $V(y) = V(x)$. For any given natural number T, consider a finite series of improving price vectors $p^0, p^1, p^2, \ldots. p^T$ such that $x = H(p^0)$, $x^k = H(p^k)$, $p^{k+1} x^k = p^k x^k$, but $p^{k+1} \neq p^k$, and $p^T = \lambda \bar{p}$ with $y = H(\bar{p})$. The $\lambda < 1$ must be chosen so that the conditions on the improving sequence $\{p^0, p^1, p^2, \ldots. p^T\}$ of price vectors can be met. Such $\lambda > 0$ always exists: even for $T = 1$ there exists $\lambda > 0$ so that $H(\lambda \bar{p}) > H(p^0)$. In addition, assume that

y is to the "north-west" of x and that x^{k+1} is to the "north-west" of x^k. This means that $p_1^{k+1} > p_1^k$, and correspondingly, $p_2^{k+1} < p_2^k$.

The next step: we substitute two consecutive prices for each $k = 0,1,2,\ldots T-1$ so that we now have a series of improving price vectors with the end vector $p^{2T} = \mu_2 \overline{p}$ with $\mu_2 < 1$. Note, however, we can find $\mu_2 > \lambda$, because now the ratio between income effect and substitution effect has become smaller. But the sum of the substitution effects has remained the same, because the sequence of price vectors always ends at a price vector in proportion to $\overline{p}$. Therefore, the sum of the income effects is smaller with the second improving sequence than with the first.

Indeed, if we are already at rather small values of Δp_1, we may write

$$\Delta Y = \alpha \left(\Delta p_1\right)^2 \text{ and } S = \beta \Delta p_1$$

with constants α and β. Dividing Δp_1 into two equally large parts and putting them together then leads to

$$\widehat{\Delta Y} = 2\alpha \left(\frac{\Delta p_1}{2}\right)^2 = \frac{\alpha}{2}\left(\Delta p_1\right)^2 = \frac{\Delta Y}{2} \text{ and } \hat{S} = 2\beta \frac{\Delta p_1}{2} = S$$

Thus, by doubling the number of improvement steps and thereby halving Δp_1 per step, we also halve the ratio between the income effect and the substitution effect.

By again and again doubling the number of improvement steps in this way, we thereby can obtain the result: For every $\varepsilon > 0$ there exists an improvement sequence starting at p^0 and ending at $\mu \overline{p}$ with $\mu > (1-\varepsilon)$. This implies that $y \in B(x)$ and that therefore every $\overline{y}$ with $V(\overline{y}) > V(x)$ is contained in $A(x)$.

We then can use $V(x)$ also as an "indicator function" for the existence or otherwise of an improvement sequence from x to y: if and only if $V(y) > V(x)$, there exists an improvement sequence from x to y.

Due to Theorem 1A we then conclude that the converse is also true: If $\overline{y} \in A(x)$ then $V(\overline{y}) > V(x)$. *Proof* by contradiction: if we had $V(\overline{y}) < V(x)$ then, as just derived, $x \in A(\overline{y})$. But then we could construct a cyclic improvement sequence starting at x going to $\overline{y}$ and ending at x, which under adaptive preferences is ruled out by Theorem 1A. Because $A(x)$ is an open set, we then can also rule out $V(\overline{y}) = V(x)$.

The "revealed preference" of the long-run demand function $x = H(p)$ is that its corresponding ordinal utility function $V(x)$ is an indicator function for the existence or otherwise of an improving sequence connecting any two baskets x (beginning) and y (ending).

We note that $V(y) = V(x)$ implies $A(y) = A(x)$. But the number of necessary improving steps to the same $z \in A(x)$, and thus $z \in A(y)$ can be quite different. If, for example, z lies slightly above x in both components, a single improving step from x to z is possible. On the other hand, it may require a large number of small improving steps from y to z, because with preferences induced by y we are likely to have $y(>;\rho(y))z$.

At this point we also can state the converse of Theorem 1A. It is

Theorem 2A: Assume continuity and non-satiation of all preferences in the preference space. Assume further that all improving sequences are acyclic. Then preferences are adaptive. *Proof:* We consider $y(>;\rho(x))x$ There are three possibilities: 1) $x(>;\rho(y))y$; 2) $x(=;\rho(y))y$; 3) $x(<;\rho(y))y$ 1) contradicts acyclicity of all improving sequences; in the case of 2), due to continuity and non-satiation, we can find $\varepsilon > 0$ so that $y-\varepsilon(>;\rho(x))x$ and $x(>;\rho(y-\varepsilon))y-\varepsilon$, which again contradicts acyclicity of all improving sequences. So we are left with 3) $x(<;\rho(y))y$, which is consistent with adaptive preferences. QED.

The "meaning" of the long-run demand function then is also that the property of adaptive preferences and the property of acyclicity of all improving sequences are equivalent.

There is a corollary from Theorems 1A and 2A, which serves a useful purpose for generalizing Theorems 1 and 2 to the model with n distinct goods, a topic we treat in Book III.

First I introduce a definition

Definition 4 ½: Consider a sequence of baskets $\{x^0,x^1,\dots x^T\}$ such that $\{x^0,x^1,\dots x^{T-1}\}$ are contained in $B(x^0)$. Moreover $x^T(>;\rho(x^{T-1}))x^{T-1}$. Such a sequence we call a *semi-improving sequence.*

We then can derive the following

Corollary Chapter 10: Let $\{x^0,x^1,\dots x^T\}$ be a semi-improving sequence of baskets. Then $x^T \neq x^0$. *Proof:* We simply have to evaluate the function $V(x)$: we have $V(x^t)=V(x^0)$ for $t\in\{0;1;\dots T-1\}$ and $V(x^T)>V(x^{T-1})=V(x^0)$, which implies $x^T \neq x^0$. QED.

References

Houthakker, Hendrick, 1950, Revealed Preference and the Utility Function, Economica, 17 (66), 159–174.

Samuelson, Paul A., 1938, A Note on the Pure Theory of Consumer's Behavior, Economica, 5, 61–71.

11

KALDOR–HICKS–SCITOVSKY WITH ADAPTIVE PREFERENCES

An important part of welfare economics is connected to the proposition that a higher real income generates welfare gains. This is the Kaldor–Hicks–Scitovsky (KHS) theory: Kaldor 1939, Hicks 1939, Scitovsky 1941. What about this proposition, if we look at an economy with people who have adaptive preferences? In this chapter, I show that we can maintain this proposition. Of course, I am aware of the critique against the KHS theory. I come back to this in Book V, Chapter 29. In addition, in the next chapter I go beyond the KHS criterion.

Consider an economy with m agents $i = 1, 2, \ldots. m$. Initially total consumption of good 1 is x_1 and total consumption of good 2 is x_2. Prices are p_1 and p_2. Nominal national income is equal to unity, so that we have $p_1 x_1 + p_2 x_2 = 1$. Now things change and citizens experience new consumption baskets, so that total consumption is $\hat{x}_1$ for good 1 and $\hat{x}_2$ for good 2. Correspondingly prices now are $\hat{p}_1$ and $\hat{p}_2$, again with the equation $\hat{p}_1 \hat{x}_1 + \hat{p}_2 \hat{x}_2 = 1$. Let us assume that preferences of the citizens are adapted to the original situation so that preferences of citizen i are $q_i = \rho\left(x^i\right)$, where x^i is the original consumption vector of citizen i.

We now make the KHS assumption that real national income has gone up so that we have the two inequalities

$$p_1 x_1 + p_2 x_2 < p_1 \hat{x}_1 + p_2 \hat{x}_2 \tag{1}$$

$$\hat{p}_1 x_1 + \hat{p}_2 x_2 < \hat{p}_1 \hat{x}_1 + \hat{p}_2 \hat{x}_2 \tag{2}$$

Inequality (1) is the Kaldor-Hicks part of the theory, and inequality (2) is the Scitovsky part. Should basket $\hat{x}$ be larger than the original basket x in both components it is clear that for any positive price vector $\vec{p}$ we have the corresponding inequality $\vec{p}\left(\hat{x} - x\right) > 0$. So, I now turn to the more interesting case:

DOI: 10.4324/9781032726410-13

Let $\hat{x}_1 < x_1$ and $\hat{x}_2 > x_2$. Let $\hat{p}_1 > p_1$ and $\hat{p}_2 < p_2$.

I first look at an hypothetical price vector $\tilde{p}$ such that

$$\tilde{p}_1\hat{x}_1 + \tilde{p}_2\hat{x}_2 = \hat{p}_1\hat{x}_1 + \hat{p}_2\hat{x}_2$$

and

$$\tilde{p}_1 x_1 + \tilde{p}_2 x_2 \geq \tilde{p}_1\hat{x}_1 + \tilde{p}_2\hat{x}_2$$

From inequalities (1), (2), and $\hat{x}_1 < x_1$, $\hat{x}_2 > x_2$ we then obtain the inequalities

$$\tilde{p}_1 > \hat{p}_1 > p_1 \text{ and } \tilde{p}_2 < \hat{p}_2 < p_2 \tag{3}$$

Now I turn to the change in preferences, due to the movement from the original vector x to the new vector $\hat{x}$. Faced with the new price vector $\hat{p}$ with a higher price for good 1 and a lower price for good 2, substitution occurs in the direction of more consumption of good 2 and less consumption of good 1. But because of adaptive preferences the corresponding price changes imply further substitution in the same direction, so that with price vector $\hat{p}$ and the new preferences an "overshooting" of the movement of the consumption baskets occurs, that is, away from x and beyond $\hat{p}$. Thus, to avoid this overshooting due to the preference change, the prices $\bar{p}_1$ and $\bar{p}_2$ corresponding to the goods vector $\hat{x}$ with the new preferences $s = \rho\left(\hat{x}\right)$ must be closer to the original prices p than are the prices $\hat{p}$. That is: we obtain the inequalities

$$\hat{p}_1 \geq \bar{p}_1 \geq p_1 \text{ and } \hat{p}_2 \leq \bar{p}_2 \leq p_2 \tag{4}$$

But inequalities (3) and (4) together show that the condition

$$\bar{p}_1 x_1 + \bar{p}_2 x_2 < \bar{p}_1\hat{x}_1 + \bar{p}_2\hat{x}_2$$

is fulfilled, so that the KHS theory carries over to adaptive preferences.

Note that the result just derived also includes the possibility that some citizens are worse off in the new situation than in the old one. For them the "overshooting" result also applies.

In the following graph we depict the logic of our analysis.

As we see, by the Kaldor–Hicks assumption (equation (1)), $\hat{x}$ lies above the budget line with price vector p going through x. By the Scitovsky assumption (equation (2)), x is below the budget line with price vector $\hat{p}$ going through $\hat{x}$. Corresponding to the changed preferences, the red budget line with price vector $\bar{p}$ going through $\hat{x}$ has a smaller slope than the black budget line. Therefore, a fortiori, it is above the basket x.

Let us note that the budget line going through x also corresponds to the price ratio π of the inverted long-run demand function $p = H^{-1}\left(x\right)$. Moreover, the red

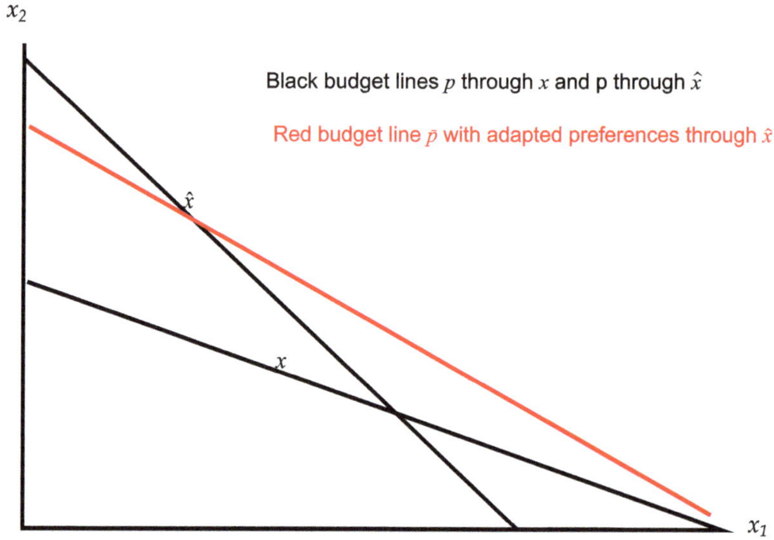

FIGURE 11.1 KHS Theory With Adaptive Preferences

budget line going through $\hat{x}$ corresponds to the price ratio $\bar{\pi}$ of the inverted long-run demand function $p = H^{-1}\left(\hat{x}\right)$. Because of $x_1 > \hat{x}_1$ and $\hat{x}_2 > x_2$ we also conclude $\bar{\pi} > \pi$. So, $\bar{\pi}$ is bracketed by π and $\widehat{\pi}$.

References

Hicks, John, 1939, The Foundations of Welfare Economics, The Economic Journal, 49 (196), 696–712.

Kaldor, Nicholas, 1939, Welfare Propositions of Economics and Interpersonal Comparisons of Utility, The Economic Journal, 49 (195), 549–552.

Scitovsky, Tibor, 1941, A Note on Welfare Propositions in Economics, Review of Economic Studies, 9 (1), 77–88.

12

SOCIAL WELFARE FUNCTION WITH ADAPTIVE PREFERENCES

Atkinson 1970 and Mirrlees 1971 have formalized Society's "preferences" for equality by means of a welfare function of the following form

$$W^*(\boldsymbol{Y}) = \sum_{i=1}^{m} W(Y^i)$$

Y^i = real annual income of citizen i, $\boldsymbol{Y} = Y^1, Y^2, \ldots\ldots. Y^m$ the corresponding real income vector, and W a concave function, rising with Y^i. As long, as real income Y^i can be measured unambiguously, the test about progress is easy in theory. If society has the choice between an existing real income vector $\boldsymbol{Y}$ and an alternative real income vector $\widehat{\boldsymbol{Y}}$ then it chooses the one with a higher value for W^*. As long as the function W^* is not affected by a change in individual preferences, upon switching from $\boldsymbol{Y}$ to $\widehat{\boldsymbol{Y}}$ there is no problem arising out of adaptive preferences.

A problem may arise from the possibility that a *project* undertaken to leave the status quo $\boldsymbol{Y}$ may be associated with uncertainty about where this project may lead the economy; in other words: uncertainty about the effective value of $\widehat{\boldsymbol{Y}}$. But this uncertainty arises even in a world with fixed preferences. Society has to cope with this uncertainty anyway. It could only be that endogenously changing preferences enhance the degree of uncertainty about this outcome $\widehat{\boldsymbol{Y}}$. This uncertainty issue leads us into deep theoretical water. We take it up later in Book IV, Chapter 21.

Here, in the classroom model I discuss the issue about the concept of real income. This issue already was at the very center of the Scitovsky critique of the Kaldor–Hicks theory. If this concept of real income is a substantial problem, we are back at the Scitovsky amendment. It is the issue of relative prices, changing endogenously as the economy changes. We know from the index number problem that it is quantitatively important, if you look at long-term changes of the economy.

DOI: 10.4324/9781032726410-14

(This is the issue of the impossibility of measuring the long-run rate of growth of an economy. It is not a topic for this book.)

So, we are back at Kaldor–Hicks–Scitovsky. As I have shown in the preceding Chapter 11, adaptive preferences do not add additional problems here. Then, we are also in the position to claim that adaptive preferences do not raise additional problems concerning the welfare function W^*. Indeed, if the price ratio between good 1 and good 2 changes due to a movement from vector x to vector $\hat{x}$ then we should test whether W^* rises in terms of the prices p, in terms of the prices $\hat{p}$ and in terms of $\bar{p}$. I now introduce the formalism for dealing with the three price vectors p, $\hat{p}$ and $\bar{p}$. It is convenient to work with the price ratio. Let $\pi = \dfrac{p_1}{p_2}$ and define $\hat{\pi}$ and $\bar{\pi}$ analogously.

In position "zero/zero" with consumption vector x and price vector p, let real income of citizen i be defined by $Y_i^0 = \dfrac{p_1 x_1^i + p_2 x_2^i}{p_1 x_1 + p_2 x_2} = \dfrac{\pi x_1^i + x_2^i}{\pi x_1 + x_2}$. Note that the sum of individual incomes equals unity.

In position "zero/one" with consumption vector x and price vector $\hat{p}$, let real income of citizen i be defined by $Y_i^1 = \dfrac{\hat{p}_1 x_1^i + \hat{p}_2 x_2^i}{\hat{p}_1 x_1 + \hat{p}_2 x_2} = \dfrac{\hat{\pi} x_1^i + x_2^i}{\hat{\pi} x_1 + x_2}$. Again, note that the sum of individual incomes equals unity.

In position "zero/two" with consumption vector x and price vector $\bar{p}$, let real income of citizen i be defined by $Y_i^2 = \dfrac{\bar{p}_1 x_1^i + \bar{p}_2 x_2^i}{\bar{p}_1 x_1 + \bar{p}_2 x_2} = \dfrac{\bar{\pi} x_1^i + x_2^i}{\bar{\pi} x_1 + x_2}$. Again, note that the sum of individual incomes equals unity.

In position "one/zero" with consumption vector $\hat{x}$ and price vector p, let real income of citizen i be defined by $\hat{Y}_i^0 = \dfrac{p_1 \hat{x}_1^i + p_2 \hat{x}_2^i}{p_1 x_1 + p_2 x_2} = \dfrac{\pi \hat{x}_1^i + \hat{x}_2^i}{\pi x_1 + x_2}$.

In position "one/one" with consumption vector $\hat{x}$ and price vector $\hat{p}$, let real income of citizen i be defined by $\hat{Y}_i^1 = \dfrac{\hat{p}_1 \hat{x}_1^i + \hat{p}_2 \hat{x}_2^i}{\hat{p}_1 x_1 + \hat{p}_2 x_2} = \dfrac{\hat{\pi} \hat{x}_1^i + \hat{x}_2^i}{\hat{\pi} x_1 + x_2}$.

In position "one/two" with consumption vector $\hat{x}$ and price vector $\bar{p}$, let real income of citizen i be defined by $\hat{Y}_i^2 = \dfrac{\bar{p}_1 \hat{x}_1^i + \bar{p}_2 \hat{x}_2^i}{\bar{p}_1 x_1 + \bar{p}_2 x_2} = \dfrac{\bar{\pi} \hat{x}_1^i + \hat{x}_2^i}{\bar{\pi} x_1 + x_2}$.

Depending on the price vector, we have three possible ratios between i's real income in state one and in state zero. They are $\hat{Y}_i^0 / Y_i^0$, $\hat{Y}_i^1 / Y_i^1$, $\hat{Y}_i^2 / Y_i^2$, respectively.

For any value of π, let $Z = \dfrac{\pi \hat{x}_1 + \hat{x}_2}{\pi x_1 + x_1}$. We then differentiate Z with respect to π

$$\frac{dZ}{d\pi} = \frac{(\pi x_1 + x_2)\hat{x}_1 - (\pi \hat{x}_1 + \hat{x}_2) x_1}{(\pi x_1 + x_2)^2} = \frac{x_2 \hat{x}_1 - \hat{x}_2 x_1}{(\pi x_1 + x_2)^2}$$

Now we know that $\hat{x}_1 < x_1$ and $\hat{x}_2 > x_2$. Therefore $\frac{dZ}{d\pi} < 0$.

Let us now remember what we have derived in the preceding chapter: The price vector $\overline{p}$ of comparison "two" tends to be "between" the two other price vectors p and $\hat{p}$. In other words: $\pi < \overline{\pi} < \hat{\pi}$. It follows

$$Z(\pi) > Z(\overline{\pi}) > Z(\hat{\pi})$$

So far, this is another way to derive what we already have derived in the preceding chapter: adaptive preferences are compatible with the KHS-calculus: If $\hat{x}$ generates a higher real national income than x with prices corresponding to x and with prices corresponding to $\hat{x}$, both with preferences induced by x, then the same is also true with prices corresponding to preferences induced by $\hat{x}$.

Using the welfare function $W^*(Y) = \sum_{i=1}^{m} W(Y^i)$ it is straightforward to give each consumer a "weight" $\beta(i)$, which, for example, is equal to the first derivative

$$\beta(i) = \frac{dW}{dY^i}$$

evaluated at Y^i. The "welfare contribution" W^i of citizen i would then look like this

$$W^i = \frac{\beta(i)Y^i}{\sum_i \beta(i)Y^i}$$

In that case the sum of all welfare contributions adds up to unity. Let us now assume that allocation $\hat{x}$ is fairly close to x. We may then approximate $\widehat{W}^i$, the welfare contribution in allocation $\hat{x}$ of consumer i, as

$$\widehat{W}^i \approx \frac{\beta(i)Y^i + \beta(i)\left(\hat{Y}^i - Y^i\right)}{\sum_i \beta(i)Y^i} = \frac{\beta(i)\hat{Y}^i}{\sum_i \beta(i)Y^i}$$

The test, whether welfare is higher at $\hat{x}$ or at x then is the sign of the expression

$$\sum_i \beta(i)\hat{Y}^i - \sum_i \beta(i)Y^i$$

In terms of the different price ratios π, $\overline{\pi}$ and $\hat{\pi}$ and their influence on the citizens' income nothing changes. Thus, if $\widehat{W}^i$ exceeds W^i at π and at $\hat{\pi}$ we then again can conclude that the same will also be the case for the intermediate case $\overline{\pi}$. The fact that these incomes have different weights in accordance with the concave welfare function $W(Y^i)$ does not invalidate the result obtained in the KHS-case.

More generally: even if $\hat{x}$ and x are too far apart for the approximation described previously, we again get the same result. This is due to the concavity of the welfare function $W^i\left(Y^i\right)$.

Due to the inequality $\pi \leq \bar{\pi} \leq \hat{\pi}$ we can find μ_i so that $0 \leq \mu_i \leq 1$ and

$$\hat{Y}_i^2 = \mu_i \hat{Y}_i^0 + \left(1-\mu_i\right)\hat{Y}_i^1$$

Because $W\left(Y_i\right)$ is concave, we then obtain

$$W\left(\hat{Y}_i^2\right) \geq \mu_i W\left(\hat{Y}_i^0\right) + \left(1-\mu_i\right)W(\hat{Y}_i^1)$$

We infer

$$W\left(\hat{Y}_i^2\right) \geq Min\left[W\left(\hat{Y}_i^0\right), W\left(\hat{Y}_i^1\right)\right]$$

and hence

$$W^*\left(\hat{\mathbf{Y}}^2\right) \geq Min\left[W^*\left(\hat{\mathbf{Y}}^0\right), W^*\left(\hat{\mathbf{Y}}^1\right)\right]$$

We thus have shown: if with initial preferences a change in allocation raises the value of the Atkinson–Mirrlees welfare function with ex ante and with ex post prices, then this change also raises that welfare function with prices corresponding to the newly induced preferences, provided preferences are adaptive.

Concluding remark concerning the classroom model. Economics is very much a science of trade-offs between two objectives, keeping other things the same. The modeling approach in this Book II then should be useful for many applications. It is therefore of interest to note that we can generalize our budget constraint, which we assumed to be a straight line from northwest to southeast. Our calculus goes through if instead we assume that the set of feasible consumption baskets is a convex set. For example, let the transformation curve between income and leisure be concave, we then can apply Theorems 1A and 2A to show that the corresponding trade-off calculus remains valid under variable preferences, provided they are adaptive.

References

Atkinson, Anthony B., 1970, On the Measurement of Inequality, Journal of Economic Theory, 2 (3), 244–263.

Mirrlees, James A., 1971, An Exploration in the Theory of Optimum Income Taxation, Review of Economic Studies, 38 (2), 175–208.

BOOK III

The Real-World Model (Continuous Time Model)

13

INTRODUCTION, THEOREM 1B FOR $n \geq 2$

The classroom model of Book II is unrealistic in two respects: 1) in the real world, but also in an Arrow–Debreu world, there are more than just two distinct goods. 2) The real world, but also models of it in science, has a continuous time flow rather than discrete time-periods. In this Book III, I transform the classroom model, step by step, into the real-world model of adaptive preferences. This transformation comes with some mathematical effort.

The first step is the discrete time model with n distinct commodities, where n is a positive integer. We maintain the (unrealistic) assumption that preferences in the present period are induced by the consumption basket of the preceding period.

Under certain assumptions we can show that adaptive preferences imply acyclic improvement sequences. The strategy used for the proof is to use Theorem 1A of Book II, which shows that adaptive preferences imply acyclicity in the case of $n = 2$. The assumptions we now specify serve to exploit Theorem 1A for the proof of Theorem 1B. The following definition is useful

Definition 6: A preference system $\{x;q;\dot{q}\}$ may have the *property of "two-dimensional mappings of improving sequences"*. By this I mean: if $\left\{x^0, x^1, \ldots x^T\right\}$ is an improving sequence in R^n, a two-dimensional mapping of $\left\{x^0, x^1, \ldots x^T\right\}$ is an improving sequence $\left\{x^0, z^1, z^2, \ldots . . z^S, x^T\right\}$ such that all $z^t \in R^2\left(x^0, x^T\right)$, where $R^2\left(x^0, x^T\right)$ is a two-dimensional subspace containing 0, x^0 and x^T. The number of in-between steps, S, in $R^2\left(x^0, x^T\right)$ need not coincide with the number of in-between steps of the original improving sequence.

DOI: 10.4324/9781032726410-16

To derive this property of two-dimensional mapping I replace Assumption 3 ("single crossing") of Theorem 1A by

Assumption 3e: ("e" for "extended"). Assumption 3 (single crossing) for $n=2$ applies to any two-dimensional subspace of R^n defined by the origin and any two linearly independent positive baskets x and y. Moreover, the following "triangle inequality assumption of preferences" holds: Consider any three baskets x, y, z such that they form an improving sequence, that is, $y(>;\rho(x))x$ and $z(>;\rho(y))y$. Then there exists some $\hat{y}$, which is a weighted average of x and z, such that $x, \hat{y}, z$ also form an improving sequence. In other words: there exists μ with $0<\mu<1$ such that $x, \hat{y}, z$ form an improving sequence with $\hat{y}=\mu x+(1-\mu)z$.

Theorem 1B: For a discrete time model with baskets in R^n and a preference system $[x;q;\dot{q}]$ defined with $q(t)=\rho(x(t-1))$ assume continuity (Assumption 1), non-satiation (Assumption 2), Assumption 3e, and adaptive preferences. Then any improvement sequence (Definition 4) $\left(x^0;x^1;x^2;\ldots\ldots x^T\right)$ of finite length is acyclic.

Proof: First Step. We define $R^2\left(x^0;x^T\right)$ as the two-dimensional subspace spanned by the origin and the two baskets x^0 and x^T. If the two baskets x^0 and x^T are not linearly independent, take any two-dimensional subspace which contains the two baskets. For each basket $y \in R^n$ we denote the Euclidean distance $d(y)$ of y from $R^2\left(x^0;x^T\right)$. We then start with the original improvement sequence $\left(x^0;x^1;x^2;\ldots\ldots x^T\right)$ and the corresponding vector of distances $\left(d\left(x^0\right);d\left(x^1\right);d\left(x^2\right);\ldots\ldots d\left(x^T\right)\right)$. Obviously $d\left(x^0\right)=0$ and $d\left(x^T\right)=0$. Now we form a sequence of improving sequences with gradually declining distances. Let s be the running number of the sequence of improving sequences: $S(0);S(1);\ldots\ldots S(s)\ldots\ldots$ Let $S(0)$ be the original improving sequence: $S(0)=\left(x^0;x^1;x^2;\ldots\ldots x^T\right)$. For $S(s)=(y^0(s);y^1(s);\ldots\ldots y^T(s))$, let $t(s)$ be the index of element $y^\tau(s)$ of the sequence $S(s)$, which maximizes $d\left(y^\tau\right)$ for $\tau \in (0;1;\ldots\ldots T)$. If there are more than one τ which maximize $d\left(y^\tau\right)$, then choose the largest maximizing τ. For $S(s+1)=y^0(s+1);\ y^1(s+1);\ldots\ldots y^T(s+1))$, we then define $y^{t(s)}(s+1)=\mu y^{t(s)-1}(s)+(1-\mu)y^{t(s)+1}(s)$, where μ with $0<\mu<1$ is chosen so that $y^{t(s)-1}(s);\ y^{t(s)}(s);y^{t(s)+1}(s)$ form an improving sequence. By Assumption 3e, such a μ is always available. Except for $\tau=t(s)$, we define $y^\tau(s+1)=y^\tau(s)$. We then observe that $d\left(y^{t(s)}(s+1)\right)<d(y^{t(s)}(s))$. This is so, because $d(y^{t(s)}(s)) \geq d(y^{t(s)-1}(s))$ and $d(y^{t(s)}(s))>d(y^{t(s)+1}(s))$. For any $\tau \in (0;1;\ldots\ldots T)$, we then know that $d\left(y^\tau(0)\right);d\left(y^\tau(1)\right);\ldots d\left(y^\tau(s)\right);\ldots.$ is a weakly declining sequence, which remains non-negative. It has a convergence point $c(\tau) \geq 0$. It is obvious that $c(\tau) \leq c(\tau-1)$ and $c(\tau) \leq c(\tau+1)$. But, because of $c(0)=0$ and $c(T)=0$, we can infer by induction on τ that $c(\tau)=0$.

Obviously, we can form a compact subset of R^n, which contains the sequence $\{y^\tau(0); y^\tau(1);....y^\tau(s).....\}$. It follows that for each $\tau \in (0;1;......T)$ there exists an accumulation point. That accumulation point $z(\tau)$ is contained in $R^2(x^0;x^T)$, because $c(\tau)=0$. By construction of $R^2(x^0;x^T)$ and the sequences $S(s)$, we have $z(0)=x^0$ and $z(T)=x^T$.

Second Step: There is an indicator function $V(.)$ for the space $R^2(x^0;x^T)$, as it was defined in Book II for the model with $n = 2$. This follows from Assumption 3e. Now we can show the following inequality: for each $\tau \in (0;1;......T-1)$, we have $V(z(\tau+1)) \geq V(z(\tau))$. *Proof by contradiction:* Because $z(\tau)$ is an accumulation point of the sequence $\{y^\tau(0); y^\tau(1);....y^\tau(s).....\}$ and because $y^{\tau+1}(s)(>;\rho(y^\tau(s))y^\tau(s)$, continuity of preferences implies $z(\tau+1)(\geq;z(\tau))z(\tau)$. Assume the contrary; then $z(\tau)(>;\rho(z(\tau)))z(\tau+1)$. But then, by continuity, there are neighborhoods $N(z(\tau)), N(z(\tau+1)$ and $N(\rho(z(\tau)))$ such that for $a \in N(z(\tau))$, $b \in N(z(\tau+1))$ and $h \in N(\rho(z(\tau)))$, we have $a(>;h)b$. On the other hand, $z(\tau)$ being an accumulation point of the sequence $\{y^\tau(0); y^\tau(1);....y^\tau(s).....\}$, $z(\tau+1)$ being an accumulation point of the sequence $\{y^{\tau+1}(0); y^{\tau+1}(1);....y^{\tau+1}(s).....\}$ and $\rho(z(\tau))$ being an accumulation point of $\{\rho(y^\tau(0)); \rho(y^\tau(1));....\rho(y^\tau(s)).....\}$, we know that these neighborhoods contain relations $b(\geq;h)a$, thereby generating a contradiction. Therefore $z(\tau+1)(\geq;z(\tau))z(\tau)$. But then, by the definition of the indicator function $V(.)$, we also have $V(z(\tau+1)) \geq V(z(\tau))$.

From this follows $V(z(T)) \geq V(z(0))$, and therefore $V(x^T) \geq V(x^0)$.

Final Step: Concerning $z(T)=x^T$, we have two possible cases.

Case 1: $V(z(T)) > V(z(0))$. It is then obvious that $z(T) \neq z(0)$ and thus $x^T \neq x^0$.

Case 2: $V(z(T)) = V(z(0))$. Here we replace x^T by some $\hat{x}$ with the following properties: 1) $\hat{x}(>;\rho(x^{T-1}))x^{T-1}$ and 2) $x^T(>;\rho(\hat{x}))\hat{x}$. Due to continuity of preferences, such an $\hat{x}$ exists. For example, using non-satiation, some $\hat{x} < x^T$, but close enough to x^T, fulfills both conditions. Now we apply the same sequencing procedure as before to generate accumulation points in $R^2(x^0;\hat{x})$. I now proceed with a *proof by contradiction.* Assume $x^T = x^0$. Then x^0 and x^T are not linearly independent. We then can define $R^2(x^0;\hat{x})$, which also contains $x^T = x^0$. Now note that because of the inequality $V(z(\tau+1)) \geq V(z(\tau))$ and $V(\hat{x}) = V(x^0)$, we have $V\left(z(\tau)\right)=V\left(z(0)\right)$ for all $\tau \in \left(0;1;......T-1\right)$. We then have a semi-improving sequence, as defined in Book II, Chapter 10. (Definition 4 ½).) We apply Corollary 10 from Book II, Chapter 10. So we get $x^T \neq x^0$, in contradiction to the assumption $x^T = x^0$. This proves Theorem 1B. QED.

A further discussion of Assumption 3e follows. With the three assumptions and adaptive preferences, we have a set of sufficient conditions for acyclicity of improvement sequences. Although I consider Assumption 3e highly plausible, I admit the possibility of other sets of sufficient conditions for acyclicity, which are just as plausible. One potential candidate is an analogy with technical progress. We could re-interpret adaptive preferences in the following way: Assume fixed preferences and look at the net social product of an economy. We may then replace the individual utility function by a net social product function. Without loss of generality, the given utility function can be written as a function with constant returns to scale. Consider an improvement of our present set-up a step of technical progress. Then, the ensuing change of preferences in our present set-up could be seen as a change in the optimal skill composition of agents induced by the new technology. Adaptive preferences in our present set-up may then be considered adaptive skills of the workforce. The a-cyclicity then would mean that the gain due to a first step of technical progress cannot be undone by further technical progress. I did not pursue this idea further.

14

THEOREM 2B FOR $n>2$

Theorem 2 generally is the converse of Theorem 1: Given continuity of preferences and non-satiation, general acyclicity of improving sequences implies adaptiveness of preferences. We have shown this in Book II for $n=2$ (Theorem 2A). In this case I can simply copy the statement and proof of Theorem 2A in order to get

Theorem 2B: Assume continuity and non-satiation of all preferences in the preference space. Assume further that all improving sequences are acyclic. Then preferences are adaptive. *Proof:* We consider $y(>;\rho(x))x$. There are three possibilities: 1) $x(>;\rho(y))y$; 2) $x(=;\rho(y))y$; 3) $x(<;\rho(y))y$. 1) contradicts acyclicity of all improving sequences; in case of 2), due to continuity and non-satiation, we can find $\varepsilon>0$ so that $y-\varepsilon(>;\rho(x))x$ and $x(>;\rho(y-\varepsilon))y-\varepsilon$, which again contradicts acyclicity of all improving sequences. So we are left with 3) $x(<;\rho(y))y$, which is consistent with adaptive preferences. QED.

An essential building block for welfare economics under adaptive preferences is the fact that acyclicity of improving sequences allows us to find "quasi-preferences" $V(x)$ which are exogenous. The function $V(x)$ does not depend on past consumption. These "quasi-preferences" are an indicator for answering the question whether some basket y can be reached from some other basket x by means of an improving sequence or not. I therefore also call it an "*indicator function*" for the existence of improving sequences: If and only if $V(y)>V(x)$ is there an improving sequence from x to y.

The ordinal indicator function or "quasi-utility function" $V(x)$ formally then looks like an ordinal exogenously given utility function, even though its precise economic meaning is different. But it also has one property in common with the

DOI: 10.4324/9781032726410-17

homo economicus model, which makes it so important for welfare economics: it links up with the person's demand behavior. Here it is "long-run demand", by which I mean the demand function, which provides the limit demand as a function of a budget that remains constant over time. It is not the demand function for given preferences q, which we call the "short-run demand function". Rather, it is the demand function, which encompasses the change in preferences induced by the budget constraint. In the tradition of revealed preference theory, we are then able to read preferences from demand behavior; only these are the fixed "quasi-preferences" $V(x)$ rather than the endogenously determined actual preferences.

I need the assumption that "long-run demand" for any given budget constraint converges to a unique point, which is independent of initial preferences $q(0)$. Throughout I assume the budget to be unity (I therefore ignore issues related to money illusion). Demand then is restricted to the inequality $px \leq 1$. Here $p \geq 0$ is the prevailing price vector. For given preferences q we then have a demand function $x = h(p;q)$. Keeping prices constant through time, we may get convergence of demand. Limit demand must have the following property

$$x = h(p;\rho(x)) = H(p)$$

For any given budget p, the demand basket must converge to a particular basket x, which also has the property that it is the "short-run demand" under the preferences induced by itself.

What are the properties of the long-run demand function? Under which conditions does it satisfy Houthakker's strong axiom of revealed preference (Houthakker 1950) and thus can be seen as the expression of an underlying utility function? The answer is given by

Corollary 2B: Under Assumption I (continuity) and Assumption II (non-satiation), assume further that all improving sequences are acyclic and that there exists a long-run demand function $x = h(p;\rho(x)) = H(p)$, which is independent of initial preferences $q(0)$. Then the long-run demand function satisfies the strong axiom of revealed preference. Thus, there exists an ordinal quasi-utility function $V(x)$ underlying the long-run demand function. Moreover this underlying quasi-utility function is continuous and has the following property: If and only if $V(y) > V(x)$, there exists an improving sequence starting at x with initial preferences $\rho(x)$ and ending at y.

An earlier version of Corollary 2B (for $n = 2$) was published in von Weizsäcker (1971). A theorem which has some similarity with Corollary 2B has been published by Munro and Sugden (2003). If I am not mistaken, Corollary 2B is more general than the Munro–Sugden theorem. The set-up of the two models and the methods of proof are quite different.

Proof of Corollary 2B: The main idea of the proof is the reference to the Samuelson–Houthakker theorem of revealed preference. This works by means of the following:

Revealed Preference Lemma of Induced Preferences: If in a sequence of baskets $\{x^0, x^1, \ldots . x^T\}$, each basket (except x^0) is revealed preferred to its preceding basket under the long-run demand function, then there exists an improving sequence from x^0 to x^T.

The proof of the Lemma is in the Mathematical Appendix of this Book III. For the case $n = 2$, I have implicitly shown the Lemma in Book II, Chapter 10.

Since, by assumption, all improving sequences are acyclic, by the Revealed Preference Lemma of Induced Preferences, all revealed preference sequences are acyclic under the long-run demand function. Therefore the strong axiom of revealed preference is fulfilled for $x = H(p)$, and we have an ordinal utility function $V(x)$ which corresponds to the long-run demand function $H(p)$. Moreover, it also follows from the Samuelson–Houthakker theorem (I use that theorem in the form given by Sondermann 1982: if and only if $V(y) > V(x)$, there exists a finite revealed preference sequence under $H(p)$ starting at x and ending at y. Then, again by the Revealed Preference Lemma of Induced Preferences, there exists an improving sequence from x to y. On the other hand, it is then obvious that for $V(y) < V(x)$ there exists no improving sequence going from x to y: for otherwise we could construct an improving sequence which starts at x, touches y and comes back to x, thereby violating the assumption that all improving sequences are acyclic. Using continuity arguments, it can also be shown that $V(y) = V(x)$ makes it impossible to construct an improving sequence from x to y. QED.

Note that the indifference curve through x corresponding to the value $V(x)$ is below the indifference curve through x corresponding to preferences $\rho(x)$, because any y with $y(>;\rho(x))x$ can be reached from x by an improving sequence, and thus by the Revealed Preference Lemma of Induced Preferences has $V(y) > V(x)$. This also immediately tells us that acyclicity of improvement sequences implies adaptive preferences.

In Figure 14.1, I depict Corollary 2B. I draw three single indifference curves corresponding to preferences induced by baskets A, B, resp. C and going through A, B, resp. C. They are in red. Then I draw a system of indifference curves, in blue, which depict the "quasi-preferences" $V(x)$. Because B is on a blue indifference curve above the one through A, Corollary 2B tells us that there exists an improving sequence from A to B.

Corollary 2B also has immediate implications for price elasticity. As we know, price elasticity of demand is higher when indifference curves have less curvature. Thus, the price elasticity of demand of the long-run demand function – corresponding to the blue indifference curves – is higher than the price elasticity of demand for those given preferences, which are induced by the basket under investigation. A change in the budget constraint generates a change in preferences, so that the total or long-run effect on demand is larger than the immediate effect holding the initial preferences constant. Preference change thus is like a *reaction amplifier*. Or we may call the interaction between consumption and preferences a *positive*

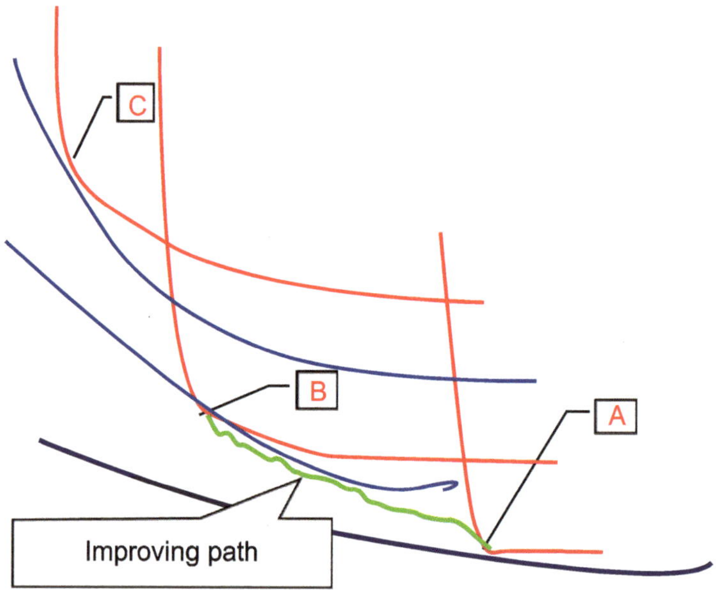

FIGURE 14.1 Short-Run Preferences, Long-Run Quasi-Preferences and Improving Paths

feedback loop, provided that preferences are adaptive. Induced preference changes thereby help the person to adapt to changes in the social or natural environment. This is a further reason I have chosen the name "adaptive preferences" for the main hypothesis of my theory. As we shall see in Book V, Chapter 22, this then also helps us to understand the "sociobiological" foundations for the empirical validity of the hypothesis.

There is the obvious symmetry of our result with the well-known fact in the theory of production: the long-run price elasticity of demand for some input is higher than the short-run elasticity of demand for the same input: the other inputs "adapt" to the new price of the input under consideration, and this adaptation takes time. In our case of flexible preferences, these preferences adapt to the new prices – and this process of adaptation takes time. We have the two ways of looking at the world: in positive economics we tend to look at the economy with "production" in our mind; thus the Stigler–Becker view and the Becker household production approach. Everything is production. Everything is "causation". In normative economics, with the aim to understand the idea of "freedom", we tend to look at almost everything as if it were derived from "tastes", from preferences. Almost everything is legitimized by "freedom". However, it is the same world: and therefore both views must have the same result concerning the quantitative difference between short-run demand and long-run demand.

References

Houthakker, Hendrick, 1950, Revealed Preference and the Utility Function, Economica, 17 (66), 159–174.

Munro, Alistair and Sugden, Robert, 2003, On the Theory of Reference Dependent Preferences, Journal of Economic Behavior and Organization, 50 (4), 407–428.

Sondermann, Dieter, 1982, Revealed Preference: An Elementary Treatment, Econometrica, 50 (3), 777–779.

15

EQUIVALENCE THEOREM 1 (THEOREM 1C)

I show an additional version of Theorem 1. This is Theorem 1C. It sheds additional light on the – as yet not fully known – set of sufficient conditions for Theorem 1–type theorems.

I repeat

Definition 6: A preference system $\{x;q;\dot{q}\}$ may have the *property of "two-dimensional mappings of improving sequences"*. By this I mean: if $\{x^0,x^1,\ldots x^T\}$ is an improving sequence in R^n, a two-dimensional mapping of $\{x^0,x^1,\ldots x^T\}$ is an improving sequence $\{x^0,z^1,z^2,\ldots..z^S,x^T\}$ such that all $z^t \in R^2\left(x^0,x^T\right)$, where $R^2\left(x^0,x^T\right)$ is a two-dimensional subspace containing 0, x^0 and x^T. The number of in-between steps, S, in $R^2\left(x^0,x^T\right)$ need not coincide with the number of in-between steps of the original improving sequence.

Theorem 1C: Assume the discrete time model with $n \geq 2$. Assumptions 1 (continuity) and 2 (non-satiation) hold. Assume further the existence of a long-run demand function $x = h\left(p;\rho\left(x\right)\right) = H\left(p\right)$. Assume adaptive preferences.

Part A: For a given preference system $\left[x,q,\dot{q}\right]$, assume that every improvement sequence has a "two-dimensional mapping". Then every improvement sequence is acyclic.

Part B: Assume that every improvement sequence of a given preference system $\left[x,q,\dot{q}\right]$ is acyclic. Then every improvement sequence of that preference system has a "two-dimensional mapping".

DOI: 10.4324/9781032726410-18

The proof of Part A is part of the proof of Theorem 1B. There we show acyclicity of improvement sequences by first deriving the existence of a two-dimensional mapping for each improvement sequence, using Assumption 3e. From this mapping we derive acyclicity, using Corollary II.5.

For the proof of Part B, I use Corollary 2B, which yields a quasi-utility function $V(x)$ as an indicator function for the existence of improvement sequences. Then we can restrict the function $V(x)$ to the subspace $R^2(x^0, x^T)$ where it serves the same indicator function for the existence of improving sequences. Thus $V(x^T) > V(x^0)$ also indicates the existence of an improving sequence in $R^2(x^0, x^T)$.

Theorem 1C indicates that any set of sufficient conditions for acyclicity of improvement sequences involve the existence of a two-dimensional mapping of the improvement sequences.

16

THEOREM 2 FOR THE CONTINUOUS TIME MODEL (REAL-WORLD MODEL)

I now define and discuss improvement sequences in a model of continuous time. By switching from a discrete time model to a continuous time model, we lose the (unrealistic) convenience that it is simply the basket of the preceding period, which induces the preferences of the present period. Now the actual preferences are induced by a flow of preceding consumption baskets. This not only changes the mathematics of the model. It also changes the meaning of improving sequences. As we shall see in detail in Book VI (on the feasibility of partial equilibrium cost benefit analysis when preferences are adaptive), the continuous time model combines the "intertemporal" nature of improving sequences with the "decentralized, but simultaneous" nature of improving sequences – and thus it lays the foundation for a welfare economics of adaptive preferences in market economies. Here, in the present Chapter 16, we prepare this transformation by admitting an intertemporal overlap of parallel sequences of improving steps. In market economies, there is a multitude of contemporaneous improvement projects.

By introducing continuous time, we not only admit that present preferences are influenced by a stream of preceding consumption baskets; we also observe that any given consumption basket implemented at some time point influences a stream of future preferences.

The preference dynamics then may be given by the vector differential equation

$$\dot{q} \equiv \frac{dq}{dt} = f\left(x;q\right)$$

We assume that $f\left(x;q\right)$ has all the properties required to make the differential equation integrable. As an example of the real-world model, assume that the mapping $\rho\left(x\right)$ of induced preferences can be inverted. Then we can write $x = \rho^{-1}\left(q\right)$.

DOI: 10.4324/9781032726410-19

We then assume a "law of motion" of preferences, such that for $z = \rho^{-1}(q)$ we have a linear vector differential equation $\frac{dz}{dt} \equiv \dot{z} = \alpha(x - z)$, which by integration leads to the equation $z(t) = e^{-\alpha t}\left(z(0) + \alpha \int_0^t e^{\alpha\tau} x(\tau)\, d\tau\right)$, with α an n times n positive definite matrix. $x(t)$ is the flow of the actual consumption basket; $z = \rho^{-1}(q)$ represents the preferences by means of a mapping from preference space to commodity space. If x remains constant through time, $z(t)$ converges to x, hence preferences q converge towards $\rho(x)$. We discussed this already in Book II, Chapter 6.

Coming back to the general case, it is useful to introduce an ordinal utility function representing the preferences involved in the analysis. Thus, $U(x;q)$ is a real-valued one-dimensional function continuous in x which represents the preferences q. Because preferences are continuous, we know that such $U(x;q)$ exists (Debreu 1959, p. 56). As before, we then also assume $U(x;q)$ to be continuous with respect to x and q in the topologies assumed to exist in commodity space and in preference space.

We now look at a path through time of the consumption basket $x(t)$. According to the differential equation above, for any given initial preferences $q(0)$, we have a movement of preferences $q(t)$, which of course depends on $x(t)$.

Consider now a movement of x through time from time zero to some finite time $T > 0$. We restrict ourselves to movements $x(t), 0 \le t \le T$, such that $x(t)$ is piecewise differentiable with K "jump points" with $K \ge 0$ a finite integer. Let $J = \{t_1, t_2, \ldots, t_K\}$ be the set of jump points. We then assume that $x(t_i)$ is the limit point of $x(t)$ as $t > t_i$ approaches t_i from above. With these restrictions we consider any path $x(t)$. Due to this restriction of piecewise differentiability (and hence piecewise continuity), and for a given $q(0)$, preferences $q(t)$ are well defined by means of the integrable differential equation $\dot{q} = f(x;q)$.

We then can describe the path by $\{x(t);q(0);T\}$.

We introduce the following definition:

Definition 7: For a given movement $x(t)$ a point in time t is an *improvement point* if for $q(t)$ there exists $\varepsilon > 0$ such that for $t - \Delta t > t - \varepsilon$ and $\Delta t > 0$, we have $U(x(t - \Delta t);q(t)) < U(x(\mathrm{t});\ q(t))$; moreover, if $x(t)$ is differentiable at t, we have $\frac{\partial U}{\partial x}\dot{x} > 0$. A point in time t is a *weakly improving point* if for $q(t)$ there exists $\varepsilon > 0$ such that for $t - \Delta t > t - \varepsilon$ and $\Delta t > 0$, we have $U(x(t - \Delta t);q(t)) \le U(x(\mathrm{t});q(t))$.

Note that in this definition of an improvement point we evaluate a consumption basket $x(\tau)$ with preferences $q(t)$ prevailing at a time t different from τ.

Definition 8: A path $\{x(t);q(0);T\}$ is a *weakly improving sequence* if $q(0) = \rho(x(0))$ and if every t is a weakly improving point for $0 \le t \le T$. A path

$\{x(t);q(0);T\}$ is an *improving sequence* if it is a weakly improving sequence and if $T = t_K$ is a jump point with $U(x(T);q(T)) > \lim_{t \to T} U(x(t);q(T))$.

Concerning this definition of improving sequences, note the following: 1) With $q(0) = \rho(\bar{x})$, a stationary path $x(t) = \bar{x}$ is a weakly improving sequence with $K = 0$. 2) The definition of improvement points only involves utility comparisons with identical preferences. Thus, we are in a purely ordinal environment. For the utility function $U(x(t);q(t))$ at time t (if $x(t)$ is differentiable at t), we note that $\frac{\partial U}{\partial x}\dot{x} > 0$ if t is an improving point. If $x(t)$ is the result of utility maximization against a budget constraint, defined by price vector p, we know that $\frac{\partial U}{\partial x} = \lambda p$ for some real number $\lambda > 0$. Thus, $p\dot{x} > 0$, which means we see a rise in real income if we are at an improvement point. We therefore can understand a weakly improving sequence as a path in which any change in real income is always upwards and never downwards. A weakly improving sequence which has strictly improving jump points or time intervals with strictly improving real income improvements could reasonably be seen as an improving sequence in the strict sense. For mathematical reasons I have defined an improving sequence somewhat more restrictively: by requiring a strictly positive utility jump at the very end. Proofs of the theorems are then much easier. But I do not think this to be a big problem, because the final jump in real income can be arbitrarily small, as long as it is positive. For any basket y which can be reached from an initial basket x by means of an "improving sequence", reasonably defined, we can find $\hat{y}$ arbitrarily close to y such that $\hat{y}$ can be reached by a sequence which I define as a strictly improving sequence. This property depends on the assumptions of continuity and non-satiation of preferences.

We now use the results from the discrete time model to derive results for the continuous time model. We first introduce the following

Definition 9: For a given preference system $\{x;q;\dot{q}\}$ in continuous time, we define the *corresponding* discrete time preference system $[x;q;\dot{q}]$ as that discrete time model which exhibits the same induced preference mapping $\rho(x)$.

We then show the following

Correspondence Lemma: Assume all improvement sequences of a continuous time preference system $\{x;q;\dot{q}\}$ are acyclic. Assume that there is a long-run demand function $x = h(p;\rho(x)) = H(p)$ for the corresponding discrete time model. For any basket x^0, let $A(x^0)$ be the set of baskets that can be reached from x^0 by means of an improvement sequence in the continuous time model. For any basket x^0, let $\hat{A}(x^0)$ be the set of baskets that can be reached from x^0 by means of an improvement sequence in the corresponding discrete time model. Then, $A(x^0) = \hat{A}(x^0)$.

The proof is in the Mathematical Annex of Book III.

Theorem 2D: Assume the "real-world model" with a given preference system $\{x, q, \dot{q}\}$. We then assume further: 1) Preferences are continuous. 2) There exists a long-run demand function $x = h(p; \rho(x)) = H(p)$ 3) Improvement sequences are acyclic. Then there exists a continuous quasi-utility function $V(x)$ with the following properties: If and only if $V(x^1) > V(x^0)$, there exists an improving sequence beginning at x^0 and ending in finite time at x^1. Thus, preferences are adaptive.

An earlier version of Theorem 2D is contained in my Thünen Lecture (von Weizsäcker 2002).

Proof: Note first that the long-run demand function is the same as the one for the corresponding discrete time model, since it only depends on the mapping $\rho(x)$. Then, by the Correspondence Lemma, the quasi-utility function $V(x)$ derived for the discrete time model from Corollary 2B is also an indicator function for the sets $A(x^0)$. As in the case of Theorem 2B, from this follows that preferences are adaptive. QED.

References

Debreu, Gerard, 1959, Theory of Value – An Axiomatic Analysis of Economic Equilibrium, New York, Yale University Press.

Von Weizsäcker, Carl Christian, 2002, Welfare Economics Bei Endogenen Präferenzen – Thünen-Vorlesung 2001, Perspektiven der Wirtschaftspolitik, 3 (4), 425–446.

17

THEOREM 1 FOR THE REAL-WORLD MODEL

For the "real-world model", we have inverted the sequence in which we prove Theorems 1 and 2. In the discrete time model, we first have obtained sufficient conditions for Theorem 1: adaptive preferences imply acyclicity of improving sequences. Then, with the same proof as in the classroom model, we show Theorem 2B. Together with the assumption that there exists a long-run demand function $x = H(p)$ and the assumption that all improving sequences are acyclic, we obtain the "exogenous" quasi-utility function $V(x)$ as an indicator function for the existence of improvement sequences (Corollary 2B). We then use Corollary 2B for the discrete time model to derive the corresponding Theorem 2 for the real-world model. The next task is to derive a Theorem 1 for the continuous time real-world model.

For the real-world model, I have so far not succeeded in showing that sufficient conditions for acyclicity of improving sequences are the same as in the discrete time model. The Correspondence Lemma only tells us that if all improving sequences are acyclic, then the quasi-utility function $V(x)$ serves as the same indicator function for improving sequences in the real-world model and in the corresponding discrete time model. However, with the additional assumption of "smoothly adaptive preferences", we can show that sufficient conditions for acyclicity of improving sequences in the discrete time model also imply acyclicity of improving sequences in the real-world model. The assumption of smoothly adaptive preferences is highly plausible.

I first define "smoothly adaptive preferences" for a cardinal utility function. Then I show that we can define a utility function which looks like a cardinal utility function but which has a completely ordinal meaning.

Definition 10: In the "real-world model", for a given preference system $\{x; q; \dot{q}\}$, assume that there exists an indicator function $V(x)$ for the corresponding

DOI: 10.4324/9781032726410-20

discrete time model for the existence of improving sequences. Thus, in the corresponding discrete time model, improving sequences are acyclic. Assume the existence of a cardinal utility function $U(x;q)$ with the following properties: 1) $U(x;q) \leq V(x)$ for all q; 2) $U(x;\rho(x)) = V(x)$; 3) $\frac{\partial U}{\partial q}\dot{q} = \frac{\partial U}{\partial q} f(x;q) \geq 0$. Then we say that preferences are *smoothly adaptive*.

I explain the economic meaning of smoothly adaptive preferences: Consider U some kind of "happiness" index. Then, for a given basket x, the person's well-being is highest with preferences induced by x, that is, with preferences $\rho(x)$. This then leads to equation 2 and inequality 1 in the definition of smoothly adaptive preferences. Condition 3 then only adds that what prevails globally (for constant x preferences converge to those which maximize utility) also prevails locally: the time derivative of utility for constant x is non-negative.

We then can show

Theorem 1D: For a real-world model preference system $\{x;q;\dot{q}\}$, assume that in the corresponding discrete time model improvement sequences are acyclic and that there exists an indicator function $V(x)$ for improving sequences of the discrete time model. Assume for the real-world model that preferences are smoothly adaptive. Then improving sequences are acyclic in the real-world model.

Proof: By the definition of an improving sequence we have $\frac{\partial U}{\partial x}\dot{x} \geq 0$ wherever $x(t)$ is differentiable. Where there is a jump point of $x(t)$ utility jumps upward. Because of smoothly adaptive preferences, we thus have $\dot{U} = \frac{\partial U}{\partial x}\dot{x} + \frac{\partial U}{\partial q}\dot{q} \geq 0$ wherever there is differentiability, and thus U is a non-decreasing function of time. Moreover, at time T, utility makes an upward jump, because we look at an improving sequence. Thus, $U(x(T);q(T)) > U(x(0);\rho(x(0))) = V(x(0))$. On the other hand, $V(x(T)) \geq U(x(T);q(T))$ and thus $V(x(T)) > V(x(0))$, which implies $x(T) \neq x(0)$ and so proves acyclicity. QED.

Theorem 1D is of particular interest, because there is great potential for transforming purely ordinal preferences into an "as if cardinal" expression. If we can then also derive smoothly adaptive preferences, we can use Theorem 1D to show acyclicity of improving sequences in the real-world model.

As an example, we introduce the following ordinal utility function. We are in a world in which the corresponding discrete time model implies acyclicity of improving sequences. We then have from the discrete time model an indicator function $V(x)$. For any x and q, consider the indifference hyper-surface $I(x;q)$ of baskets z which are indifferent to x, given preferences q. Thus, in a formula $I(x;q) = \{z : z(=;q)x)\}$. We then define $U(x;q) = \min_{z \in I(x;q)} \{V(z)\}$. The "utility" of x, given preferences q, is the smallest value of $V(z)$ reachable within the indifference hyper-surface containing x. We assume that such minimum always exists. First, we have to show that this is a utility function which represents the preferences for any given q. For $y(>;q)x$ we know that $I(y;q)$ lies above $I(x;q)$. Therefore we also have $U(y;q) = \min_{z \in I(y;q)} \{V(z)\} > \min_{z \in I(x;q)} \{V(z)\} = U(x;q)$. This proves that $U(x;q)$ is a utility function representing preferences q.

Obviously, since $x \in I(x;q)$, we know that $U(x;q) \leq V(x)$. On the other hand, due to Theorem 2D, we know that for $z \in I(x;\rho(x))$, we have $V(z) \geq V(x)$, and therefore $U(x;\rho(x)) = V(x)$. Thus, for given x, "utility" is maximized across preferences q at the point $\rho(x)$. So the conditions 1 and 2 of smooth adaptiveness are fulfilled. Concerning condition 3 we observe the following. We look at preferences which are induced by some basket z, that is, $\rho(z)$. Note that in this case the defined $U(x;\rho(z)) = V(z)$. Normally it will be the case that the defined minimum $U(x;q) = \min_{z \in I(x;q)} \{V(z)\}$ declines as the distance between z and x rises. For $n = 2$, we then have a map of "isoquants" for $U(x;\rho(z))$, which look like a map of a single peaked mountain with the peak at $z = x$. This "Mount Utility" may be connected with a vector differential equation for the movement of preferences, which is linear in commodity space. Since for constant x, preferences converge towards $\rho(x)$, the time derivative of preferences points from z to x and thus points in the direction of rising utility. This, then, is condition 3 of smoothly adaptive preferences, which reads $\frac{\partial U}{\partial q} f(x;q) \geq 0$.

To generalize from $n = 2$ to $n \geq 2$, we may assume that in the real-world model, the preference system also has the property of "two-dimensional mappings of improving sequences"(see Definition 6). For any given improving sequence (or weakly improving sequence) $x(t)$ beginning at $x(0)$ and ending at $x(T)$, there exists an improving sequence (or weakly improving sequence) $z(t)$ beginning at $x(0)$ and ending at $x(T)$, such that for $0 \leq t \leq T$ the basket $z(t)$ is contained in a two-dimensional subspace $R^2(x(0), x(T))$ containing the beginning and the end of the improving sequence (or weakly improving sequence). We can assume this property of "two-dimensional mappings of improving sequences", because we know from Theorem 2 that it is valid whenever all improving sequences are acyclic.

We then understand that smoothly adaptive preferences are the "canonical case" of adaptive preferences, like a single-peaked mountain is the "canonical case" of a mountain. Moreover, I am convinced that further mathematical effort will enable me or somebody else to show that a condition quite similar to Assumption 3e in the discrete time model is sufficient to demonstrate that under adaptive preferences improvement sequences are acyclic.

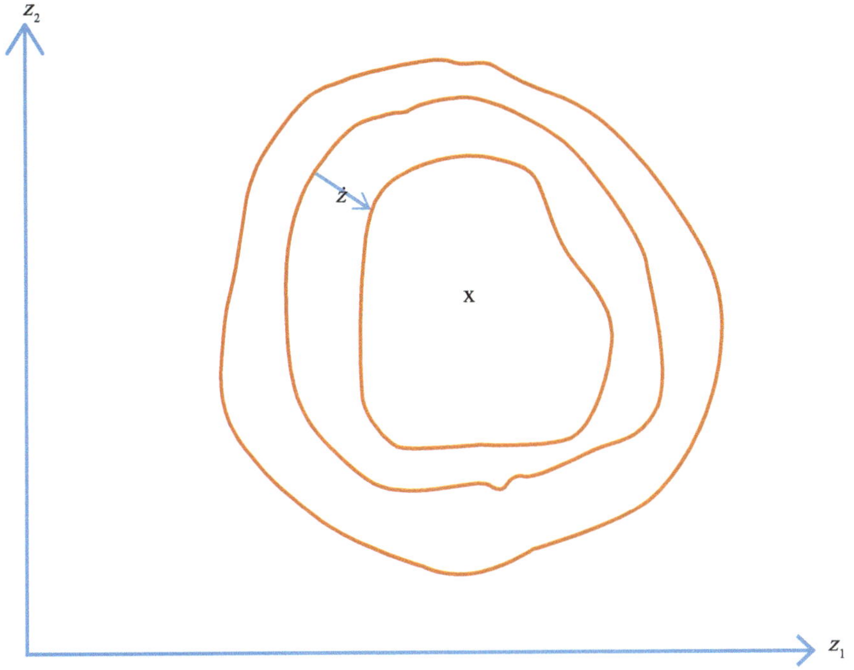

FIGURE 17.1 Smoothly Adaptive Preferences. For some given x, the indifference curves in terms of the inverted mapping $z = \rho^{-1}(q)$. Arrow indicates the movement of z through time.

Whatever the results for an "ordinal" preference theory are, the "cardinal" utility proof is a nice heuristic to understand intuitively why the theorems work. We see this in the quite simple and intuitive proof of Theorem 1D above.

The term "single peakedness" reminds us of social choice theory. If preferences of different people are single peaked along a one-dimensional curve majority voting works, despite the Arrow impossibility theorem in the more general case. It may be of interest to investigate the applicability of adaptive preferences to social choice problems, particularly by looking at interpersonal influences on preferences. The latter are the general topic of Book V below. However, there I don't address the social choice issues.

Summary of Books II and III

Here, I summarize the results of the model of adaptive preferences, which are contained in Books II and III. If preferences generally have the property of continuity, non-satiation and satisfy Assumption 3e, then adaptive preferences imply that improvement sequences are acyclic, that is, are improvement paths (Theorem 1). Moreover, if in a preference system, all improving sequences are acyclic, then there exists an indicator function $V(x)$, which looks like an ordinal utility function and which indicates which basket can be reached from which other basket by means of an improvement path. In addition, it then also follows that preferences are adaptive. (Theorem 2). Since fixed preferences are a special case of adaptive preferences, we can understand the present theory as a true generalization of traditional neoclassical preference theory. As will be seen in Book VI, we can thereby develop the foundations of a welfare economics of market economies under the assumption that preferences are adaptive. In addition, it lays the foundation for the proposition that adaptive preferences are a necessary condition for a functioning system of decentralized decision-making.

BOOK IV

Freedom and the Phenomenology of Adaptive Preferences

18

FREEDOM AND COMPOSSIBILITY

As a concept used in normative economics, "preferences" are the modeling mirror image of liberty or freedom. We describe a free society as a society in which, within certain boundaries, society legitimizes actions of its citizens simply because free citizens perform them. These actions are legitimized actions irrespective of the causes that lead up to these actions.

An example are free elections of candidates for a political office. Votes of citizens count irrespective of the reasons they voted as they did. When the votes are counted, the causal chain leading up to the voting decision is irrelevant. In order to consider such voting compatible with a truly free society, institutional arrangements are needed which grant easy and equal access to the voting box and which grant absence of outside pressure on those who have the right to vote. Secret balloting and controls over vote counting belong to the typical mode of elections in democracies. Then the election of the candidates simply is the result of the vote count. In a free society, typically there is disagreement about the causes of the election result. Nevertheless, immediately after the election, typically there is agreement on the outcome of the election.

In Book I, Chapter 3, I discussed the concept of compossibility of rights. In a free society, every citizen is constrained in his/her behavior, because without these constraints, he/she could damage the well-being of other citizens. Compossibility of rights is an architecture of rights so that actions of citizens do not destroy the legitimate use of rights by other citizens. In the social philosophy literature there is an intensive discussion about the structure of compossible rights. Compare Steiner 1977, Christmas 2019, and further contributions cited by Christmas. Here I refrain from entering into this ongoing debate. Rather I take a pragmatic approach, an economist's approach.

DOI: 10.4324/9781032726410-22

For a free society, it is obvious that citizens' behavior must be constrained so that other citizens can execute their legitimate rights. There are, however, at least two different forms of "compossibility" of rights. One form we may call "strict compossibility"; another form we may call "pragmatic compossibility". The idea is that within the realm of the individual rights, the agent is free to act as he/she pleases.

Strict compossibility, as I define it, means that the architecture of individual rights is such that, in whichever way each agent makes use of his/her freedom, these actions do not interfere negatively with the freedom of the other citizens.

Pragmatic compossibility is a weaker form of compossibility. Its definition is somewhat more complicated. But, as I shall argue, it is the form of compossibility which we reasonably can ask for. Here, even before defining it precisely, I want to point out the following: since pragmatic compossibility is a much weaker requirement than is strict compossibility, the rights that can be held by the different citizens under pragmatic compossibility can be much broader than the rights that can be granted under strict compossibility. Indeed, under strict compossibility, people would only have very few rights.

Take the use of cars with a given road infrastructure. If people who have a car can use it as they like without interfering with other people's rights, then very few people indeed could own the right to drive a car. This would be the case of strict compossibility. If the use of the roads for car drivers is subject to certain rules like obeying the commands of traffic lights, speed limits, prohibition to drive a car after having consumed alcohol and so on, many more people can use a car. Even then, there are certain negative externalities which one car driver imposes on other car drivers. If very many people drive at the same time, there will be traffic jams. Experience tells us: traffic jams are a rather regular occurrence. There may be accidents, even fatal accidents, affecting people who have obeyed all traffic rules. The actual driving rules, as experience shows, make it possible to grant driver's licenses to a large number of people, thereby enhancing rights to act legitimately within one's constraints defined by these rights. Provided we consider them satisfactory, we then see the actual rules of the road as an example of "pragmatic compossibility". It is an example for the proposition that pragmatic compossibility generates much greater freedom of action for citizens than does strict compossibility. However, it does so by accepting the fact that there *are* negative externalities suffered by any one driver from other drivers.

Traditionally, economics has made the distinction between physical and pecuniary externalities. The latter were considered immaterial concerning the goal of an efficient allocation of resources. The former were considered to be detrimental for an efficient allocation of resources. That theory was "pre-Coasian". Markets in that model operated competitively and did not generate any transaction costs. Following Coase (1960) and taking account of transaction costs, we no longer can consider the existence of physical externalities necessarily an indicator of inefficiency. On the other hand, pecuniary externalities in real life may cause inefficiencies

(Greenwalt and Stiglitz 1986). For many questions, it is then no longer adequate to draw this sharp distinction between physical and pecuniary externalities.

Before defining pragmatic compossibility, I refer to the well-known paradigm of the Walras–Arrow–Debreu general equilibrium and its property of Pareto optimality. We note that "rights" allocated to the agents in this model do not satisfy "strict compossibility". Each agent has the "right" to buy and sell as many goods as he/she wants, provided the budget constraint is satisfied. But of those different budget-wise feasible consumption baskets of any given agent, only a small subset – generally only one basket of those exhausting the budget – is "compossible" with the consumption baskets of the fellow citizens. The general compossibility of the actions of the agents in the Walras–Arrow–Debreu world is only provided for those actions of the agents which they actually choose in equilibrium, given their constraints and given their preferences. Thus, already the basic paradigm of traditional welfare economics rejects the strict compossibility criterion.

To come to the definition of pragmatic compossibility, I further observe the following property of the Walras–Arrow–Debreu general equilibrium and its associated allocation. An easy way to show this general property is to assume a pure exchange economy. For ease of presentation, I assume that for any given set of initial allocations and any given set of preferences there exists a unique Walras general equilibrium. For any given preferences, the corresponding Walras general equilibrium is Pareto-optimal. Assume now a set of preferences, called "preferences 1". The corresponding Walras equilibrium may be called "equilibrium 1". Assume further alternative preferences for citizen A, different from those she/he has in the "preferences 1" case. We then define a set of "preferences 2": here, citizen A has those alternative preferences, and all the other citizens have the same preferences as in "preferences 1". We then have a different Walras equilibrium, called "equilibrium 2". We compare the (ordinal) utilities in the two equilibria, that is, we compare the "real incomes" of the citizens. Let p^1 be the price vector prevailing in equilibrium 1. Let p^2 be the price vector prevailing in equilibrium 2. Since equilibrium prices are only defined as relative prices in a Walras equilibrium, we always can set the two equilibrium price vectors such that the equation $p^1 x = p^2 x$ is fulfilled, where x is the total consumption vector of the economy, which is the same in the two equilibria.

In terms of price vector p^2, let Δy_i be the change in real income of citizen i as the economy moves from equilibrium 1 to equilibrium 2. By this, we mean the negative of the change in income citizen i would require to keep his/her utility constant. Let $x^i(1)$ be the demand basket of citizen i in equilibrium 1. It is then clear that $\Delta y_i \geq \left(p^1 - p^2\right)x^i(1)$. For, if Δy_i were equal to $\left(p^1 - p^2\right)x^i(1)$, then, if citizen i would receive $-\Delta y_i$ as compensation for the change in prices, then he/she could buy the old consumption basket he/she consumed in equilibrium 1. The inequality $\Delta y_i \geq \left(p^1 - p^2\right)x^i(1)$ also applies to citizen A if we apply his new preferences. Let

$\Delta y = \sum_{i=1}^{m} \Delta y_i$ be the sum of real income changes for all citizens. We then obtain the inequality $\Delta y \geq \sum_{i=1}^{m} \left(p^1 - p^2\right) x^i\left(1\right) = \left(p^1 - p^2\right) x = 0$. Thus, applying "preferences 2", we see that the changeover from equilibrium 1 to equilibrium 2 raises real income of the economy in terms of prices prevailing in equilibrium 2.

Similarly, however, we show that this result also obtains if we define real income changes in terms of prices prevailing in equilibrium 1. In deriving that result, we simply have to replace the consumption basket consumed in equilibrium 1 used previously by the consumption basket consumed in equilibrium 2. Obviously, it is then also possible to show that real income rises from equilibrium 1 to equilibrium 2 in terms of any price vector $p^{\lambda} = \lambda p^1 + \left(1 - \lambda\right) p^2$, $0 \leq \lambda \leq 1$, which is a mixture of the price vectors of the two equilibria.

We then see that changes in demand of one agent due to her/his change in preferences raise real income in the economy. The loss in real income resulting for the other agents is smaller than the gain (in terms of the "new" preferences) in real income of the agent whose preferences have changed.

Within the Arrow–Debreu framework of general equilibrium, we can generalize this result to the case of production. Indeed, this follows from the fact that we can consider producing firms in this model add-ons of consumers. We may see production as "negative consumption". The shareholder of the producing firm, who is an agent with an ordinal utility function, is then an "extended" consumer with an "enriched" initial endowment where the "enrichment" consists of his proportional share of that firm. In a sense, we turn the idea of "household production" (of the positive economics approach developed by Becker) upside down by looking at production as if it were (negative) consumption.

But the generalization can also be shown directly by working through the Arrow–Debreu calculus of consumption and production. A special case, which is easily understood, is the case of a single original factor of production, which we may call labor. Moreover, we assume absence of joint production of different goods. This, then, is the "labour theory of value" economy where final consumption goods bear prices in proportion to the direct and indirect labor content of their production. Here, a change in tastes by any one consumer does not affect market prices of consumption goods. Only the quantities of the goods will change in accordance with the new preferences. People whose preferences have not changed are not affected by this change in demand. And the change in demand by the others raises their income relative to the equilibrium that prevailed before the change in tastes and demand took place.

For our aim to find a reasonable definition of "pragmatic compossibility", we now can conclude. In the paradigm of Walras equilibrium and Pareto optimality, we find that changes in the behavior of any given agent A within his/her realm of granted "rights" have an impact on other members of society that is more favorable than the negative of the gain for agent A from this change of behavior. I then use this criterion as the general criterion of "pragmatic compossibility" of rights. But pragmatic compossibility has further to be construed to be compatible with the constitutionally granted "basic rights". They are an additional barrier against interference of one citizen with another one. I then define

Definition 11: Granted the basic rights of every citizen, a sufficient condition for the rights of the citizens of a society to be *pragmatically compossible* is satisfied if the following holds. A change of behavior of any given citizen within the realm of his/her rights provides at least as great an advantage to this citizen as the negative of the byproduct of this change to his/her fellow citizens. Advantages and disadvantages are measured in terms of economic values with prevailing prices.

Note that this is a *sufficient* condition for compossibility in the pragmatic sense. We would not expect the concept of freedom (in terms of compossibility) to be completely captured by this income criterion.

To put this sufficient condition of compossibility in different words: Citizen A changes her/his choice within the realm of her/his rights. She/he does so, because her/his preferences have changed – and the new choice suits the changed preferences. The sum of side effects she/he thereby imposes on others may either be positive (in monetary terms) or, if it is negative, it is so small in absolute value that her/his own benefit from the change is larger than the absolute value of the sum of side effects on others.

We thus do not require that any change in behavior of a given person only have positive or at least non-negative effects on all other citizens. Negative effects on others of any change in behavior remain compatible within a pragmatic regime of free people, and they are justified within the realm of compossible rights if the benefits of this change of behavior outweigh the costs.

This idea of pragmatic compossibility of rights is of course related to earlier work by economists, in particular their critique of Hayek's definition of liberty as the absence of coercion (1960). One example of this critique is Stigler 1978. See also Schmidtchen 2004, where a more detailed argument is developed.

Common sense tells us that pragmatic compossibility as just defined is more in line with the common meaning of freedom than the strict compossibility criterion would be. Any society, and a free society in particular, is characterized by lots of competitive situations. This does not only hold in economic matters in the narrow sense of this word. It is a characteristic of everyday life. If John loves Mary and Robert loves Mary, we would consider it Mary's freedom to decide whether to live with John or with Robert or with neither. If she decides to live with Robert, then John suffers a setback, as compared to the situation where Mary has not yet made up her mind. This kind of "negative externality" in matters of personal life is unavoidable in a free society. Note that we discuss this matter under the assumption that you cannot simply "buy" your preferred partner by outbidding all competitors. In our western culture, for good reasons, we have certain quantifying valuation taboos. I return to this taboo issue in Chapter 27 in Book V.

In economic matters, economists and many other people consider it a good thing that suppliers compete with each other. Indeed, anti-trust law is here to promote competition. Typically, and in contradiction to the model of perfect competition, competing suppliers sell at prices which are above marginal cost of production. They make substantial efforts to sell their wares (advertising, marketing, hiring a sales force, etc.). If customer C has to make up her mind whether to buy from supplier A or from supplier B, then we are in a typical situation where the freedom of the customer to decide which supplier to prefer will end up in disappointment for that supplier who has not been chosen.

Whenever the freedom of choice of an agent involves the choice between different persons eager to be chosen, any given decision of the agent causes harm to those persons who were not chosen.

The distinction between actions that are within the boundaries of pragmatically compossible rights and actions that are not within these boundaries, then, is equivalent to the criterion of gain or loss to society at large. Thus, in contrast to economic competition, robbery is not within those boundaries. The monetary gain obtained by the robber is not larger (probably smaller) than the loss of the person being robbed; moreover, there are incremental costs of preventing being robbed, if robbery were legal. Robin Hood is a fake story. However, it may have a certain seductive appeal for people who abhor the "injustice" of this capitalist world. After all, viewed in isolation without the general equilibrium implications following from Robin Hood, such robbery may contribute to more wealth equality.

Also, unregulated monopoly does not fit the criterion of pragmatic compossibility. More on this in Book V, Chapter 28.

It is obvious to the economist that this principle of pragmatic compossibility essentially is the same as the well-known efficiency criterion by Kaldor–Hicks–Scitovsky. They apply this criterion to government legislation or executive action. Here, I apply the criterion of net gain in terms of real national income to derive a definition of pragmatic compossibility. As will be seen later, this confluence of criteria helps us to develop a foundation of welfare economics within the framework of a market economy.

An important point concerning this concept of pragmatic compossibility is that society or its appointed agents do not own a calculating machine that allows them to compute gains and losses of all kinds of actions and thereby would allow them to define rights, which are compossible. The reason I call this compossibility criterion "pragmatic" is that it is mainly by experience, as society evolves, that lawmakers obtain some reasonable but never perfect judgment about the kind of arrangements that are compossible according to this criterion of net social gain from any change in a person's behavior.

I want to emphasize that a free society is characterized by many unalienable rights, be they in the form of legally adopted human rights, be they in the form of constitutionally protected rights like the USA's "Bill of Rights" of the first ten Amendments or like the "Basic Rights" of the German Constitution. These rights serve as a protection of citizens against encroachments of their liberty by government. As such, they are important constituents of a free society. Yet they may be seen as a limitation of the principle of pragmatic compossibility, as defined here: a particular government action or law may violate one of these basic liberties and yet raise total real income in this state. Such conflict between these basic rights and the principle of pragmatic compossibility can be interpreted differently.

Either we say: pragmatic compossibility is one limit of rights of individuals, but there are others like the basic constitutional rights, which further limit one person's right to interfere with the affairs of other persons, or we say: given the complexity of social life and the inability to reach consensus about the probable effects of action by government, basic rights are a safeguard against erroneous majority beliefs about the benefits and costs of any change in law instituted by government. Thus, we can see these basic constitutional individual rights as being consistent with the principle of pragmatic compossibility – taking account of the obvious difficulty of reaching consensus about the effects of any new legislation. Both interpretations have the effect that my theory definitely is not a plea to abolish constitutionally protected individual rights against encroachments by the government.

I consider constitutionally protected individual rights a feature of a society that follows Karl Popper's incrementalism, which he calls "piecemeal engineering" (1945, Chapter 9). In an open society, we do not have a consensus about a total picture of an ideal society. According to Popper, belief in such consensus would be totalitarian and thus would be the opposite of an "open society" or a free society. The way a free society runs its common affairs is by incremental steps away from the status quo, by piecemeal engineering. Such steps may turn out to be in error and may turn out to be the opposite of improvement. Then, society must have the opportunity to reverse such incremental steps. The open society is a society guided by the principle of reversibility. Then constitutionally protected individual rights may be a safeguard against steps that violate the principle of reversibility in a profound sense.

Moreover, constitutionally protected individual rights serve an important function of stabilizing democracy. There is, as experience tells us, always the danger that the majority in power uses its power to suppress political opposition in order to maintain its dominant position. To prevent such abuse of power freedom of speech, freedom of the press and other basic rights are important. On freedom of speech, see, for example, Cooter and Gilbert 2022, pp. 243–264.

Freedom includes the right "not to cooperate". And this is a right which is fundamental. However, it may be in conflict with the income criterion for compossibility that we discussed above. Because of this conflict, I say that the income criterion is only a sufficient condition of compossibility, not a necessary one. Assume the paid work of a person – for example, a physician – generates positive externalities. Then, his/her decision to reduce or to end the supply of this work may reduce the economy's real income. Here "real income" understood to include the money equivalent of the enjoyment of more leisure. Nevertheless, our understanding of personal freedom would obviously consider it the right of the person to reduce his/her workload. Economists may argue that this inconsistency of freedom with the income criterion is due to a "false" wage system. The physician is underpaid, they could say. But this counterargument only would be valid if it were possible for everybody in the economy to obtain a monetary income that equals his/her marginal product. This may not be the case. We may be in a world in which even at a macro-level economies of scale prevail, particularly due to the production of public goods like new knowledge. It is then impossible to internalize all positive externalities – even if we were able to use non-linear pricing on a large scale. However, even without such macroeconomic economies of scale the tax system imposes a wedge between the marginal product of the person's work and his/her income after taxes. Within certain limits, the right to withdraw from the labor market should be part of the citizens' rights.

This right of non-participation may find its limits, where participation causes quite large positive externalities. Think of vaccination against a highly contagious disease.

Policy debates frequently concern distributional issues. As I have shown in Book II, Chapter 12, a welfare function taking account of income distributional issues is compatible with adaptive preferences. I return to the distributional issues in Book V, Chapter 29.

References

Christmas, Billy, 2019, A Reformulation of the Structure of a Set of Compossible Rights, Philosophical Quarterly, 69 (275), 221–234.

Coase, Ronald, 1960, The Problem of Social Cost, Journal of Law and Economics, 3, 1–44.

Cooter, Robert D. and Gilbert, Michael D., 2022, Public Law and Economics, Oxford, Oxford University Press, 581 pages.

Greenwalt, Bruce C. and Stiglitz, Joseph E., 1986, Externalities in Economies with Imperfect Information and Incomplete Markets, Quarterly Journal of Economics, 101 (2), 229–264.

Hayek, Friedrich A., 1960, The Constitution of Liberty, Chicago, IL, University of Chicago Press, 570 pages.

Popper, Karl, 1945, The Open Society and Its Enemies, Vol. 1 Plato, Vol. 2 Hegel and Marx, London, Routledge and Kegan Paul, 361 pages and 420 pages.

Schmidtchen, Dieter, 2004, Recht, Eigentum und Effizienz: Zu F.A. v. Hayeks Verfassung der Freiheit, ORDO, 55, 127–151.

Steiner, Hillel, 1977, The Structure of a Set of Compossible Rights, Journal of Philosophy, 74, 767–775.

Stigler, George J., 1978, Wealth and Possibly Liberty, The Journal of Legal Studies, 7 (2), 213–217.

19

PHENOMENOLOGY OF ADAPTIVE PREFERENCES AND PRAGMATIC COMPOSSIBILITY

As I have already written in the last chapter, a free society learns about "pragmatic compossibility" by experience. This is at the very core of the "Open Society" as presented by Karl Popper 1945. The laws and institutions providing the rights of citizens have to take account of the actual behavior of its citizens. At any given time, experience about human behavior results from observations in the past. Only by extrapolating past observed behavior into the future can society develop ideas how to improve the laws that assign pragmatically compossible rights to the citizens.

This extrapolation from the past into the future only works if human behavior is reasonably stable. This precondition of experience-based legislation requires human preferences, which are stable ("fixed preferences") or which are adaptive. As we discussed already in Book II, Chapter 6, adaptive preferences are equivalent to a certain "preference conservatism". Provided external constraints remain reasonably stable, adaptive preferences make human behavior reasonably predictable. This allows a liberal form of pragmatic compossibility.

As an example, I again take traffic rules for car driving. I discussed this example already in the preceding chapter. Here I add a discussion about the way society changes these traffic rules. These changes are experience based. Authorities and citizens observe what happens on the roads. For example, government imposes speed limits in order to reduce the number and the graveness of traffic accidents. Drivers who violate the speed limits risk fines to be paid to some government agency. If observed driver behavior gradually changes, the point may come so that the administration raises speeding fines and/or invests in equipment so that violators are caught more often. Thereby, the "price" (in terms of expected value) of transgressing speed limits goes up. The background for a changed behavior of drivers may be rising average incomes or a changed age composition of drivers or

DOI: 10.4324/9781032726410-23

a changed composition of the car types driven by the population, to mention just three causes among many more.

Other reasons for changing traffic rules may be technological advance in road construction and maintenance or in traffic control. Thereby, driver behavior may change, and government may consider it an adequate reason for a change in traffic rules.

As a rule, traffic rules change at a slow pace – frequently after long discussion in the public. Experience with present rules is the dominant argument for specific change proposals. The public implicitly assumes that observed past behavior can be extrapolated into the future. Such extrapolation is an implicit acknowledgement of adaptive preferences.

For anti-adaptive preferences, there exist mirror images of Theorem 1 and Theorem 2. These are theorems about deterioration sequences. Mathematically we can show that a sequence of baskets, which deteriorate from one to the next one is acyclic (mirror image of Theorem 1) and: if all deteriorating sequences are acyclic, then preferences are anti-adaptive (mirror image of Theorem 2). From the point of view of economic policymaking, these mirror images are useless. Nobody wants to pursue an ever-deteriorating sequence of baskets.

Extrapolating past observations into the future is an animal instinct and thus a human instinct. Even very small babies extrapolate. Adapting to other creatures' behavior is a necessity for survival. Moreover, making one's own behavior predictable raises the chance of participating in productive cooperation with others. Productive cooperation is of tantamount importance for everybody. Thus, whatever their "true" preferences are, people act as if they had adaptive preferences. From our freedom perspective we explicitly refrain from distinguishing between "true" preferences and "as if" preferences. However, even if we wanted to investigate this distinction we should refer to the instinctive basis of human behavior. Being accepted in the group, by behaving predictably, has always, even many thousand years ago, been such a great advantage for survival that making oneself predictable is deeply ingrained in human (and animal) instincts. It goes much beyond rational strategic behavior. People, including small children, want to be loved – and they adapt their behavior accordingly.

I provide a name for this partial description of human behavior. I call it the *extrapolation principle*. Human actors (leaving aside animal behavior) extrapolate observed behavior of others into the future. Moreover, due to the benefits of productive cooperation with others, human actors adapt their own behavior to make it predictable for others. This "strategic" component of behavior reinforces extrapolation of observed behavior of others. Human behavior thus consists of an extrapolation equilibrium. As seen from the pragmatic compossibility perspective of a free society, the extrapolation equilibrium is a society of people with adaptive preferences.

Only in adversarial encounters with others is predictability a disadvantage.

The general idea of pragmatic compossibility corresponds to some trade-off thinking in terms of the ideal of freedom. As many philosophers and economists have pointed out, the freedom of contract and the freedom of exchange generates cooperative activities, which enhance the well-being of the people involved. Taking this advantage of cooperation for granted, we find a trade-off between the average extent to act (i.e. the extent of the rights of the average citizen) on the one hand and the protection against disturbance generated by the actions of others, on the other hand. The following graphs may explain what I mean.

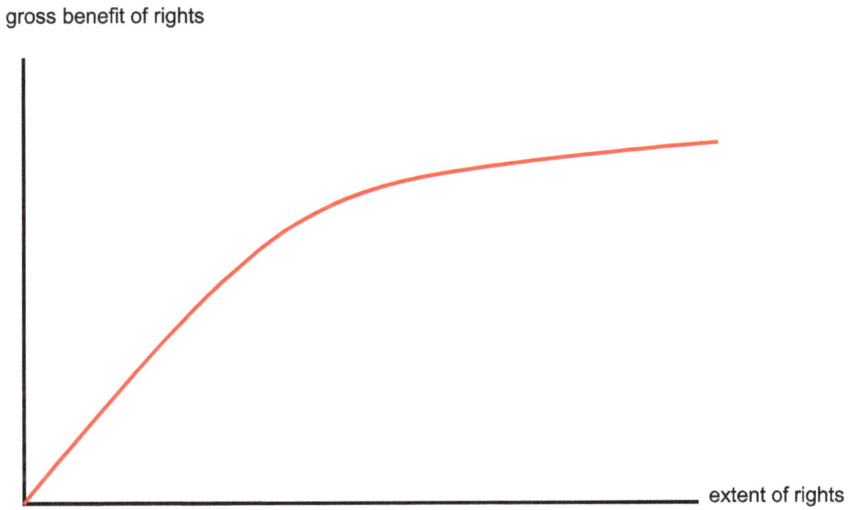

FIGURE 19.1 Gross Benefit of Rights Depending on Rights Extension

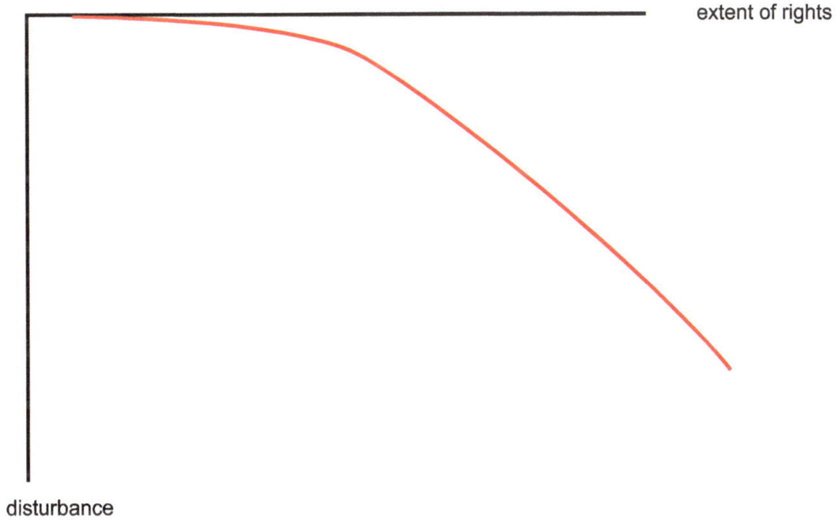

FIGURE 19.2 Disturbance Depending on Rights-Extension

Other things equal, a greater extent of a citizen's rights generates a greater benefit for this citizen. I call these benefits "gross benefits", because they tend to come with some costs, which one has to deduct before one obtains the net benefits. These "costs" arise because, by legislation or custom, a greater extent of rights of one citizen come with a greater extent of rights for other citizens. And these additional rights of other citizens raise the degree to which the actions of other citizens disturb the first citizen. So, for the first citizen we have a disturbance curve, which rises with the common extent of rights. This, then, is the second graph above.

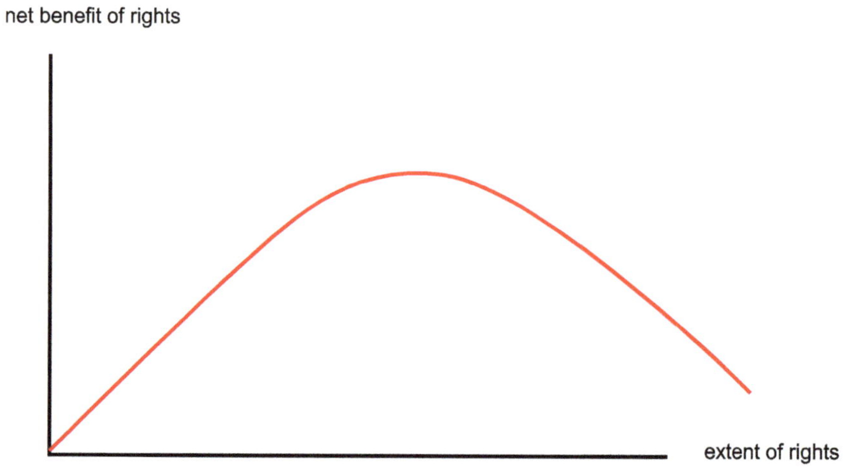

FIGURE 19.3 Net Benefit of Rights Depending on Rights Extension

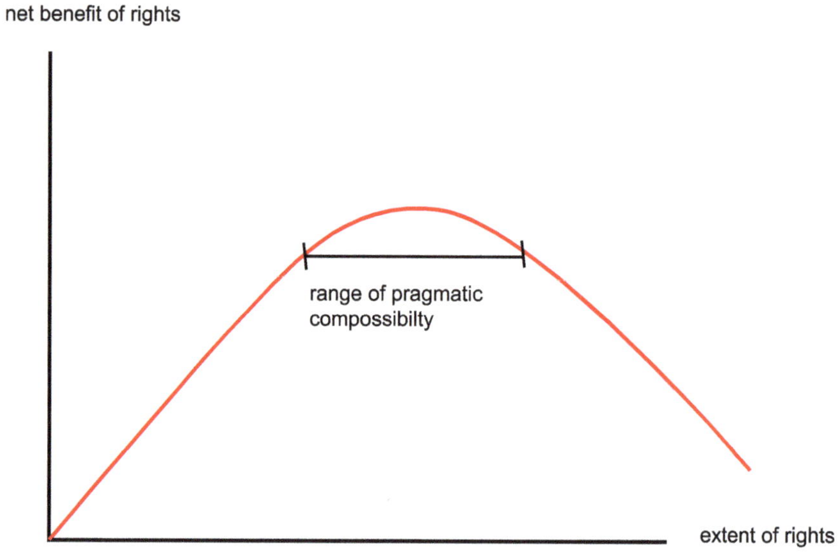

FIGURE 19.4 Net Benefit of Rights: Range of Pragmatic Compossibility

Next, we subtract the disturbance from the gross benefit and we get the net benefit as a function of the extent of rights

Now we should be aware that society and its agents responsible for the definition of rights are not wise enough to exactly find the net benefit maximizing extent of rights. On the other hand, around the "true maximum" the slope of the net benefit curve is rather small, be it positive or negative. It is then reasonable to indicate a "range of pragmatic compossibility" as an answer to our compossibility issue of civil liberty. This range develops through time thanks to the experience of people living with those rights.

As mentioned before, my concept of "freedom" corresponds to Karl Popper's "piecemeal engineering" philosophy in his book on the "Open Society". This has also been called "incrementalism": we start from a given "status quo" of society, and from there we attempt to find improvements, by, for example, changing the law or by investing in infrastructure or by introducing a new product in the market. What I add to this general idea of "piecemeal engineering" is a definition of "improvement": the attempted "breakaway" from the status quo should raise real national income, as evaluated by market prices. This concept of pragmatic compossibility makes sure that, granted fundamental rights, there remains no tradeoff between the idea of greater freedom and the idea of enhanced efficiency.

I want to add that this proposed incrementalism in defining "freedom" by "pragmatic compossibility" is in good company: as you read Amartya Sen's great book, *The Idea of Justice* (2009), you will again find this incrementalist approach.

References

Popper, Karl, 1945, The Open Society and Its Enemies, Vol. 1 Plato, Vol. 2 Hegel and Marx, London, Routledge and Kegan Paul, 361 pages and 420 pages.

Sen, Amartya, 2009, The Idea of Justice, Cambridge, MA, Belknap Press of Harvard University Press, 468 pages.

20

PHENOMENOLOGY OF ADAPTIVE PREFERENCES

Intertemporal Complementarity

In this chapter, I discuss several real-world phenomena which are examples of intertemporal complementarity of consumption baskets. This means that they correspond to the hypothesis of adaptive preferences. We thus derive these real-world phenomena from the assumption of adaptive preferences. In Chapter 21, we turn this analysis around: there we derive adaptive preferences from the real-world phenomena under investigation.

Concerning intertemporal complementarity, observe the following. If preferences are adaptive, then a higher consumption of some specific good last year raises the attractiveness of that good in the current year. So more of it will be consumed this year. It means that consumption of a specific good last year and consumption of the same good this year are complements. This is intertemporal complementarity.

1 *The appetite-satiation cycle.* Before we eat a meal, we are hungry; after the meal, we are satiated, as far as food is concerned. Then we gradually get hungry again. This cycle, which we share with almost all animals, comes about because our body uses energy continually, but opportunities for the intake of energy by nourishment are not available continually. For survival, the body just needs storage possibilities of energy. Our tastes then are geared to this fact. The hunger instinct signals the need for replenishment of the energy stock in our body and lets us intensify our search for food and our urge to eat.

   We thus observe an inter-temporal substitutability in terms of food intake. A higher level of food consumption a short while ago induces lower demand for food now. However, economists know that this observation does not contradict the traditional assumption of fixed preferences. We simply have to take the average of food consumption over a period, like a day, which is long enough to

DOI: 10.4324/9781032726410-24

include a full cycle of appetite and satiation. Between two neighboring periods of such length, the demand for food is no longer a close substitute.

Apart from purely physiological appetite-satiation cycles, there are such food-related cycles due to "taste" rather than simply hunger. A person who has one meal a day with meat or fish may want to alternate between the two. Thus, after he/she has consumed meat for a few days in a row, he/she will have a preference for fish today and vice versa. People have a preference for variety and thereby exhibit a certain degree of inter-temporal substitutability of any given kind of food: for given prices today, a lower price of meat yesterday may induce a lower demand for meat today. Or, to put it this way: meat yesterday and fish today are complements, whereas meat yesterday and meat today are substitutes.

Concerning food, adaptive preferences then show up in the phenomenon that for unit periods long enough to accommodate the preference for variety we see an inter-temporal complementarity of demand for any given kind of food. People in Argentina get used to a food mix with a substantial share of meat. Vegetarians do not eat meat at all. Children do not like to drink alcoholic beverages – and adults who never have consumed alcohol tend to dislike the taste of an alcoholic beverage. However, a person who – for whatever reason – did drink alcohol as an adolescent tends to like alcoholic beverages as an adult: habit formation. It did take the Prussian kings quite some effort to induce or force their subjects to consume potatoes. Once this was achieved, Prussian subjects, given their choice, preferred potatoes over other forms of caloric intake. Ever since Duesenberry's path-breaking book (1949), economists have been familiar with the empirically well-established phenomenon of habit formation.

The appetite-satiation cycle applies to many other goods beyond food. There is a universal taste for variety. Alfred Marshall already understood very well that this was not in contradiction to what I call adaptive preferences. Concerning the "law of diminishing marginal utility", he writes in his *Principles of Economics*:

> The marginal utility of a thing to anyone diminishes with every increase in the amount of it he already has. There is however an implicit condition in this law which should be made clear. It is that we do not suppose time to be allowed for any alteration in the character or tastes of the man himself. It is therefore no exception to the law that the more good music a man hears, the stronger is his taste for it likely to become; that avarice and ambition are often insatiable; or that the virtue of cleanliness and the vice of drunkenness alike grow on what they feed upon. For in such cases our observations range over some period of time; and the man is not the same at the beginning as at the end of it. If we take a man as he is, without allowing time for any change in his character, the marginal utility of a thing to him diminishes steadily with every increase in the supply of it.
>
> *(Marshall 1920, p. 94)*

Marshall was interested in the law of diminishing marginal utility and wanted to show that habit formation, that is, adaptive preferences, do not interfere with this law. I am interested in the hypothesis of adaptive preferences, and thus I show that the taste for variety (which corresponds in ordinal terms to the – cardinal – law of diminishing marginal utility) does not contradict the hypothesis of adaptive preferences.

2 *Random or foreseen changes in consumption constraints.* When it rains, our consumption basket is different from the one we consume when there is sunshine. Our consumption basket in winter is different from the one we demand in summer. This is, of course, no contradiction to the hypothesis of fixed preferences. What changes through time is the set of baskets we can consume. For the case of fixed preferences, all this is well understood. Given that fixed preferences are a special case of adaptive preferences, weather- or season- or age-dependent consumption baskets are no contradiction to the general hypothesis of adaptive preferences either.

Moreover, it is interesting to observe the following: Assume there are two states of the world: rain (R) and sunshine (S). We assume the "discrete time model". We keep the price vector the same across the two states of nature R and S. We designate by the real number y the budget available in state R. We designate by the real number z the budget available in state S. For simplicity of presentation, we call $[y;R]$ and $[z;S]$ a "basket", thereby ignoring the fact that with a given state R (or S) and a given budget y (or z), it takes time until the actual commodity basket converges to some basket corresponding to the preferences induced by that basket. For simplicity of presentation, I further assume that for this given price vector preferences induced by $[y;R]$ are the same for different levels of y, and, similarly, preferences induced by $[z;S]$ are the same for different levels of z. Thus, induced preferences $\rho(R)$ and $\rho(S)$ can be written without adding the budget as an argument.

Assume that in period Zero it rains; that is, the state R prevails and the person has a consumption budget of y_0. We want to construct an improving sequence. Thus, if in period 1 R prevails, the available budget must satisfy the inequality $y_1 > y_0$. If in period 1 S prevails, income must be above $\hat{z}(y_0)$, where the function $\hat{z}(y)$ is defined by $\left[\hat{z};S\right](=;\rho(R))[y;R]$. Thus, $z_1 > \hat{z}(y_0)$. Symmetrically let $\hat{y}(z)$ be defined by $\left[\hat{y};R\right](=;\rho(S))[z;S]$. Assume now that the state of period 2 is again R. For an improving path, we then have the condition $y_2 > \hat{y}(z_1) > \hat{y}(\hat{z}(y_0))$.

Assume now that we have adaptive preferences. This implies that $\left[\hat{z}(y_0);S\right](\geq;\rho(S))[y_0;R]$. Since, on the other hand $[y_2;R](>;\rho(S))\left[\hat{z}(y_0);S\right]$ we see that $y_2 > y_0$. Let $y^*(y_0)$ be the infimum value for a budget in period 2 such that it is compatible with an improving sequence, provided that the state of nature is R in periods 0, 1 and 2. Obviously we have $y^*(y_0) = y_0$. Let $y^{**}(y_0)$

be the infimum value for a budget in period 2, such that it is compatible with an improving sequence, provided the states of nature are R in period 0, S in period 1, and R in period 2. Then, due to the inequality $y_2 > y_0$ derived above for this sequence of states, we can infer $y^{**}(y_0) \geq y_0$ and thus $y^{**}(y_0) \geq y^{*}(y_0)$.

The symmetric result can be derived if we start with state of nature S.

The important point is that changing states of nature do not violate the proposition of Theorem 1B, which says that adaptive preferences imply the acyclicity of improving sequences. On the contrary, if distinct states of nature really matter for the baskets that are being bought, and if in addition preferences are not fixed but adaptive in the narrower sense of the word, which excludes fixed preferences, then continuity and non-satiation and regularity assumptions imply that improving sequences are even "more acyclic" than in the case that states of nature remain the same or are irrelevant for the basket bought with a given budget. In our example, in that case we have $y^{**}(y_0) > y^{*}(y_0)$.

It is my conjecture that this property is a general one: in a wide class of circumstances, variation in the feasibility of consumption baskets – not only variation in available budgets – maintains the conclusion of Theorem 1: adaptive preferences imply acyclicity of improving sequences.

3 *Inter-temporal allocation of consumption, that is, saving and dissaving.* The standard model of saving and dissaving assumes the existence of a life utility function, which is a weighted sum of period utilities. The problem then to be solved by the consumer is to maximize this life utility for a given inter-temporal budget constraint. In an economy in which consumers can rely on the existence of markets for all goods, they can postpone the decision which particular goods to buy in the future. Then, the relevant parameters for an optimal saving decision today are the inter-temporal prices (derived from real interest rates) and the income flows, which jointly form the inter-temporal budget constraint together with an appropriate price index of the goods available in the future.

In this model, there exists no inter-temporal complementarity of demand for any given good. If the world were like this model and thus all consumption goods could be bought – without further transaction costs – at the time they are consumed, then the computational effort to maximize the life utility would be insubstantial and thus one could realistically assume that this maximization exercise would be performed.

In real life, things are more complicated. For example, many purchases come in the form of consumer durables. Relative to buying the services of the durables every period again, transaction costs are substantially lower if one buys these durables. This then generates an inter-temporal complementarity of demand for the services of the consumer durables. If the person has consumed the services of a vacuum cleaner in the preceding period, it is much more likely that she will consume these services again in the present period than if she had not consumed the vacuum cleaner services in the last period.

This is known in economics and does not contradict the hypothesis of fixed preferences. Here we can exemplify the difference between the traditional approach and our approach encompassing the hypothesis of adaptive preferences. Gary Becker, one of the authors of the Stigler-Becker paper quoted in Book I, has pioneered the household production approach, which has been very fruitful for many theoretical and practical topics in economics; see, for example Becker 1993. Using this household production approach, one can then try to explain the inter-temporal complementarity of consumption in terms of transaction costs of market transactions. In my approach of adaptive preferences, I simply state that consumer behavior is in line with the hypothesis of adaptive preferences; that is, it exhibits inter-temporal complementarity of consumption.

We may consider this a waste of knowledge about consumer behavior. However, in normative individualism, we stick to the proposition that within a certain realm a decision or choice of an agent is legitimate simply due to the fact that it is the person's choice. It is on purpose that we look at the person with "a veil of ignorance", as was discussed in Book I. We do not have to find out why the person makes this choice rather than any other choice within his/her choice set, because the choice taken by the person is legitimate irrespective of the causes for this particular choice. Society's agent, the State, operates here in the "freedom mode".

Once we have accepted this point of view, we then are also able to accept much more easily that – in their inter-temporal allocation decisions – people do not exactly maximize a life utility function, which consists of a weighted sum of period utilities. One reason they do not act in that way is the fact that in real life the corresponding optimization calculus is much too complicated. Even with the enormous simplification of life by means of the institution of "money" and by means of the existence of a large array of reliably functioning markets, there is a large gap between the real-life situation and the previously mentioned model of a maximization of a life utility function. One reason for this gap is a kind of "self-destroying" tendency of the low transaction cost assumption behind this simple model: the easier it is to transact on goods markets in a money economy, the more such goods markets come into being. As Adam Smith told us, markets enable the social organization of the highly productive division of labor, Smith (1776), Book I, Chapters 2 and 3. Transaction costs – in terms of human time expenditure – generate a "rebound effect": the lower the costs of transacting on any given market are, the more such markets arise. Thereby, in sum, transaction costs may not decline at all through historical time for the persons benefitting from these markets. The complexity of life generated by the wealth-producing division of labor then makes it implausible for people to pursue their optimization in such a simple way as the additive period utility model of maximizing a life utility function suggests.

Taking account of this link-up with what I consider Adam Smith's most important proposition, it is then also more productive to describe human behavior in terms of endogenously changing preferences rather than in terms of fixed preferences or fixed meta-preferences. On the latter, see the important work of Gary Becker; Becker 1996, including the Becker-Murphy "theory of rational addiction".

Inter-temporal complementarity of demand for any given good then means that choice in the future is constrained by certain choices taken in the past. To the extent that these choice constraints are not imposed by society based on "compossibility" considerations, we may see them as an expression of the preferences of the citizen. Due to the inter-temporal complementarity, we then recognize them as an expression of adaptive preferences. But, apart from the "durables effect" discussed above, this inter-temporal complementarity may result from simplification strategies of the person: in order not to have to make consumption decisions anew every morning for the day the person decides to arrange his/her things in such a way that certain earlier consumption decisions are also binding for consumption baskets consumed later.

Thus, apart from hardware durables (or, indeed, software durables in the literal sense of that word – in an age of notebooks and smartphones), we also encounter many "decision durables" to reduce the amount of effort needed to make decisions. The hypothesis of adaptive preferences is supported also by the phenomenon of "decision durables" as a device to simplify one's life. I pursue this consideration in Chapter 21 under the topic of "rational inattention".

Moreover, there is the well-known fact of limited mobility of people. Generally, once a person has settled in a particular town, the probability is very high that he/she will still be living in this town ten years hence. Immobility is a great device to simplify your life! Seen from the perspective of normative individualism and adaptive preferences, it is not so important whether this resistance against changing your hometown is for emotional or for purely rational reasons.

In economics, the hypothesis of bounded rationality (Simon 1956, Gigerenzer and Selten 2001) is, of course, well accepted by now. It ties in very well with this phenomenon of inter-temporal complementarity that I subsume under the hypothesis of adaptive preferences.

4 *Information acquisition as a byproduct of consumption or by search.* Real life is characterized by incomplete information about the existence, the availability and the quality of goods and services. For decades, the economics of incomplete information has been a thriving field of inquiry. It is obvious that under conditions of incomplete information markets do not show the same efficiency performance as under perfect information and perfect competition. The classic contributions by Stigler 1961, Arrow 1963, Akerlof 1970, Stiglitz 1975, Spence 1973 and others are known by every economist.

Economists have also thought about the consequences of the fact that consumers are aware of their imperfect knowledge concerning consumption goods. One particular point, the evolution of trademarks and reputation as an asset, was emphasized by Hayek 1946 long ago. He then argued that the build-up of a reputation for good quality was an answer to the problem of incomplete information and that this build-up was a productive part of the competitive process and thus trademarks and brands should not be seen as an obstacle to competition.

Here I do not go into the details of the welfare analysis of actual and potential markets with incomplete customer information. I am interested in the relation of incomplete information to the hypothesis of adaptive preferences. First, I point to the simple fact that one way that information is gathered about products is by using them. Of those products, which the consumer considers to be satisfactory, the likelihood of repeat buys is very high. The industrial organization literature talks of "experience goods".

Some people will buy a new product introduced by a supplier into the market; others are not among the pioneer customers. If the product is satisfactory to those who have obtained it early on, they will be repeat buyers, and this then provides a positive correlation between the distributions of purchases of that product among people yesterday and today. This then is again intertemporal complementarity, that is, the phenomenology of adaptive preferences.

Moreover, psychologically, this observed inter-temporal complementarity is supported by an effect, which is well established empirically: avoidance of cognitive dissonance, Festinger 1957, Akerlof and Dickens 1982, Schlicht 1984. Once a person has decided that the product was a good buy he or she will raise his or her emotional attachment to the product. The marketing literature agrees on this point – and, of course, marketing practitioners exploit it in real life. Thus, even apart from the statistically observed inter-temporal complementarity, if you ask people about their subjective preference concerning a particular product, they will give answers which are proof of the hypothesis of adaptive preferences, here understood as an expression of customer emotions.

We then see strong support for inter-temporal complementarity of consumption from the information acquisition process going on as a by-product of consumption. This is in line with the hypothesis of adaptive preferences.

Incomplete information also stimulates search activities. Economics has investigated quite a few aspects of search. I only mention the work underlying the 2010 Nobel Prize for Peter Diamond 1984, Mortensen and Pissarides 1994. Here I am interested in the relation of search activities to the hypothesis of adaptive preferences. Search is not without cost. And search costs limit the search activities. People may want to avoid search costs by putting a (subjective) premium on those goods they know by having consumed them. This, then, is exactly in line with the hypothesis of adaptive preferences.

5 *Education and schooling.* Education and schooling are social activities organized by the grown-ups for their children. Children thereby acquire useful skills – one hopes – and, of course, thereby become –one hopes – better-informed citizens than they otherwise would be. Parents also want to influence children's attitudes and preferences. Without going into detail, I simply state that the belief of most parents in the fruitfulness of education rests on an implicit assumption

that their children have adaptive preferences. Children imitate their parents. It is therefore generally accepted that parents' own attitudes and behavior are important for the success of education. However, imitation is part of the hypothesis of adaptive preferences. More on imitation in Book V, Chapter 26. Moreover, parents generally try to induce their child to perform activities which they believe will make the child's adult life a "better life" if they continue performing those activities. By inducing (forcing?) them to play the piano as children, they expect to influence children's tastes so they will like to play the piano when grown up. Obviously, this expectation rests on the implicit assumption of adaptive preferences. If preferences were "anti-adaptive", education, as our civilization knows it, would be inconceivable. If parents had to expect that inducing children to acquire the skill of playing the piano would induce them to dislike the piano when grown up, how could they expect to succeed in their wish that the children will play and like to play the piano when grown up? Those people who, as children, did acquire the skill do not like to use it. Those people who, as children, did not acquire the skill would like to use it but cannot because they did not acquire it.

More generally: The human species is a species whose individuals live and even survive on acquired skills. That species would not exist with anti-adaptive preferences. The success of education and of training skills builds on adaptive preferences.

6 *Switching costs and the "default option"*. For individual decisions, economists and psychologists have established the quite robust fact that the "default option" has a much higher probability of being chosen as compared to a different scenario with the same choice menu but a different alternative being the default option. We can easily identify this quite general observation with our hypothesis of adaptive preferences. We only have to define the "default option" as the "basket" that is actually consumed. Moreover, as is usually the case, if the default option remains the same through time it is very likely that we observe a strong inter-temporal complementarity of choices.

Another phenomenon frequently discussed in economics is "switching costs". They were introduced into the academic literature in Von Weizsäcker 1984a. On switching costs, see the survey article by Farrell and Klemperer 2007. If a consumer has the choice between different products for fulfilling a certain task, switching from one product to another may involve "switching costs". If you move from one flat to another one, you incur moving costs. Obviously, to avoid switching costs, consumers will continue to consume the same item that they consumed before, unless a competing offer is so much superior that it is worth switching and thereby incurring the switching costs. Again, we then observe strong inter-temporal complementarity of consumption.

I put switching costs under the same heading as the "default option", because they quite naturally define a default option. It is the product consumed so far, which therefore can be further consumed without incurring switching costs.

And the other way round: deviating from the default option in a decision situation implies "psychic switching costs". Again, for the result of substantial inter-temporal complementarity, it is immaterial whether switching costs are "objective" costs (whatever that may mean) or "subjective" costs which we also may call "psychic" costs or reasons for "serendipity".

References

Akerlof, George A., 1970, The Market for Lemons: Quality Uncertainty and the Market Mechanism, Quarterly Journal of Economics, 84 (3), 488–500.
Akerlof, George A. and Dickens, William T., 1982, The Economic Consequences of Cognitive Dissonance, American Economic Review, 72 (3), 307–319.
Arrow, Kenneth J., 1963, Uncertainty and the Welfare Economics of Medical Care, American Economic Review, 53 (5), 941–973.
Becker, Gary S., 1993, A Treatise on the Family, Cambridge, MA, Harvard University Press, Paperback Edition, Xii + 424 pages.
Diamond, Peter A., 1984, Money in Search Equilibrium, Econometrica, 52 (1), 1–20.
Duesenberry, James S., 1949, Income, Saving, and the Theory of Consumer Behavior, Cambridge, MA, Harvard University Press, 128 pages.
Farrell, Joseph and Klemperer, Paul, 2007, Coordination and Lock-In: Competition with Switching Costs and Network Effects, in: Armstrong, Mark and Porter, Robert A. (eds), Handbook of Industrial Organization, Vol. 3, Amsterdam, Elsevier, pp.1967–2072.
Festinger, Leon, 1957, A Theory of Cognitive Dissonance, Stanford, CA, Stanford University Press, 291 pages.
Gigerenzer, Gerd and Selten, Reinhard (eds), 2001, Bounded Rationality – The Adaptive Toolbox, Cambridge, MA, MIT Press, XV + 377 pages.
Hayek, Friedrich A., 1946, The Meaning of Competition (Princeton Lecture 20 May 1946), in: Hayek, Friedrich A. (ed.), Individualism and Economic Order, Chicago, IL, Chicago University Press, 1948, pp.92–106.
Marshall, Alfred, 1890, Principles of Economics (1920 eighth ed.), London, Macmillan, 858 pages.
Mortensen, Dale T. and Pissarides, Christopher A., 1994, Job Creation and Job Destruction in the Theory of Unemployment, Review of Economic Studies, 61, 397–415.
Schlicht, Ekkehart, 1984, Cognitive Dissonance in Economics, in: Todt, H. (ed.), Normengeleitetes Verhalten in den Sozialwissenschaften, Berlin, Duncker & Humblot, pp.61–81.
Simon, Herbert, 1956, Rational Choice and the Structure of the Environment, Psychological Review, 63, 129–138.
Smith, Adam, 1776, Inquiry into the Nature and Causes of the Wealth of Nations, 2 volumes, London, W. Strahan and T. Cadell.
Spence, Michael, 1973, Job Market Signaling, Quarterly Journal of Economics, 87 (3), 355–374.
Stigler, George J., 1961, The Economics of Information, Journal of Political Economy, 69, 213–225.
Stiglitz, Joseph E., 1975, The Theory of Screening, Education and the Distribution of Income, American Economic Review, 65, 283–300.
von Weizsäcker, Carl Christian, 1984, The Costs of Substitution, Econometrica, 52 (5), 1085–1116.

21

DIGGING DEEPER INTO ADAPTIVE PREFERENCES

Introduction and Adaptive Preference Lemma

In Chapter 20 I discussed several selected patters of individual behavior which are the consequence of adaptive preferences and thus of intertemporal complementarity of demand for specific goods. In this Chapter 21 I show that many observed patterns of individual behavior imply that preferences are adaptive. The preceding chapter derives patterns of behavior from adaptive preferences. The present chapter derives adaptive preferences from observed patterns of individual behavior.

As we discussed in Book III, the "real-world model" is a model with continuous time. Do we take a conscious decision every moment of time? The answer clearly is "no". Without going into the psychic and physical details of decision-making, we as economists have decided that it is reasonable to stipulate the existence of a "default option": it is what happens at any given moment of time without an explicit decision taken by the agent. Assuming that we only take a finite number of explicit decisions in any given finite stretch of time, it is the case that the set of time moments without a decision has a measure (in the sense of mathematical measure theory) which equals the measure of the stretch of time we are looking at. We may write: "most of the time the default option prevails".

Let us now assume that the agent is in state $x(t)$ in time t. Moreover, preferences are $q(t)$. If t_0 is a moment of time in which the agent takes a decision, this decision may change his/her state from a time flow $x(t)$ to a time flow $y(t)$ for $t > t_0$. This then also could mean that due to endogeneity of preferences the time flow of preferences switches from $q(t)$ to some $r(t)$ for $t > t_0$. We may now stipulate the two preference inequalities

$$y(t)(>;q(t))x(t)$$

DOI: 10.4324/9781032726410-25

$$y(t)(>;r(t))x(t)$$

The agent takes the decision at time t_0, because he/she expects to be better off with this decision rather than without that decision. And this, he/she expects, to be the case also with the then-different flow of preferences. However, given the extensive treatment in Book VI on cost-benefit analysis, I here refrain from a detailed model building. The important point is the universal presence of a default option, that is, an option not to take any decision at some particular time t.

Let us then proceed to look further behind the government's "veil of ignorance", which characterizes the idea of civil liberty or freedom. As discussed in Chapters 18 and 19 of Book IV, it is only due to the principle of compossibility that the government has the duty to look at people's actual behavior. There I argue that adaptiveness of preferences is a precondition for a successful implementation of a free society. Here in Chapter 21, I further explore the causes of adaptive preferences. For this exploration, I need the observation that there always exists a default option.

To explain my narrative, take first the following analogy: If I move from point x to point y on the earth's surface, I incur an effort, a traveling effort. I may have the option not to move. Staying at x is the default option. "Choosing" the default option comes with a traveling effort of zero. The size of the traveling effort depends, say, on the distance between x and y.

Correspondingly, we may talk about a "decision effort". The default option of staying with the flow of "baskets" $x(t)$ then is the option without any "decision effort". The decision effort to leave basket flow $x(t)$ then may depend on the range Y of choices y taken into account as an alternative to the basket flow $x(t)$. The larger this range Y, the greater the "cost" of deciding about which y to choose within that range.

This phenomenon of a non-zero decision cost leads directly into the idea of adaptive preferences. Provided that I decide at time t_0 to switch from basket x to basket y, I reveal $y(t)(>;q(t))x(t)$. However, once this decision has been implemented, further decision costs are zero, as long as we stay with $y(t)$. On the other hand, moving back to $x(t)$ would again come with additional decision costs. To the extent that the preference stream $r(t)$ induced by $y(t)$ differs from $q(t)$ only by the change in decision costs, it then follows $y(t)(>;r(t))x(t)$.

Note that this is not a mathematical proof but only an intuition. For the discrete time model developed in Book III, we do obtain a mathematical proof:

Adaptive Preference Lemma: In a discrete time model, assume that preferences in period t are induced by the basket $x(t-1)$ of the preceding period $t-1$. Assume that preferences are continuous and satisfy the condition of non-satiation. Assume further that there exists a mapping $f(x:y)$ from the doubled commodity space $\mathcal{X}\, times\, \mathcal{X}$ into commodity space $\mathcal{X}$, which we may call the "friction mapping". The friction mapping has the following properties: 1 for $y \neq x$ and for components i with $y_i > 0$, we have $0 < f_i < y_i$; 2 for $y \neq x$ and for components i with $y_i = 0$, we have $f_i = 0$; for $y = x$, we have $f(x;x) = 0$. Assume now that there exists an underlying preference ordering represented by a continuous utility function $V(x)$. The preference system of induced preferences then is assumed to be the following

$y(>;\rho(x))x$ if and only if $V(y - f(x;y)) > V(x)$

$y(=;\rho(x))x$ if and only if $V(y - f(x;y)) = V(x)$

Proposition: Then the preference system exhibits adaptive preferences

Proof:

$y(>;\rho(x))x$, due to non-satiation, implies for $y \neq x$

$$V(y) > V(y - f(x;y)) > V(x) > V(x - f(y;x))$$

which means

$$y(>;\rho(y))x$$

This means that preferences are adaptive. QED.

In other words: if the inducement mapping $\rho(.)$ can simply be explained by the friction mapping together with an underlying exogenous preference ordering $V(.)$, then preferences are adaptive.

For a moment, let me exploit the name "friction function" for the mapping $f(.)$. Isaac Newton discovered the force of gravitation because he could exploit the measurements by his predecessors of friction free planetary motion. Here we have stipulated the underlying friction free preference ordering $V(.)$. On the other hand, as in Chapters 18 and 19, taking again the example of car traffic, we know that it only can work due to functioning brakes in all cars on the road. But brakes depend on physical friction. Analogously, preventing excessive variability of preferences requires adaptive preferences, which we here derive from the friction cost of changing consumption baskets.

To come back to the "real-world model" of continuous time, we should note why we cannot provide a similar Lemma of Adaptive Preferences. The reason is that neither $x(t)$ nor $q(t)$ (which is associated with $x(t)$) are constant through time. The same is the case with $y(t)$ and $r(t)$. Therefore, it is typically not the case for any given time t that $q(t)$ is induced by $x(t)$, and it is typically not the case for any given time t that $r(t)$ is induced by $y(t)$. However, if we made the additional (unrealistic) assumption that the inducement of preferences by any basket occurs without any delay, then a similar Lemma of Adaptive Preferences would hold. As we shall see in our book on cost-benefit analysis (Book VI below), we can cope with time delays of the inducement process of preferences. However, in that book, we do not derive adaptive preferences in a mathematical sense. We assume it – and then "show" indirectly that adaptive preferences prevail, because otherwise an economy with decentralized decision-making could not have worked as successfully as it actually did.

To which extent can we generalize our "Adaptive Preferences Lemma"? The remainder of this chapter is devoted to this question.

Reference Dependence: The Example of Loss Aversion and Adaptive Preferences

There is a large literature on the quite general phenomenon of reference-dependent preferences. Using our language introduced in Book I, we may say: the reference point "induces" the preferences. Moreover, the vast literature on the topic agrees that, empirically, the reference point is a strong attraction point for the choice taken by the agent. The formal model introduced below is on a particular example of reference-dependent preferences, namely "loss aversion". By this model, I show that loss aversion is an example of adaptive preferences. One could develop analogous models for other forms of reference-dependent preferences – to show that they also indicate adaptive preferences – and thereby, by our calculus in Books II and III, they have the property that every improvement sequence is acyclic. Here I only mention the following examples of reference-dependent preferences: "prospect theory" by Kahneman and Tversky 1979, "status quo bias" described by Samuelson and Zeckhauser 1988, the "endowment effect": see the survey article by Morewedge and Giblin 2015 and Fehr and Kübler 2022, reference dependence Reck and Seibold 2022, and especially in the housing market: Andersen et al. 2022.

Experimental and other empirical evidence indicates the fact that many people are loss averse. In terms of a von Neumann–Morgenstern expected utility function, loss aversion comes down to a kink in the utility function at the actually prevailing level of wealth. However, this kink is a moveable kink as the actual level of wealth changes over time. It thus changes the von Neumann–Morgenstern expected utility function. This is like a change in preferences. The prevailing wealth "induces" a particular von Neumann–Morgenstern expected utility function. We then can test whether loss aversion corresponds to the assumption of adaptive preferences.

Consider the following model. A consumer can buy a lottery ticket. He/she can choose any quantity q of that lottery ticket. The price p of the lottery ticket is exogenous. The consumer wants to maximize a von Neumann–Morgenstern expected utility function V. It is given by the formula

$$V = \int_0^\infty f(z)U(z)dz \text{ with } \int_0^\infty f(z)dz = 1$$

The function $f(z)$ is a probability-density function; $U(z)$ is a von Neumann–Morgenstern utility function, where z is the person's wealth. Provided the initial wealth is $\bar{z}$ the function V then is this

$$V = \int_0^\infty \pi(x)U[\bar{z} - pq + qx]dx$$

Here $\pi(x)$ is the probability density function of the lottery ticket. Without loss aversion, maximization of V with respect to q, by differentiation leads to the equation

$$\frac{dV}{dq} = \int_0^\infty \pi(x) U'[\bar{z} - pq + qx](x - p)\,dx = 0$$

Here $U'[z]$ is the marginal von Neumann–Morgenstern utility of wealth.

Now I look at the demand function for the lottery ticket as a function of its price. I differentiate the last expression with respect to p. We then obtain

$$\int_0^\infty \pi(x) U''[\bar{z} - pq + qx](x - p)\left(-q + (x - p)\frac{\partial q}{\partial p}\right) dx$$

$$-\int_0^\infty \pi(x) U'[\bar{z} - pq + qx]\,dx = 0$$

Remembering the distinction between income effect and substitution effect, we also can obtain an equation for the compensated demand curve. We introduce the compensation by means of changed initial wealth $\bar{z}$. Obviously, the corresponding marginal compensation must read $\frac{d\bar{z}}{dp} = q$. The previous equation then changes, because the $-q$ in the first integral drops out so that the compensated demand function reads

$$\int_0^\infty \pi(x) U''[\bar{z} - pq + qx](x - p)\left((x - p)\frac{\partial q}{\partial p}\right) dx$$

$$-\int_0^\infty \pi(x) U'[\bar{z} - pq + qx]\,dx = 0$$

This implies

$$\frac{\partial q}{\partial p} = \frac{\int_0^\infty \pi(x) U'[\bar{z} - pq + qx]\,dx}{\int_0^\infty \pi(x) U''[\bar{z} - pq + qx](x - p)^2\,dx}$$

The numerator is positive, because U' is positive. The denominator is negative, because with risk aversion U'' is negative and $(x - p)^2$ is positive, except at $x = p$, where it is zero. Thus, we know that the slope of the compensated demand curve for the risky asset is negative.

This situation is a special case of the two-commodity model discussed in Book II. The quantities of two commodities are the quantity q of the lottery ticket and "wealth minus expenses for the lottery ticket", denoted by $s = \bar{z} - pq$. The price p of the lottery ticket is the price ratio of the two-commodity model. The budget constraint is $\bar{z}$, the initial level of wealth. With fixed preferences an improvement from position 0 to position 1 simply consists of the inequality $V(position1) > V(position0)$.

Consider now the change in preferences due to loss aversion. We can define the loss aversion function in the following way

$$L(\bar{z},p,q) = \int_0^p \pi(x)\lambda[\bar{z},-pq+xq]dx \text{ for } q \geq 0 \text{ and}$$

$$L(\bar{z},p,q) = \int_p^\infty \pi(x)\lambda[\bar{z},-pq+xq]dx \text{ for } q < 0$$

Here we assume the function $\lambda[.,.]$ to be twice differentiable, with $\lambda[\bar{z},0] = 0$, $\lambda' = \frac{\partial\lambda}{\partial(-pq+qx)} > 0$ for $-pq+qx < 0$ and $\lambda'' = \frac{\partial^2\lambda}{\partial(-pq+qx)^2} < 0$. Note that $L(\bar{z},p,q) \leq 0$.

The expected utility $\hat{V}$ then is

$$\hat{V} = \int_0^\infty \pi(x)U[\bar{z} - pq + qx]dx + L(\bar{z},p,q) = V + L(\bar{z},p,q)$$

Let $\vec{V}(\bar{z},p) = \max_q \int_0^\infty \pi(x)U[\bar{z} - pq + qx]dx$ be the indirect utility function without loss aversion.

Let $\vec{\hat{V}}(\bar{z},p) = \max_q (\int_0^\infty \pi(x)U[\bar{z} - pq + qx]dx + L(\bar{z},p,q))$ be the indirect utility function with loss aversion.

We now observe that despite the "preference change" induced by a change in the initial endowment $\bar{z}$ the function $\vec{\hat{V}}(\bar{z},p)$ looks like an ordinary fixed preference indirect utility function. As opposed to the two-commodity model of Book II, I have so far assumed that there is no time delay of the inducement of new preferences: $\bar{z}$ induces simultaneously the appropriate loss aversion. To make the loss aversion compatible with the Book II model, I now introduce a one-period time delay of the change in loss aversion due to a change in the consumption basket.

Consider now two periods "zero" and "one". In period "zero", the indirect utility function is equal to

$$\vec{\hat{V}} = \vec{V}(\bar{z},p) + L(\bar{z},p) = \vec{V}(\bar{z}(0),p(0)) + L(\bar{z}(0),p(0))$$

To this allocation corresponds for the other good s a value $s(0)$

$$s(0) = \bar{z}(0) - p(0)q(0)$$

For period "one" now consider an allocation $q(1)$ and $s(1)$ such that

$$\hat{V}_1(q(1), s(1)) > \vec{V}(\bar{z}(0), p(0))$$

By forming the inverted demand function we can find the values $\bar{z}(1)$ and $p(1)$, which correspond to the given values $q(1)$ and $s(1)$. We then know that

$$\vec{V}(\bar{z}(1), p(1)) > \vec{V}(\bar{z}(0), p(0))$$

What is the economic meaning of this little exercise in inequalities? $\vec{V}(\bar{z}(0), p(0))$ and $\vec{V}(\bar{z}(1), p(1))$ are the maximum obtainable utility levels for the exogenously given values $\bar{z}(0), p(0)$, resp. $\bar{z}(1), p(1)$. We can understand the loss aversion function (i.e. the preferences) in period "zero" to be induced by the allocation $q(0), s(0)$ and the loss aversion function (i.e. the preferences) in period "one" to be induced by the allocation $q(1), s(1)$.

Let us now assume that there is a one-period delay of the inducement. We then may understand the allocation $q(1), s(1)$ to be an improvement, which came about by a better combination $\bar{z}, p$ but still with the loss-aversion function induced by $q(0), s(0)$. So it is an improvement. Yet because of the inequality $\vec{V}(\bar{z}(1), p(1)) > \vec{V}(\bar{z}(0), p(0))$, it also remains an improvement after the loss aversion function induced by the new allocation prevails. This means that the preference change in the form of loss aversion obeys the condition of adaptive preferences. It is then possible to apply our calculus derived in Book II.

We then know, by Theorem 1A that any improvement sequence under loss aversion is acyclic. Moreover, the von Neumann–Morgenstern utility function without loss aversion is the upper envelope of all von Neumann–Morgenstern utility functions with loss aversion.

Why is loss aversion so common among people? It corresponds to the "friction function" $f(.)$ discussed in the preceding section. The actual consumption basket x is geared to the agent's present wealth level $\bar{z}$. Whereas a rise in wealth does not force a change in the consumption pattern, a wealth reduction forces a rearrangement of consumption plans – and it thereby generates the need to incur decision effort. To put the same phenomenon the other way round: one of the privileges of sufficient wealth is that it enables the agent to avoid making hard decisions.

Rational Inattention

> In an information rich world, the wealth of information means a dearth of something else: a scarcity of whatever it is that information consumes. What

> information consumes is rather obvious: it consumes the attention of its recipients. Hence a wealth of information creates a poverty of attention and a need to allocate that attention efficiently among the overabundance of information sources that might consume it.
>
> (Simon 1971)

With this Herbert–Simon quotation, the authors Mackoviak et al. 2023 begin a survey article on "Rational Inattention". The basic idea of the theory of rational inattention is contained in the Simon quotation: if (non-artificial) intelligence and attention is a scarce resource, it is rational to be quite selective in taking account of available information. It was Christopher Sims who pioneered model-building for the theory of rational inattention. Using a Bayesian approach, he developed a theory of optimal choice of those information pieces which the agent uses in his/her decisions. In macroeconomics, for example, he thereby could substantially improve the explanation of the observed inertia in price movements. In this case, the default option for the price setter consists of maintaining the selling price of the recent past; Sims 1998, 2003.

As the survey article by Mackoviak et al. 2023 tells us, there is by now a vast literature on rational inattention. The idea has been applied in many areas of economics research: macroeconomics, finance, oligopolistic settings (using game theory), "thinking fast and slow" theory of behavior (Kahneman 2011), labor economics (for example, discrete choice models, McFadden 1974), trade, migration and development and political economy.

There is an obvious vicinity between our Adaptive Preference Lemma introduced above in Section 1 of this chapter and the rational inattention approach. I then hypothesize that adaptive preferences can be derived from rational inattention models. Given the vast array of rational inattention models, there should be plenty of work to check this out. However, the intuition behind this hypothesis is very straightforward: "Rational inattention" is just the shadow image of the "friction mapping" I discussed in Section 1. Avoiding friction effort by sticking to the default option, by serendipity, is simply an extreme case of rational inattention: disregarding any publicly available hunches for improvement. Generally: the optimal decision effort for leaving the default position corresponds to the optimal degree of rational inattention. On the relation between rational inattention and adaptive preferences, scc also Welsch 2005.

Thus, if we stylized the model economy by using the assumptions of the Adaptive Preference Lemma, we then also would have shown that rational inattention implies adaptive preferences.

However, the real world is more complicated than is the stylized model economy. And, concerning "liberty", we may return to John Stuart Mill. In his *Essay on Liberty* (1859), we can read:

> The human faculties of perception, judgment, discriminative feeling, mental activity, and even moral preference, are exercised only in making a choice. He

> who does anything because it is the custom, makes no choice. He gains no practice either in discerning or in desiring what is best. The mental and moral, like the muscular powers, are improved only by being used.
>
> *(I am indebted to Malte Dold for this Mill quotation)*

Following Mill's philosophy we then should expect that most people do attend to some information, do search for improvement.

As we discussed already in Book II, Chapter 9, error is a possibility. By inattention, even by rational inattention, it may turn out that the agent erroneously saw the movement from x to y as an improvement, and only after arriving at y felt himself/herself cheated and thus now considers x superior to y. However, here I can add the following: The possibility of error is one of the driving motives for expanding the attention range in the "wealth of information". We would expect that a clever way of implementing rational inattention makes regretting a seeming improvement from x to y the exception rather than the rule. In this sense, we conclude: most of the time rational inattention comes with adaptive preferences.

"A risk assuming decisiveness – betting on an alternative, even before all the evidence is in – is the supreme mark of character" (William James). This may not be a realistic description of everyday life. However, it expresses an ideal which pervades every country with free citizens. It is difficult to imagine that this ideal could have persisted, if it were not true that most of the time preferences would adapt to decisions taken.

"Use It or Lose It": Habit Formation

> If a person doesn't exercise his or her physical body, he or she will likely lose strength, stamina and endurance. The same applies to a person that doesn't practice a new skill, whether it is learning to drive, speaking a foreign language, etc. he or she may forget or lose those skills.
>
> *(Oxford Learners Dictionary)*

This is one description of "use it or lose it" if you google that expression. We know that this fact does not only apply to human but also to animal nature. It is one of the laws of evolution of life.

The future is not known, but, given a reasonably stable environment, extrapolating the experienced environment from the past into the future is a good survival tactic for any living organism. However, the environment is not exactly stationary. For an organism with a substantial life expectancy, it is therefore useful to be able to adapt to changed circumstances. A species may adapt to an environmental change by "mutation and selection", i.e., by the "survival of the fittest". But provided that this fitness also encompasses a substantial individual life expectancy, an individual adaptation of capacities to their experienced use in the past is part of this survival fitness.

Thus, the architecture of the muscle system of any given individual is not only determined by the organism's DNA but also by the actual use of these muscles in the recent past. There is a feedback from the actual use of the body to its architecture. This feedback enhances those capabilities which were in past intensive use and, for saving energy requirements, reduces those capabilities which were not used in the recent past.

"Use it or lose it" then is part of the animal nature of the human species. And it then also applies to the human brain, to its memory in particular. The human memory only has a limited storing capacity. Science has shown that one important function of sleep is to make sure that the memory can get rid of useless content, of content that may have been useful for a short while in the preceding waking periods but now is simply waste. There seems to be an implicit Bayesian calculus in the subconscious part of our brain, which decides which memory content now is waste and which memory content is worth being kept. Thus, for example, practicing a foreign language enables our brain to improve our corresponding language skills: the subconscious Bayesian calculus concludes from the frequent use of the language that it is useful for the future individual fitness to memorize its words and its grammar.

Economists have intensively studied the behavioral pattern called "habit formation", for example: Houthakker and Taylor 1970, Hall 1978, 1988, Mankiw 1982, Becker and Murphy 1988, Bolle 1990, Constantinides 1990, Dynan 2000, Koehne and Kuhn 2015. Habit formation is one form of the "use it or lose it" pattern. The person who starts running develops a body which is more suitable for running, and he/she enjoys this activity more and more. It becomes a habit. Darwin 1856 observed: "Men are called 'creatures of reason', more appropriately they would be called creatures of habit".

"Use it or lose it" means that preferences are adaptive in the sense I use this word in this book. If, with preferences induced by x, the agent prefers y over x and has the opportunity to go from x to y, he/she experiences a change in preferences, which eventually are the ones induced by y. By this change, be it physical or be it psychic, the agent a fortiori prefers y over x. Indeed, "running" can become an obsession. Indeed, enjoyment of conversing in a foreign language rises as the use of the language improves this language skill. Here we then observe "habit formation" and, equivalently, adaptive preferences.

Uncertainty Aversion and Ambiguity Aversion

As Frank Knight 1921 taught us, uncertainty is everywhere. I argue that uncertainty is a driving force towards adaptive preferences. In his path-breaking book, Knight emphasizes human uncertainty aversion. Given that uncertainty cannot be avoided for society at large, individual uncertainty aversion generates an equilibrium premium for people who take on tasks which involve substantial uncertainty. This premium then is what people – including economists – call "profits". Profits as a reward for bearing with an above-average degree of uncertainty are a “sure thing” only in the aggregate. Obviously, for the individual agent there is no profit guarantee. It would be a contradiction in terms if such guarantee existed.

Uncertainty aversion is a natural consequence of the fact that people plan for the future. Planning works better if there is less uncertainty about the future state of affairs. On the level of the individual agent, you find uncertainty-avoiding strategies everywhere. These are on top of risk-avoiding strategies, which, for example, you observe when people diversify their stock portfolio. Uninsurable risk frequently is uncertainty. Many people, perhaps a large majority, choose an education and further on a job which is associated with a highly predictable income – or at least with a highly reliable minimum income guarantee. Despite the fact that “difficult” training courses, like math, certain sciences or engineering, promise substantially higher life incomes, a majority of those who should be able to master these courses shy away from them – for the fear that they may drop out without a degree. In a sense, then, the higher income of the graduates of these “difficult” fields contains a “profit component” for having accepted the uncertainty of obtaining the degree.

“Schumpeterian” innovation profits contain a large portion of profits for accepting the uncertainty that comes with an attempted “innovation career”. More on Schumpeter and innovation in Book VI, Chapter 34.

However, uncertainty aversion again corresponds to induced preferences, which are adaptive. If $x(t)$ is already the result of strategies to minimize relevant uncertainty, then a substantial hurdle has to be overcome before the agent departs from $x(t)$ in favor of $y(t)$. Once this decision has been taken, even though thereby raising uncertainty, the outlook of the world is likely to change: having become more accustomed to $y(t)$, it is likely to go with reduced uncertainty. On the other hand, the details of former $x(t)$ gradually evaporate in the agent's memory. Thereby, the expected uncertainty associated with $x(t)$ rises. Uncertainty aversion then generates a rising attractiveness of $y(t)$ and a declining attractiveness of $x(t)$. This then implies $y(>;\rho(y))x$.

In a similar way, we could deduce adaptive preferences from ambiguity aversion. On the latter, see, for example, Baillon et al. 2022 and von Gaudecker et al. 2022.

Religion

Historical evidence, even pre-historical evidence, tells us that every society co-exists with strong religious beliefs and religious organizations, for example, Christian churches or Islamic mosques. Typically, children are born into a religion because their parents belong to that religion. For a child, it is an uncertainty-avoiding and conflict-avoiding instinct simply to accept the religious teachings and rituals in which they grow up. The simple belief in the truth of the prevailing religion shuts out many doubts and fears about the true nature of the world one has to cope with. Successful religious organizations know how to educate their flock, how to make pragmatic answers to the vicissitudes of life compatible with the traditional teachings and rituals of their religious community. Indeed, their adherents are happy thereby to cut out too many alternatives in place of the received doctrine and the received commandments. There is great variety in the teachings and rituals of religious organizations. But there is almost no variety between societies in terms of the existence or absence of religious organizations. Religion then is a universal institutional answer to the strong individual abhorrence against perceived uncertainty.

Religions may have beneficial and may have destructive effects on society. Economics, as a child of the Enlightenment, is critical of the narrowness of thought associated with many traditional forms of religious life. Intolerance is not only a restriction for advances in research and entrepreneurial activity. It is, obviously and primarily, a restriction of liberty. Today nobody would deny that the sanctions of the Church against free research were an impediment for advances in science. On the other hand, to the extent that religion generates imagined transcendental sanctions against anti-social behavior of people, it can serve as a substitute for worldly sanctions, which themselves may endanger individual freedom. If citizens, to a degree, follow the Ten Commandments, the world is a better place than a world without these Commandments – other things equal.

It is obvious that religion, as described, corresponds to the assumption of adaptive preferences. After an improvement from x to y, the believer will thank God, and this reinforces his satisfaction with this move. In a more abstract way: the universal propensity to avoid uncertainty attaches people to the well-established beliefs, customs, ways of thought. Whatever their specific content is, they adhere to it, they adapt to it, because they thereby avoid uncertainty.

Even beyond religion we can see the "rational inattention" function of customs and tradition. As Karl Popper 1949 argues in his article "Towards a Rational Theory of Tradition", it is unavoidable and highly productive that society and the scientific community let tradition guide people, including scientists, in their decisions. This is the case as long as such coordination of activities is open to change induced by new knowledge ("falsification") and innovation.

Intertemporal Choice Again

In Chapter 20, Section 4, I discussed intertemporal choice, arguing that – with variable but adaptive preferences – intertemporal choice is too complicated to be described by maximization of an integral over period utilities. The implication is rational inattention. In this section, I return to the topic of intertemporal choice, because there is plenty of evidence which appears to contradict the hypothesis that people are rational in their intertemporal behavior. I mention "hyperbolic discounting" and "present bias". There is a large literature on insufficient retirement saving.

However, recent literature pursues the following question: Could it be that it is the complexity of the decision problem which accounts for "hyperbolic discounting" and for "present bias"? Are these phenomena then simply an outgrowth of complexity reducing rational inattention? The paper by Enke et al. 2023 provides evidence in that direction. The authors report an experimental setup in which they can compare results in an intertemporal setting with results in an atemporal mirror setting. The complexity of the two settings, by design, is the same. In the atemporal mirror setting, they obtain approximate mirror results of the temporal hyperbolic discounting and present bias phenomena. It is then a preliminary corroboration of the hypothesis that hyperbolic discounting and present bias are results of complexity reduction rather than of "irrational" intertemporal behavior.

It would mean "rational complexity reducing inattention" replaces "irrationality" as an explanation of hyperbolic discounting and present bias. However, as we argued in Section 3 of this chapter, rational inattention goes with adaptive preferences. Thus, "hyperbolic discounting" and "present bias" would be part of a world with adaptive preferences.

Gabaix and Laibson 2022 have a different approach. Nevertheless, their results point in a similar general direction. In their paper "Myopia and Discounting", they come to the conclusion "that behavior that arises from imperfect foresight is hard to distinguish from behavior arising from time preference" (p. 3). In their calculation they compare a Bayesian imperfect foresight model with a quasi "neoclassical" model including time preference à la Irving Fisher. The latter model, like every non-stochastic model with fixed preferences, can be generalized to include induced preferences and thereby adaptive preferences. See our Books II and III. It thus appears that there is no contradiction between an imperfect foresight model and models of adaptive preferences.

Both papers, Enke et al. 2023 and Gabaix and Laibson 2022, are pioneering first attempts to understand the rationality or otherwise of decisions in an intertemporal framework and under conditions of uncertainty. The results appear to be consistent with a welfare economics of adaptive preferences.

A third point of view is expressed by Bernheim et al. 2021. The authors call their approach "A Theory of Chosen Preferences". Again, to my understanding, their theory of intertemporally, endogenously changing preferences is consistent with the hypothesis of adaptive preferences.

Nudging

As we work with continuous time and with a default option of "non-decision", it is natural to have a look at the "nudging" philosophy, made popular by Thaler and Sunstein 2008. The authors recommend public intervention into the way the default option for decision makers should be designed. The authors themselves call their interventionist philosophy "Libertarian Paternalism". The paternalist part, according to their philosophy, is the government intervention into the design of the default option. The "libertarian" part is the non-intervention into the "menu" of choices available for the decision maker.

In this book, I do not go into the detailed merits or de-merits of this nudging philosophy. However, I want to state that this philosophy is compatible with my welfare economics of adaptive preferences as presented here. As I described it in Chapters 18 and 19 of this Book IV, I believe it to be States' obligation to provide a framework of pragmatic compossibility of citizens' rights. This means that the lawmaker should take account of externalities in the actions of the citizens. Another justification for nudging is irrationality of human behavior, as perceived by the analyst.

Let me take up one of many nudging examples: grocery shops should place their wares in the shelves to make it easy for the customer to pick up healthy products and to make it harder for the customer to pick up "unhealthy" products. Such a shelf policy may not be profit maximizing for the shop; it would require government regulation. The externality may be the load for the universal health insurance system. Provided that for other reasons a country has such a universal health insurance system, it is the case that unhealthy food consumed by the people raises the health costs which have to be covered by the health insurance system. Encouraging person 1 to consume healthy food tends to lower the health insurance costs of every insured citizen. However, unhealthy food is still available in the shops so that people remain free to disregard the health effects of their food preferences. In terms of their time effort, it gets more expensive for them to pursue their unhealthy food preferences. This may change their habits in the direction of more healthy food consumption. It is obvious that this nudging philosophy presupposes that preferences are adaptive.

In a more recent book with the title *On Freedom*, Sunstein 2019 argues that there is always a default option. For a good life in freedom, he says, it is then obligatory for society to consider how to improve the architectures of default options. Intelligent proponents of nudging policies clearly know about the limits of this kind of interventionism: We should be aware that "nudging" can be misused by the state authorities. In an authoritarian regime, a lot of nudging is likely to happen with the goal of stabilizing the position of those in power. It is therefore also advisable to look for alternative means for the same policy aims. In the example of encouraging healthy food, the tax system might achieve the same result as can be expected from the described nudging policy. There is also the possibility to differentiate health insurance premiums in order to encourage people switching to health-promoting food.

Another interesting topic on nudging is the choice of an appropriate default option concerning provision for old age. Almost every member country of the OECD has a social security system. Given that people also can save money in addition, the pensions provided by the social security system are a "nudge" concerning the provision for old age. Very few people indeed want to borrow money against the promise to repay the debt from their pensions in the future. Thus, for many people, a higher pension simply means that they "save" more for old age. On this topic, using German data, see Seibold 2021.

A nudge can have an architecture so that people can accept a particular proposal, or they can reject it by "opting out". The idea came up that an optimal nudge is that one which minimizes the frequency of opting out. In a recent paper Bernheim and Mueller-Gastell 2021 show under which general conditions this opting out minimization criterion is indeed the optimum.

For the main topic of my book, I repeat that the philosophy of nudging only makes sense if their proponents accept the idea of habit formation and thereby implicitly accept that preferences are adaptive.

The Elasticity Test for Adaptive Preferences

What happens with the price elasticity of demand in the short run and in the long run under adaptive preferences? And what would happen with these two price elasticities if preferences were not adaptive?

As a simple example, consider a person confronted with a constant budget constraint. Take the discrete time model. As we know from Book II and from Book III, under adaptive preferences and a constant budget constraint, demand converges to some long-run demand vector by means of an improvement path. If preferences are anti-adaptive (in the strict sense, i.e. excluding fixed preferences), demand jumps around all the time, and the corresponding improvement sequence is cyclic. Even under such simple constraints as a fixed budget constraint, demand does not settle down to some basket. In this sense, long-run demand remains unpredictable.

Using the simple two-goods model from Chapter 9 in Book II, we can show in a few lines what happens with the consumption ratio under anti-adaptive preferences. We there had the demand function

$$\chi = b\omega^{\mu}\pi^{-\frac{1}{\gamma}}$$

with χ the demand proportion of the two goods, b a weight parameter for the two goods, ω the demand proportion of the preceding period, μ a parameter indicating the strength and the sign of the influence of past consumption on present consumption, π the price ratio of the two goods and γ the inverse of the price elasticity of demand for the two goods. In Chapter 9 we chose the following values for the exogenous parameters: $b = 1$, $\gamma = 2$, $\mu = \frac{1}{2}$, which implies for the long-run price elasticity, $1/\left((1-\mu)\gamma\right) = 1$. The short-run price elasticity is $\frac{1}{2}$. The value $\mu = \frac{1}{2}$ implies adaptive preferences. A value $\mu = -1$ would imply anti-adaptive preferences. I now again assume that the long-run elasticity of demand $1/\left((1-\mu)\gamma\right) = 1$ equals unity, which implies a short-run price elasticity of 2, or $\gamma = \frac{1}{2}$. With these anti-adaptive preferences, the short-run price elasticity exceeds the long-run price elasticity. A constant demand proportion through time requires $\chi = \omega$. Applying the chosen numerical values for the parameters then leads to $\chi\omega = \chi^2 = \pi^{-2}$ or $\chi\pi = 1$. In the long-run "equilibrium" then both goods have an expenditure share of one half.

However this "equilibrium" is unstable. Once the past consumption ratio diverges from today's consumption ratio we perpetually have $\chi\omega = \pi^{-2}$ with $\chi \neq \omega$, and therefore χ jumps around between two values. If, for example, one of the two prices is reduced, the demand ratio of the present period differs from the previous one, and we have $\chi \neq \omega$. Because the price level has declined, the consumption bundle of today is an improvement over the last period's consumption bundle. As from now on the consumption changes in every period, despite a constant budget constraint, each consumption bundle is an improvement over the preceding one. So we have an improvement sequence which again and again comes back to previous consumption bundles. It is not acyclic.

Can we generalize this observation? Here I do not present a general mathematical model. I provide an intuition that the relation between short-run and long-run price elasticity indicates the presence or absence of adaptive preferences. Theorems 1 and 2 tell us that. Let $Y(x)$ be the set of baskets y better than x with preferences induced by x, that is, $Y(x) = \{y \mid y(>;\rho(x)\} x$. Let $A(x)$ be the set of baskets z, which can be reached from x by means of an improvement sequence. We then know that $Y(x) \subseteq A(x)$, because the move from x to $y \in Y(x)$ is itself an improvement sequence, albeit a very short one. Moreover, if preferences are adaptive and if the other assumptions of the theorems hold, there are baskets z such that z is contained in $A(x)$ but not in $Y(x)$, except for the case of fixed preferences. In the case of $n = 2$, the indifference curve passing through x with preferences $\rho(x)$ lies above the curve, which is the lower bound of $A(x)$. Let us give the lower bound of $A(x)$ the name "quasi-indifference curve". At the point x then the quasi-indifference curve has a lower curvature than the indifference curve. This implies that the long-run price elasticity of demand is higher than the short-run price elasticity. The short-run price elasticity being formed with fixed preferences $\rho(x)$, the long-run price elasticity takes account of the change in preferences along the improvement path induced by some initial price reduction.

On the other hand, if preferences are universally anti-adaptive, then, as the numerical example previously indicates, the short-run price elasticity exceeds the long-run price elasticity if, indeed, we can find a value for the long-run price elasticity. Typically, there is no well-defined long price elasticity, because there exists no unique limit for the time series of baskets after an initial price reduction, despite the fact that this time series forms an improvement sequence.

We can generalize from the two-goods case to the n-goods case. Because of Theorem 1B, derived in Book III, we know that for any basket x the indifference surface through x with preferences induced by x lies above the quasi-indifference surface passing through x. I define the "directional price elasticity of demand" at x. Consider the generation of an improvement sequence by an initial price change Δp,

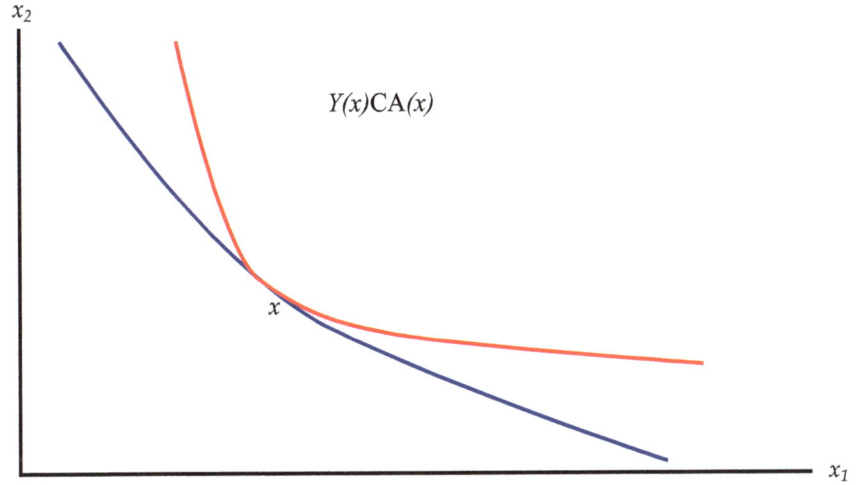

FIGURE 21.1 Indifference Curve and Quasi-Indifference Curve Under AP

which allows for a higher real income. To derive Theorem 1B I introduced Assumption 3e. As I showed in the proof, it is then always possible to replace the actual improvement sequence $S = x^0, x^1, \ldots.\ x^T$ with an improvement sequence $S^* = x^0, z^1, z^2, \ldots\ x^T$ which starts at the same basket and ends at the same basket but which is contained with all its baskets in the two-dimensional subspace $R^2\left(x^0, x^T\right)$, which is spanned by the origin and by x^0 and x^T. By appropriately chosen composite commodities, we then can interpret the improvement sequence S^* as an improvement sequence in a two-commodity world. We then know from the preceding argument that the long-run price elasticity exceeds the short-run price elasticity.

As I discussed in Book I and again later, we have two forms of analysis for the same object. The object is the economy at large or perhaps, really, society at large. The two forms of analysis are positive economics and normative economics. In both forms of analysis we adhere to "methodological individualism". Positive economics adheres to causal analysis: the purpose is to find the causal relations between the different objects: by theoretical and empirical research. Normative economics in the form of normative individualism searches for a well-functioning of a society of free citizens. Freedom or liberty then is at the center stage of such a project. Freedom is represented by the concept of preferences. In its extreme form as formulated by Stigler and Becker 1977, the causal analysis of positive economics can dispense with the concept of "preferences", as it has the aim of explaining everything by means of the causes of observed phenomena. On the other hand, in its extreme form, as formulated in this book, normative economics "explains" as much as possible by means of the preferences of the people. Only the requirement of "compossibility" imposes limits to this way of explaining facts by preferences.

In this Section 9 of the present Chapter 21, I have argued that an excess of the long-run price elasticity of demand over the short-run price elasticity of demand is an indicator for the prevalence of adaptive preferences. Now we can turn to our hat as "positive economists", and we can ask the question: in the real world, is the long-run price elasticity of demand generally higher than the corresponding short-run price elasticity of demand? We know the answer: "Yes". The textbook explanation comes from the theory of production: a higher relative price of an input induces substitution away from this input in the direction of inputs, which now may have become more attractive. Thus, for example, higher wages induce a substitution of labor for capital. However, additional capital goods need time to become available.

We then see that the "positive" and the "normative" views on the economy are complementary to each other: one view may provide results for the other view. Here we find that well-known and familiar facts observed by the "positive" view provide evidence for the hypothesis in the "normative" view that actual flexible preferences are predominantly adaptive.

Rationality vs Irrationality

Common sense as well as behavioral economics tell us that human nature neither is all rational nor is all irrational. In a democracy, the system of citizens' rights and obligations takes account of this mixture, guided by experience and by public debate. In Book V on interpersonal influences on preferences, we go much deeper into this distinction between the rational and the irrational part of human nature.

Here, I conclude this chapter by pointing to its quintessence: to the extent that people behave in a rational way, most of the time their preferences appear to be adaptive.

The eminent biologist Edward O. Wilson 1998 has written an impressive book: *Consilience*. By the term consilience, he means that discoveries in different corners of our knowledge and research come to similar conclusions. Thereby they enable us to arrive at new theories, which one expresses by means of new concepts that are more general. Wilson provides many examples from the sciences. Here I suggest that the many observations which support the concept of "adaptive preferences" are such a case of consilience.

Summary of Book IV

In Chapter 18, I introduce the concept of "pragmatic compossibility" as a framework for the individual rights which are compatible with each other – in a free society. Pragmatic compossibility is also compatible with the Kaldor–Hicks–Scitovsky criterion for improving changes in the society. Chapter 19 then shows that the "pragmatism" inherent in "pragmatic compossibility" presupposes that preferences are adaptive. Only then can one extrapolate past experience to predict effects of changes in legislation, infrastructure or innovations. A society of free citizens works on the extrapolation principle, thereby implicitly accepting the hypothesis of adaptive preferences. Chapter 20 gives several examples of the phenomenology of adaptive preferences: 1) the appetite-satiation cycle, 2) random or foreseen changes in the behavioral constraints, 3) saving and dissaving, 4) information acquisition as a byproduct of consumption or by search), 5) education and schooling and 6) switching costs and the default option. In Chapter 21, I investigate several known phenomena, and I show that they confirm the hypothesis of adaptive preferences. These are "decision costs", "loss aversion", "rational inattention", the "use it or lose it" phenomenon, "habit formation", "uncertainty aversion", "ambiguity aversion", "reference-dependent preferences", "religion", "hyperbolic discounting", "present bias", the "default option" in the context of the "nudging" philosophy and the universal fact that long-run demand price elasticities are higher than short-run price elasticities.

References

Andersen, Steffen, Badarinza, Cristian, Liu, Lu, Marx, Julie and Ramadorai, Tarun, 2022, Reference Dependence in the Housing Market, American Economic Review, 112 (10), 3398–3440.

Baillon, Aurélien, Halevy, Yoram and Chen, Li, 2022, Randomize at your Own Risk: On the Observability of Ambiguity Aversion, Econometrica, 90 (3), 1085–1107.

Becker, Gary S. and Murphy, Kevin M., 1988, A Theory of Rational Addiction, Journal of Political Economy, 96 (4), 675–700.

Bernheim, B. Douglas and Mueller-Gastell, Jonas, 2021, Optimal Default Options: The Case for (Weighted) Opt-Out Minimization, NBER Working Paper 28254.

Bernheim, B. Douglas, Braghieri, Luca, Martinez-Marquina, Alejandro and Zukerman, David, 2021, A Theory of Chosen Preferences, American Economic Review, 111 (2), 720–754.

Bolle, Friedel, 1990, Habit Formation and Long Term Contracts, Journal of Consumer Policy, 13, 273–284.

Constantinides, George M., 1990, Habit Formation: A Resolution of the Equity Premium Puzzle, Journal of Political Economy, 98 (3), 519–543.

Darwin, Charles, 1856, Quotation in Charles Darwin, Metaphysics, Materialism, and the Evolution Mind: Early Writings of Charles Darwin, Transcribed, and Annotated by Paul H. Barrett with a Commentary by Howard E. Gruber, Chicago, IL, Chicago University Press, 1974.

Dynan, Karen, 2000, Habit Formation in Consumer Preferences: Evidence from Panel Data, American Economic Review, 90 (3), 391–406.

Enke, Benjamin, Graeber, Thomas and Oprea, Ryan, 2023, Complexity and Time, CES-Ifo Working Paper 10327, 67 pages.

Fehr, Dietmar and Kübler, Dorothea, 2022, The Endowment Effect in the General Population, CES-Ifo Discussion Paper 10150, 16 pages plus Appendix.

Gabaix, Xavier and Laibson, David, 2022, Myopia and Discounting, unpublished, 50 pages.

Gaudecker, Hans-Martin von, Wogrolly, Axel and Zimpelmann, Christian, 2022, The Distribution of Ambiguity Attitudes, CES-Ifo Working Paper 10079, 38 pages.

Hall, Robert E., 1978, Stochastic Implications of the Life Cycle Permanent Income Hypothesis: Theory and Evidence, Journal of Political Economy, 86 (69), 971–987.

Hall, Robert E., 1988, Intertemporal Substitution in Consumption, Journal of Political Economy, 96 (2), 339–357.

Houthakker, Hendrick S. and Taylor, Lester D., 1970, Consumer Demand in the United States, Cambridge, MA, Harvard University Press.
Kahneman, Daniel, 2011, Thinking, Fast and Slow, New York, Farrar, Straus and Giroud, 499 pages.
Kahneman, Daniel and Tversky, Amos, 1979, Prospect Theory: An Analysis of Decision under Risk, Econometrica, 47 (2), 263–292.
Knight, Frank H., 1921, Risk, Uncertainty and Profit, Boston, MA and New York, Houghton Mifflin Company, 381 pages.
Koehne, Sebastian and Kuhn, Moritz, 2015, Optimal Taxation in a Habit Formation Economy, Journal of Public Economics, 122, 31–39.
Mackoviak, Bartosz, Matejka, Filip and Wiederholt, Mirko, 2023, Rational Inattention: A Review, Journal of Economic Literature, 61 (1), 226–273.
Mankiw, N. Gregory, 1982, Hall's Consumption Hypothesis and Durable Goods, Journal of Monetary Economics, 10 (3), 417–425.
McFadden, Daniel, 1974, Conditional Logit Analysis of Qualitative Choice Behavior, in: Zarembka, Paul (ed.), Frontiers in Econometrics, New York, Academic Press, pp.105–142.
Mill, John Stuart, 1859, On Liberty, London, Walter Scott Publishing Company, 1903, with an Introduction by W. L. Courtney, LLD, XXVIII + 219 pages.
Morewedge, Carey K. and Giblin, Colleen E., 2015, Explanation of the Endowment Effect: An Integrative Review, American Psychological Association Psych Net, 19 (6), 339–348.
Popper, Karl, 1949, Towards a Rational Theory of Tradition, in: Popper, Karl (ed.), Conjectures and Refutations, London, Routledge, pp.162–182.
Reck, Daniel and Seibold, Arthur, 2022, The Welfare Economics of Reference Dependence, CES-Ifo Working Paper 9999, 82 pages.
Samuelson, William and Zeckhauser, Richard, 1988, Status Quo Bias in Decision Making, Journal of Risk and Uncertainty, 1, 7–59.
Seibold, Arthur, 2021, Reference Points for Retirement Behavior: Evidence from German Pension Discontinuity, American Economic Review, 111 (4), 1126–1165.
Simon, Herbert, 1971, Designing Organizations for an Information Rich World, in: Greenberger, H. (ed.), Computers, Communications, and the Public Interest, Baltimore, MD, Johns Hopkins Press, pp.37–72.
Sims, Christopher A., 1998, Stickiness, Carnegie-Rochester Conference Series on Public Policy, 49, 317–356.
Sims, Christopher A., 2003, Implications of Rational Inattention, Journal of Monetary Economics, 50 (3), 665–690.
Stigler, George J. and Becker, Gary S., 1977, De Gustibus non est Disputandum, American Economic Review, 67 (2), 76–90.
Sunstein, Cass R., 2019, On Freedom, Princeton, NJ, Princeton University Press, 127 pages.
Thaler, Richard H. and Sunstein, Cass R., 2008, Nudge – Improving Decisions about Health, Wealth, and Happiness, New Haven, CT, Yale University Press, 312 pages.
Welsch, Heinz, 2005, Adaptation of Tastes to Constraints, Theory and Decision, 57, 379–395.
Wilson, Edward O., 1998, Consilience – The Unity of Knowledge, New York, Knopf, 367 pages.

BOOK V

Interpersonal Influences on Preferences

22

ADAPTIVE PREFERENCES AS A RESULT OF EVOLUTION

Assume – contrary to empirical evidence – that preferences are anti-adaptive. Take the following example. I own a piano. I am prepared to sell the piano for € 500. I sell it for that price. Now, because my preferences are anti-adaptive, I value a piano of the same quality at more than € 700. So I go and buy a similar piano for € 700. I am now back at my original state – except that I am € 200 poorer than I was originally. Now somebody comes along and gives me € 200. Thus, I am now back at the point from where I started. Each transaction was an improvement. Otherwise, I would not have agreed to it. So I have walked an improvement sequence and came back to my original position. That improvement sequence was cyclic.

Not only does this sequence of events shed some light on my limited degree of rationality, it also implies that others have made a profit at my expense. Someone has pocketed the € 200 which I lost in selling and then buying again my piano. If preferences generally were anti-adaptive we would expect that a large class of arbitrageurs arises who make a living out of exploiting the anti-adaptiveness of the preferences of the public.

We would not expect this to be a stable state of affairs. Anti-adaptive preferences are unlikely to survive. We expect at least two mechanisms by which anti-adaptive preferences disappear. One is individual and social learning. A person repeatedly experiencing downward-spiraling "improvement sequences" eventually understands that, in some sense, his/her behavior is not rational. He/she would expect to be a happier person if he/she changed his/her behavior. From the outside, from the point of view of normative individualism, we consider this change in behavior (due to learning) a change in preferences. In our language, there is a tendency for a change in the "law of motion" of preferences in the direction of adaptive preferences.

DOI: 10.4324/9781032726410-27

The other, much slower mechanism that drives out anti-adaptive preferences is evolution in the biological sense of that word. Through the history of mankind up until, but excluding, very modern times, there was a competition for survival similar to the Darwinian principle of the "survival of the fittest". High birth rates and high infant and adult mortality due to under-nourishment, infectious diseases, violence and civil war were the rule rather than the exception. The "laws of motion" of preferences must have been formed very much by this competition for survival. In this competition among different laws of motion of preferences, anti-adaptive preferences must have been rather unfit for promoting the survival of its human bearers and their offspring. As such, humans equipped with anti-adaptive preferences were potential prey of clever exploiters; their lot – other things equal – must have been much worse than that of people with adaptive preferences. Their and their offspring's chances of survival must have been inferior to those of people with adaptive preferences.

Fixed preferences are the borderline case between adaptive and anti-adaptive preferences. Consider some parameter γ which indicates the degree to which preferences are adaptive ($\gamma > 0$) or anti-adaptive ($\gamma < 0$) or in between, that is, fixed ($\gamma = 0$). Assume now that the basic unconstrained genetic development of γ is a random walk with expected value of zero for the rate of change $\Delta\gamma$. But different values of γ have different survival values for its bearers. Let the survival value $\lambda(\gamma)$ be small for $\gamma < 0$, large for a range of positive values of γ and then again small for very large values of γ. We then could compute the ergodic frequency distribution of γ. Its main mass will be in the positive range of γ, and its average will be positive.

In the case of two commodities ($n = 2$), we can define γ in the following way: Let σ be some kind of appropriately weighted average of the elasticity of substitution of the indifference curves corresponding to preferences q and baskets x. Let σ^* be some kind of appropriately weighted average of the elasticity of substitution of the quasi-indifference curves for given baskets x. These are the

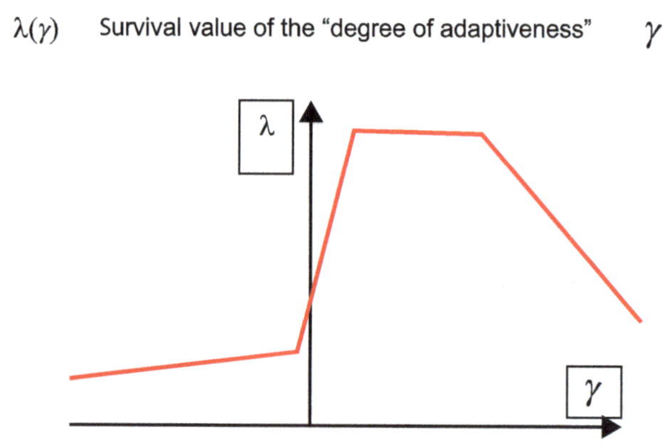

FIGURE 22.1 Survival Value of the Degree of Adaptiveness

quasi-indifference curves derived in Theorem 2. They can also be constructed for anti-adaptive preferences. Here, their economic meaning is "the opposite" of the meaning in the case of adaptive preferences: it indicates which basket can be reached from which other basket by means of a "deterioration path". We can show in the case of "smoothly anti-adaptive preferences" that deterioration paths are acyclic. The adaptation parameter γ can then be defined by the following formula

$$\gamma = \frac{\sigma^*}{\sigma} - 1$$

With adaptive preferences, the indifference curve going through some point x with preferences $\rho(x)$ induced by x lies above the quasi-indifference curve going through x. Hence the long-run demand function is more elastic than the short-run demand function, which means that σ^* is greater than σ at this point. The adaptation parameter then is a kind of average of the coefficient between the long-run and the short-run demand elasticity, minus one.

In the case of anti-adaptive preferences, the long-run demand function is less elastic than the short-run demand function. If, due to a change in relative prices, demand for one good goes up and demand for the other good goes down, anti-adaptive preferences have the effect that the relative taste for the good now more consumed goes down, and hence there is a swing-back of demand due to the preference change. This then implies that $\sigma^* < \sigma$ and therefore $\gamma < 0$.

The survival value λ is not a monotonically increasing function of the degree of adaptiveness. γ may rise because the long-run elasticity of substitution σ^* rises, or it may rise because the short-run elasticity of substitution σ declines. If adaptive preferences prevail and λ already is substantially above zero, a further rise in γ is very likely to be due to a declining short-run elasticity of substitution. However, in an ever-changing environment, it is a disadvantage for survival if the short-run ability to substitute is very small.

The upshot of this Chapter 22 then is this: there are strong "Darwinian" causes for adaptive rather than anti-adaptive preferences and fixed preferences.

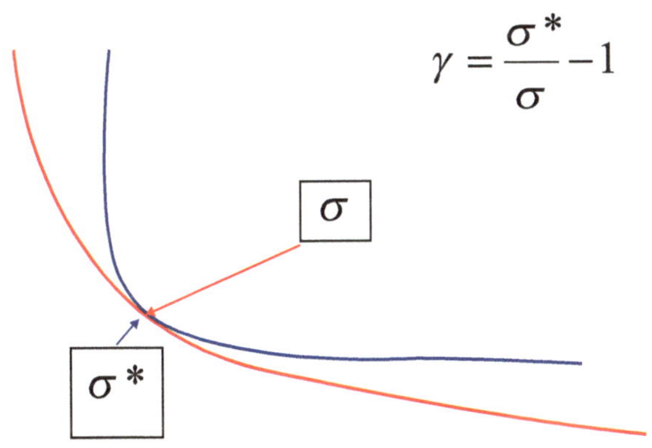

FIGURE 22.2 Short Run and Long Run Elasticity of Substitution: Adaptive Preferences

23

NON-CONVEXITY OF PREFERENCES

Phishing for Phools

In an important book, Akerlof and Shiller (2015) present their theoretical framework for the "economics of manipulation and deception". The book title, *Phishing for Phools*, tells us that manipulation and deception are not matters of the past. Modern telecommunication and the internet not only provide great advantages; they also create new opportunities for profitable exploitation of other people by manipulation and deception. And it is the strong belief of the authors that there are many opportunities for government intervention to protect people from such exploitative attempts by others.

The book is full of empirical case studies. In addition, it provides stories of how government, including legislators, answered to such phenomena by regulation and other forms of market intervention. The theoretical framework comes down to the following: people do not always act in their own best interest. If they don't, there will be others who exploit the profit opportunities arising out of such irrational or uninformed behavior. Wherever there are fools ("phools") there are fishers ("phishers") who fool ("phool") them. There arises then a "phishing equilibrium". The reason people do not always act in their own interest is a general psychology of the two persons encapsulated in the same body: one person, the rational forward-looking one, and another person: the "monkey" sitting on the shoulders of the other one, striving for immediate satisfaction of wants. Often the "monkey" wins in a conflict situation. Then the agent gives in to some vice, disregarding the future costs of such action. "Addiction" to smoking, alcohol, gambling, drugs, chatting on Facebook is a class of such behavior.

The theory of the "phishing equilibrium" is important for an understanding of the government role in this context. Most "phishers" work in a competitive environment. The world does not change very much if a particular "phisher" shuts down his operation. Competitors take over his "customers". There may exist two

DOI: 10.4324/9781032726410-28

possible equilibria: a "good" equilibrium and a "bad" one, the "bad" one being the "phishing equilibrium". Government intervention then has the function to move people from the bad to the good equilibrium or to keep people from wandering from the good equilibrium to the bad one.

To my understanding, the two authors do not consider this government intervention "paternalistic". They point to the fact that addicted people themselves are unhappy with their state of affairs – and wish for a liberation out of their psychic prison.

I provide a link between my normative individualism approach and the Akerlof–Shiller philosophy. In a book review, I generally agreed with the two authors (Von Weizsäcker 2016). I now show that their book and the present book are compatible. We should note that their "two-persons-within-one" set-up is incompatible with the assumption of fixed preferences. The latter mean utility maximization for a utility function, which is independent of the choice taken by the agent. It leaves no room for two persons within the agent's body or brain.

However, adaptive preferences allow for "two-persons-in-one". To show this graphically, I return to the classroom model with two goods. Consider a person who in period $t = -1$ has been in a stationary state $\overline{x} = x(p;\overline{q})$ with $\overline{q} = \rho(\overline{x})$. Now, in period $t = 0$, the price vector changes to $\widehat{p}$, which is different from the previous p, but the previous consumption vector $\overline{x}$ is still obtainable; that is, $\widehat{p}\,\overline{x} \le 1$. From now on, the price vector remains the same. So we obtain a series of consumption vectors $(0) = x(\widehat{p};\rho(\overline{x}))$; $x(1) = x(\widehat{p};\rho(x(0))$;......$x(t+1) = x(\widehat{p};\rho(x(t))$; . . . This sequence is an improving sequence. Because preferences are adaptive, it is a monotonically rising or monotonically falling sequence in terms of, say, the first component x_1 of the demand vector x. This monotonicity derives from the fact that adaptive preferences have the property of intertemporal complementarity for each component for improving sequences. But since the two components within the budget constraint are bounded from below and above, the improving sequence has a convergence point $\hat{x} = x(\widehat{p};\rho(\hat{x}))$.

However the location of this convergence point may depend on the initial value $\overline{x}$. Only if the set $A(x)$ of baskets, which can be reached from x by an improving sequence, is a convex set can we be sure that the convergence point described above is independent of the initial point.

Otherwise, we may get a figure like the following one: For a given stationary budget constraint we have two convergence points **A** and **B**. At the convergence point **A** there is the blue indifference curve touching the budget line and corresponding to the equation $\hat{x} = x(\widehat{p};\rho(\hat{x}))$ with $\hat{x} =$**A**. The green curve is the lower bound of the set $A(\hat{x})$ of baskets, which can be reached from $\hat{x}$ by means of a finite improving path. If that set $A(\hat{x})$ is not convex, a subset of it may be below the budget constraint. However, even if this is the case, the beginning of any improving path lies above the budget constraint. This is significant for the economic interpretation of our model.

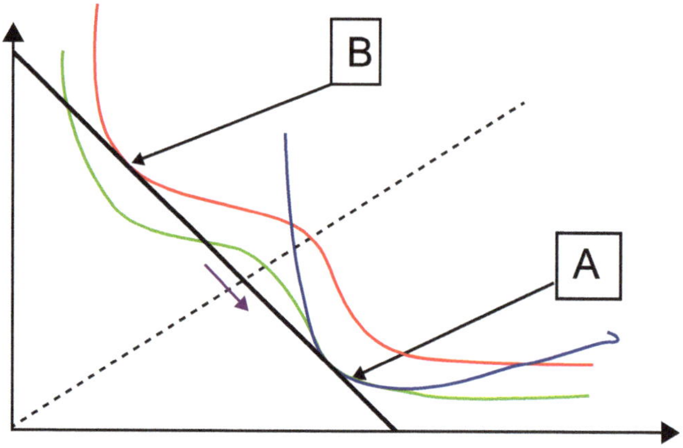

FIGURE 23.1 Path Dependence of Long-Run Demand

Then there is the other convergence point **B**. Let $\breve{x}$=**B**. Then here also $\breve{x} = \breve{x}\left(\hat{p}; \rho\left(\breve{x}\right)\right)$. The red curve touching the budget line at **B** is the lower bound of the set $A\left(\breve{x}\right)$ of baskets, which can be reached from **B** by means of a finite improving path.

As we have drawn the figure, the red curve lies above the green curve. This means that the basket **B** can be reached from basket **A** by an improving path. In this sense basket **B** is "better" than basket **A.** There is a point on the budget line, which separates the initial baskets converging to **A** from the initial baskets converging to **B.** The crossing point between the dotted line and the budget line may be that separating point. This graph is an example of non-convex improvement sets.

Non-convex improvement sets allow the combination of normative individualism with the common sense for government intervention in a "phishing for phools" situation, in particular in the context of addiction. The picture above contains an arrow from "north-west" to "south-east". It symbolizes the "phishing" part of the story. Assume that by some activity of the "phisher" the starting point $x\left(-1\right)$ of the improving sequence shifts from the north-west of the separating point to the southeast of the separating point. This then means that the agent converges to the basket **A** rather than to the basket **B.** The "phisher" thereby pushes the agent to a convergence point, which is inferior to another possible convergence point. He thereby may make a profit.

Why is this a case for government intervention? The agent himself/herself could pull himself/herself out of the swamp of basket **A** either by sacrificing present enjoyment in favor of much larger gains in future enjoyment or by following an improving path from **A** to **B**. In the latter case, he/she would initially have to borrow money, because the first steps of the improving path lead to baskets, which are beyond the budget. However, at a sufficiently low rate of interest, he/she can repay the loan, because the improving path eventually lies below the budget.

However, anthropology and simple experience teach us that a large majority of addicted agents are unable to master the foresight and willpower for such journey from **A** to **B**. Here common sense lets us deviate from the standpoint of liberty, that is, from the view that agents' actions are socially legitimized, simply because they are their actions (within the compossibility constraints). It appears to be wise to let government prevent potential "phishers" from inducing other agents to switch from convergence point **B** to convergence point **A**.

As with the nudging philosophy, the "phishing" theory argues for government instructions and prohibitions to its citizens in the interest of third parties.

References

Akerlof, George A. and Shiller, Robert J., 2015, Phishing for Phools: The Economics of Manipulation and Deception, Princeton, NJ, Princeton University Press, 288 pages.

von Weizsäcker, Carl Christian, 2016, Book Review on Akerlof, George A. and Shiller, Robert J.: Phishing for Phools: The Economics of Manipulation and Deception, Journal of Economics, 118 (1), 91–96.

24

FREEDOM MODE AND CAUSAL MODE OF GOVERNMENT ACTION

In the preceding Chapter 23, we discussed a class of cases, where common sense leads us to the conclusion that government should overrule the principle that agents' actions are legitimized simply because they are free actions within the compossibility boundaries. I suggest that we define two modes of government action. One mode is freedom mode: it means government non-interference with citizens' actions beyond the government obligation to implement the rules of compossibility. The other mode is causal mode: in this mode, government may interfere with citizens' actions, if a causal analysis of the situation – together with common sense – strongly indicates such interference.

For a free society, such government interference in the causal mode should be the exception rather than the rule. Nevertheless, we should acknowledge that such exceptions do exist. This is because not everybody behaves in an autonomous mode. Experience and common sense tell us that small children will not always act in their own self-interest. Nobody in his/her right mind denies parents the right (and the obligation) to impose constraints on actions of their own small children. Society, as a rule, expects from parents that love of their children induce them to impose appropriate behavioral rules for their small children. Society, as a rule, also expects from parents that they educate their children in an appropriate way. The background for this worldwide government attitude towards their citizens in their role as parents is the well-established experience that small children do not act as autonomous human beings. Human nature has to *learn* autonomy. This learning takes years. On this, see also Witt 2001.

Moreover, if parents massively fail to perform their educational role, there is agreement in modern free societies that government should interfere with the parents' action or non-action. Here, obviously, government acts in the causal mode.

DOI: 10.4324/9781032726410-29

One could try to subsume such intervention by parents and by government under the heading of compossibility. If parents fail to appropriately constrain their children's behavior at the peril of the children's health or life, we might say that such non-action of parents violates the principle of pragmatic compossibility, because the damage for children weighs more than the cost of appropriate behavior on the parents' part. However, such subsumption is problematic. Constraints on a person's activity due to compossibility are in the interest of other citizens. Here we discuss behavioral constraints in the interest of the person himself/herself, that is, in the interest of the small child.

There exists a large literature on child-raising by parents. As a recent example I refer to Sutter et al. 2022. Here the authors show empirically the parental influence on the "grit" of the child.

For a free society, we then distinguish two classes of constraints on citizens' actions. One class of constraints is due to the compossibility requirement; the other class consists of constraints due to lacking autonomy of people. The criterion for recognizing this autonomy deficit must be overwhelming evidence that the person does not act in his/her own interest.

The case of addiction discussed in the preceding chapter is different from the case of small children. However, here also we can argue that addiction is inconsistent with autonomous behavior. As we have shown, there exists an improvement path from the addiction equilibrium **A** to the non-addiction equilibrium **B**. This means that a longer journey of many small improvements out of the addiction equilibrium is possible if preferences are adaptive. The lack of autonomy in this case consists of the inability of the addicted person to pursue this long journey without external help.

Realistically, we should assume that human agents are able to optimize locally but not globally. This is all right for the case of a convex improvement space $A(x)$. Then, for any linear budget constraint, there exists only one local optimum – and therefore it is a global optimum. Within the budget constraint there exists then no improving path away from this optimum. There is then a connection between the idea of autonomy and the convexity property of the improvement set $A(x)$.

There are, of course, many cases where equilibria for given budget constraints are path dependent. One example is the collection of natural languages which people speak. Today there are still thousands of such spoken languages, even though their number is on a secular decline. Children acquire their language from their parents – and thus in most cases speak the same "mother tongue" throughout their life as did their mothers. There is no compelling reason the government should intervene in the individual "choice" of the spoken language. However, there are exceptions. In a country with a large heterogeneity of spoken languages, the schools and the political system may require that all children learn the same "national" language. Thus, for example, English is the national language of the United States of America, even though many inhabitants have an immigration background and speak another "mother tongue".

To know and to speak a particular language is more useful if more other people speak the same language. Indeed, a language only spoken by me and not by anyone else is almost useless for me. Therefore, there is a general social pressure imposed on most people to acquire the ability to communicate in a largely used language. This is the background for the secular trend of increasing language conformity. One may speak of language competition. As far as I can see, there are three characteristics which are important for the adoption of one language rather than another. The first characteristic may be the "object adequacy" of the language: those things the speaker (or writer) wants to express about the real world should be conveyable by means of the language. This concerns the available vocabulary and the available grammatical forms. The second characteristic may be the number of relevant speaking partners who speak the language. The third may be the ease of learning the language. English as a world language performs well on all three characteristics. Most English-speakers speak it as a second language; however, the number of people speaking it as their mother tongue is also quite large. In the European Union English is the by far most frequently used language for communication between people of different mother tongues. And this despite the fact that after Brexit only a very small minority of EU citizens speak English as their mother tongue.

Here I do not dwell more deeply on the fascinating topic of languages. I have touched on it because language use is a prime example of adaptive preferences. If two persons with different mother tongues so far have used, say, Russian as their communication language and now try out English, once they find out that it works, they will tend to stick with English. This conforms to the formula

$$y(>;\rho(x))x \rightarrow y(>;\rho(y))x$$

with x =Russian and y =English.

Language use, obviously, is path dependent. We may surmise that different equilibrium points have different improvement sets $A(x)$ (for different equilibria x). However, we do not explain this by a lack of autonomy. Government intervention is not necessarily called for. However, governments have frequently intervened, in most of the cases by promoting or even enforcing the use of a national language. Indeed, a person's main language use (or mother tongue) has frequently been seen as a signal for the nationality of that person. From a freedom point of view, such a "nationalistic" policy must be viewed as highly problematic.

Another example of non-convex improvement sets is the letter type ordering on typewriters and today, personal computers. On this example, read David 1985.

References

David, Paul, 1985, Clio and the Economics of QWERTY, American Economic Review, 75, 332–337.

Sutter, Matthias, Untertrifaller, Anna and Zoller, Claudia, 2022, Grit Increases Strongly in Early Childhood and Is Related to Parental Background, Scientific Reports, 12, 35–61.

Witt, Ulrich, 2001, Learning to Consume – A Theory of Wants and the Growth of Demand, Journal of Evolutionary Economics, 11, 23–36.

25

IMITATION OF OTHERS

A Case of Adaptive Preferences; Advertising

People imitate the behavior of others. This means that other people have an influence on their preferences. Such imitation is consistent with the hypothesis of adaptive preferences. Here I derive this result by means of the classroom model. We then have two goods and one price ratio, with a normalized budget of unity: $p_1x_1 + p_2x_2 = 1$. Let $x = (x_1, x_2)$ be the quantity vector, and let $p = (p_1, p_2)$ be the price vector. Let $z = (z_1, z_2)$ be an appropriately weighted average quantity vector of other consumers. They are the group of people whom our agent tends to imitate. Let w be a vector of nominal incomes of this group of people. We then have a demand function for this group average

$$z = z(p; w)$$

We construct a vector of compensated demand by stipulating that the budget vector w marginally changes with marginal changes of p so that "real income" of the other people remains constant. So, we write for the compensated demand function

$$z = z(p, w(p)) \equiv g(p)$$

Consider now two price vectors p^0 and p^1 such that for the initial quantity vector x^0 the following equation holds

$$p^1x^0 = p^0x^0 = 1$$

or, with $\Delta p = p^1 - p^0$,

$$x^0\Delta p = x_1^0\Delta p_1 + x_2^0\Delta p_2 = 0$$

DOI: 10.4324/9781032726410-30

Let us now look at the demand function of our agent. It is

$$x = f(p;z)$$

Because z enters by the imitative behavior of the agent, we know that for given p demand for good 1 rises with rising z_1; and demand for good 2 rises with rising z_2. But with the compensated demand function g, it is the case that z depends on p. So we can write

$$x = f(p;z) = f(p;g(p)) \equiv F(p).$$

In order to test for adaptive preferences we distinguish between the demand function without the imitation effect and the demand function with the imitation effect. We first look at the demand function $\hat{x} = f\left(p;g\left(p^0\right)\right)$. Here we treat $g\left(p^0\right)$ as a constant. Given that we assume $p^1x^0 = p^0x^0$, we know that $\hat{x} = f\left(p^1;g\left(p^0\right)\right)$ is an improvement for the preferences which have been induced by x^0. Assume that $\Delta p_1 > 0$ and thus $\Delta p_2 < 0$. For $\Delta\hat{x}_i = \hat{x}_i - x_i^0$ with $i = 1;2$ it then follows that $\Delta\hat{x}_1 < 0$ and $\Delta\hat{x}_2 > 0$.

But, at the same time, because of the identical price change $\Delta p_1 > 0$ and thus $\Delta p_2 < 0$, we have for the compensated demand curve $g(p)$ that $\Delta g_1 < 0$ and $\Delta g_2 > 0$. Because of the imitation effect, we then can conclude that

$$\Delta x_1 \le \Delta\hat{x}_1 < 0 \text{ and } \Delta x_2 \ge \Delta\hat{x}_2 > 0$$

This means that $\hat{x}$ is located between $F\left(p^0\right)$ and $F\left(p^1\right)$. We then look at the inverted demand function $p = F^{-1}(x)$ evaluated at $\hat{x}$. Because of the convexity of the set of "preferred baskets" we can infer

$$\Delta p_1 > \Delta\hat{p}_1 > 0 \text{ and } \Delta p_2 < \Delta\hat{p}_2 < 0$$

Figure 25.1 provides a graphical proof that interpersonal imitation is a case of adaptive preferences. We compare two different consumption baskets x and $\hat{x}$. As described, x is the demand vector for the budget constraint p^0. The black budget constraint represents the price vector p^0, and x is a point on that black line. The green budget constraint represents the price vector p^1, and the corresponding demand vector (keeping the consumption baskets of the other consumers the same) is $\hat{x}$. We have assumed that the green line also touches x, but it is steeper, because Δp_1 is positive and Δp_2 is negative. The basket $\hat{x}$ therefore lies to the "north-west" of x, and it lies above the black budget line. This means that $\hat{x}$ is revealed preferred over x.

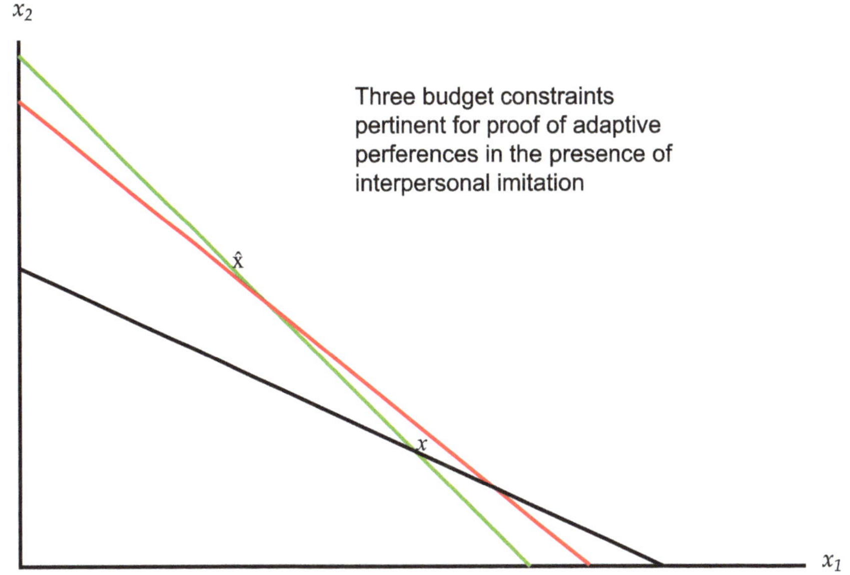

FIGURE 25.1 Imitation Is a Case of Adaptive Preferences

Now we introduce interpersonal imitation. As shown, if the price change Δp also applies to the people our agent imitates, then including this imitation effect the change Δp has an even stronger change effect on the agent's consumption basket. But this means that the price change required to let the agent consume $\hat{x}$ is smaller with the imitation effect than without the imitation effect. The red budget line passing through $\hat{x}$ thus is not as steep as the green budget line. The red budget line represents the price vector $\hat{p}$, which generates demand $\hat{x}$, taking account of the imitation effect. Being less steep than the green budget line, the red budget line lies above x. And this proves that the preference change induced by imitation results in a demand vector $\hat{x}$ which is preferred over x. This result corresponds to the hypothesis of adaptive preferences, because from $\hat{x}\left(>;\varrho\left(x\right)\right)x$ follows $\hat{x}\left(>;\varrho\left(\hat{x}\right)\right)x$.

We may also express this result in terms of reaction elasticities: Because people imitate each other in their consumption habits, the price elasticity of demand is higher than it would be without such imitation.

Because people on average are ill informed about the suitability and quality of products, they look around to see what their neighbors buy. And they talk to their neighbors, relatives or friends about consumer products. If these other people have experience with some product and if they seem to be satisfied with it, this may induce them to buy the product. Imitation then is a method to replace (lacking) direct product information by indirect product information. Its effect is better-informed customers.

Like adaptive preferences in general, imitation thereby raises the price elasticity of demand.

In the context of imitation, it is interesting that it also applies to time, risk and social preferences. This, it seems to me, can be read from the results of a worldwide empirical study by Kotschy and Sunde 2023. They show that these preference characteristics become more similar worldwide through time. This can be explained by the fact that worldwide interaction of people becomes less costly and thereby more frequent due to technical progress.

In this imitation context, let us have a look at advertising. Economists have an ambivalent view on government intervention into the activity of advertising. I refer the reader to the survey article by Kyle Bagwell 2007. We can understand advertising and other forms of sales effort best by reminding ourselves of the typical market structure for produced goods: even under competitive conditions, the typical transaction is of the monopolistic competition type: supply is offered at prices above marginal production cost, and typically, it is the demand side which determines the quantity sold and bought. After this transaction, the buyer is "transaction satiated" on this market, whereas the seller remains "transaction hungry". If the seller believes that advertising raises his/her sales volume, and if the advertising cost is sufficiently low, it pays him/her to advertise.

We can assume that enduring advertising is profitable for the advertising seller. Let us now look at the interaction between imitative behavior of the customer and advertising by the seller. It reminds one of a "double helix" of successful selling. The background is "incomplete information" and "agency cost of geographical distance between production and consumption". Due to the division of labor, production of any manufactured commodity is much more concentrated in space than is consumption of that commodity. So typically, the manufacturer uses the service of agents, who are distributed over the country and thus closer to the end consumer of the product. The distributor sells goods from many manufacturers and frequently has the choice whom of several manufacturers of similar products to serve. Given the agent's outlet with limited space, there is an opportunity cost of using part of the shelves for storing the product of any given manufacturer. Given a particular margin, a higher turnover of the product makes it more profitable to sell that particular product. Thus, the selling agent of the manufacturer profits from the product advertising by the manufacturer. By advertising, the manufacturer makes it more likely that the agent will put his product on the shelves.

This old and well-known story is reinforced by the fact that consumers tend to imitate each other, as described. As we have seen, there is an "imitation multiplier" for the price elasticity of demand of any given product. To the extent that advertising can raise the "imitation multiplier" of price changes one can expect that the manufacturer's profit – maximum consumer price may be lower than it would be without advertising. This is the "double helix": Advertising pushes consumer imitation; consumer imitation pushes advertising.

This "double-helix" result of advertising-cum-imitation analysis does not fit with a strong tradition in the economics of advertising. Indeed, many economists for a long time considered advertising-supported brand loyalty of customers as a barrier to entry into the relevant market. See in particular Bain 1956. Indeed, if there is competition among suppliers, it is very likely that the countervailing advertising of competitors could destroy the double-helix result of greater price elasticity of demand. A cartel agreement among suppliers to stop advertising (but to maintain price competition) could possibly raise the intensity of price competition. However, apart from the difficulty of implementing such an anti-advertising cartel (without doing harm to price competition), it is not clear that such non-advertising equilibrium with lower average prices is a welfare improvement for customers. It could very well be that advertising has an informative effect for consumers so that in the non-advertising equilibrium customers too frequently buy the "wrong" brand or, due to lacking information, do not benefit from this market at all.

As Bagwell 2007, Chapter 2, summarizes, economists have wavered between the "persuasive", the "informative" and the "complementary" view of advertising. The "double helix" characterization described previously belongs to the "informative" view. The view of advertising as providing useful information in an imperfect information environment leads to a "laissez-faire" policy recommendation. However, the informative view traditionally has based its theory on the assumption of fixed preferences – other than my "double helix" story. The "persuasive" view considers advertising as a distortion of preferences: the preferences prevailing with a ban on advertising are considered somehow superior to those induced by advertising. It also follows from the persuasive view that advertising is a waste of resources. The consumer pays too high a price for the product. He/she is worse off than he/she would be with a government-enforced ban on advertising.

For adherents of the persuasive view, a move from non-advertising to advertising is the opposite of an improvement. Thus, we can test on adaptive preferences only by looking at the opposite move: from laissez-faire advertising to a ban on advertising, which in this worldview is an improvement. By the very preference value judgement involved in the persuasive view, people must be happier under a ban on advertising than on laissez-faire advertising. This corroborates the hypothesis of adaptive preferences if we accept the ban on advertising as a public good of collective action as a replacement for the unfeasible individual choice to prefer the state of affairs without advertising to the laissez-faire of advertising. It is then an empirical question whether with preferences induced by laissez-faire advertising people do accept the public good of a ban on advertising. In a positive answer to this question, we can consider it highly plausible that with the preferences induced by a ban on advertising, people a fortiori prefer this ban to the advertising laissez-faire. Therefore, we would have adaptive preferences.

However, it appears highly implausible that with preferences induced by advertising laissez-faire, people prefer a general ban on advertising. To understand this,

I refer to the third variant for the economist's view on advertising: the "complementary" view. Here the economist considers the good in question and the advertising of it as two different goods, which are complements. They may be complements as seen from the consumer, or they may be complements, because the supplier only offers the good if the consumer also accepts some advertising coming with this good. In this latter case, as a rule, the advertisement promotes another good than the one to which the advertisement is tied. We of course talk about media like newspapers or television or Google. They operate on two-sided markets. The complementary view of advertising works with the basic assumption of fixed preferences. It is an extension of the informative view. This complementary view makes it highly implausible that people living in an advertising laissez-faire world would prefer to live in a world of an advertising ban. The latter would mean that people could not consume those media which live on the two-sided markets of offering media-news consumption and of providing an advertising outlet.

It is then likely that people prefer remaining in the state in which they are, be it a government ban on advertising (call it **B**) or an advertising laissez-faire (call it **A**). This in itself would not be a proof of adaptive preferences, but at least it comes close to a proof that preferences are not anti-adaptive. If we assume adaptive preferences then, in all likelihood, there exists an improving path either from **A** to **B** or from **B** to **A**. But, without substantial further information, we would not know which of the two improving paths really exists. How can we decide?

At this point, it is useful to return to Popper's theory of the Open Society (Popper 1945). We referred to it already in Book IV, Chapter 18. In Chapter 19 we also argue that adaptive preferences are a precondition for the working of the Open Society and of the principle of pragmatic compossibility. This then means that the status quo and the preferences induced by it are the starting point for any piecemeal piece of reform. In the actual world of western democratic societies, we have a somewhat regulated regime of "almost laissez-faire advertising". Not knowing whether there exists an improving path either from **A** to **B** or from **B** to **A**, we then conclude: a general ban on advertising would be against the spirit of an Open Society and of piecemeal engineering.

But the real world does have some regulation attached to the activity of advertising. It is a regime of *almost* laissez-faire advertising. There exist institutions which aim to implement "truth in advertising". To the extent that these institutions make a difference they may indeed help the effectiveness of advertising. If consumers trust the messages which advertising firms send by their advertisements, they are more likely to respond positively to those messages. "Truth in advertising", or better: "trust in advertising", may be a public good, benefitting consumers, as well as advertising manufacturers, as well as "two-sided market media".

One particular class of "truth in advertising" activities is the case of "phishing for phools", which we discussed in Chapter 23. There we analyzed the addiction problem in terms of a non-convexity of the "improvement sets" $A(x)$. The addiction equilibrium $\mathbf{A} = x$ has an improvement set $A(x)$, which contains the non-addiction equilibrium $\mathbf{B} = y$. In words: there exists an improvement path starting at $\mathbf{A} = x$ with preferences induced by x and ending at $\mathbf{B} = y$. If the addicted person were able to achieve a global optimum in an adaptive preferences set-up, he/she would walk that improvement path and would liberate himself/herself from the addiction. But people may be able to find the local optimum; however, they may be unable to find a global optimum in a world of non-convex improvement sets $A(x)$. Here a ban on advertising the good, which induces addiction, is consistent with the "truth in advertising" idea. But, here, obviously, the government acts in causal mode, not in freedom mode. And, as frequently pointed out in this book, the evidence required to let the government shift from freedom mode to causal mode must be very strong.

In this book, I do not discuss the economics of media like newspapers, television, social media and so on. I am aware of the concerns, whether a laissez-faire attitude towards the media is still appropriate for democratic life.

In the second part of this chapter I have discussed advertising, starting with the "double helix" of advertising and imitation. But, every kind of activity which intends to influence the behavior of other people could be investigated in the same manner as we did here with advertising. In a free society, we expect many diverse activities aimed at influencing the behavior of other people. It would be absurd to strive for the goal of a society without any influencing activities. With this observation in the background, a ban on all kinds of advertising appears difficult to defend. Rather, any specific government restriction on advertising can only hold up based on robust evidence concerning damage caused by such advertising.

References

Bagwell, Kyle, 2007, The Economics of Advertising, in: Armstrong, Mark and Porter, Robert A. (eds), Handbook of Industrial Organization, Amsterdam, Elsevier, Vol. 3, pp.1701–1844.

Bain, Joe S., 1956, Barriers to New Competition, Cambridge, MA, Harvard University Press, Xi + 329 pages.

Kotschy, Rainer and Sunde, Uwe, 2023, Have Preference Become more Similar Worldwide? CES Ifo Working Paper 10735, 64 pages.

Popper, Karl, 1945, The Open Society and Its Enemies, Vol. 1 Plato, Vol. 2 Hegel and Marx, London, Routledge and Kegan Paul, 361 pages and 420 pages.

26

COMPLEXITY, PRIVATE PROPERTY, DEMOCRACY, PUBLIC GOODS

Complexity and Near-Decomposability

In a classic piece, Herbert Simon 1962 argued that every complex system is a composition of "nearly decomposable subsystems". If a subsystem is again complex, it is also "nearly decomposable" into several sub-sub-systems, and so on, until one arrives at a large set of system elements, which are no longer complex. By "near decomposability", Simon means the following: he stipulates that every particular system has a well-defined measure of "intensity of interaction" between any two basic elements. Two subsystems then belong to a nearly decomposable system when the average intensity of interaction between any two elements in the same subsystem is much higher than the average intensity of interaction between any two elements belonging to different subsystems.

For example, look at temperature in a building with separate rooms. Due to strong (thermodynamic) interaction of air molecules in the same room, temperature differences between different points in the same room are on average much smaller than temperature differences between two points of the building located in two different rooms. (Second law of thermodynamics = law of increasing entropy.) Rooms in the building may have thermostats which maintain quite different temperatures from one room to the other. Nevertheless, even with more than one thermostat in a single room, temperature differences at different points of the same room are quite small.

Although, in all probability, examples from science may have inspired Simon's thinking, he insists that it is the evolution of *any* complex system which generates this property of near-decomposability. Any system is exposed to external shocks. Unless such a shock is so large that it destroys the whole system, it somehow manages to absorb this shock. This ability to absorb an external shock is, according to

DOI: 10.4324/9781032726410-31

Simon, much greater under conditions of near-decomposability than in the absence of this condition. For the latter case, take the example of a house of cards. If one of these cards is taken away, the whole house of cards collapses. On the other hand, in the case of near-decomposability, an external shock is most likely to directly affect only one of the subsystems or perhaps only one of the sub-sub-systems. The secondary or indirect effect of the local shock on other subsystems then in all likelihood is much weaker than the primary shock on the first subsystem. The other subsystems, by their interaction with the first subsystem, may then "repair" the damage made by the primary shock in the first subsystem.

Compared to a house of cards, a nearly decomposable system then also has much greater capacity of "trial and error" changes of its composition. It is then mutation prone – a characteristic allowing for further evolution. Mutations of its elements, after all, are just a specific class of external shocks. As complex systems are products of evolution, they must have a structure which is particularly suitable for evolution. Therefore, they all have the property of near-decomposability.

Figure 26.1 is a symbolic depiction of near-decomposability. It shows a quadratic matrix, where its elements a_{ij} represent the impact intensity of element i on element j. The smaller squares along the main diagonal of the large matrix contain the impact coefficients a_{ij} within any of the subsystems. Assume four subsystems of equal size, and assume that the average value of a_{ij} within any subsystem is ten times larger than the average value of a_{ij} across two subsystems. Then the total impact within the subsystems is 77% of the total impact in the large system, even though the number of impact factors a_{ij} within the subsystems is only one quarter of the total number of impact factors a_{ij} at large.

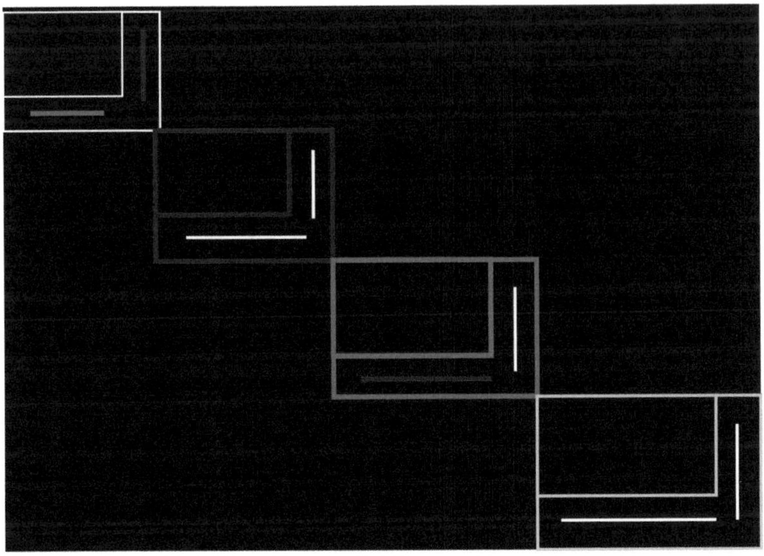

FIGURE 26.1 Near-Decomposability

We are, of course, aware of examples of system breakdown. Take a bush fire. A local fire may be the initial external shock. The fire may then spread and as a result may destroy many bushes or trees, perhaps a large forest. However, certain general conditions, for example, sufficient humidity and/or sufficient distance between trees and/or bushes, are likely to prevent the spreading of a local fire. If this natural forest is left alone one may observe an equilibrium cycle of large fires burning down many trees and bushes followed by a period of tree growth without large fires, because the last large fire has eliminated the conditions for further large fires. Much later the density of trees and bushes and grass then has become so large that a large bush fire is again to be expected.

In a similar way, Lotka and Volterra have described prey–predator cycles which exhibit population cycles with stable long-term values. Simon cites their work.

For an economist cycles of boom and bust due to financial interdependencies are a familiar topic. As Admati and Hellwig 2013 and again in the second edition 2023 show in their book, the stability of the financial system primarily rests on a sufficiently high equity ratio of bank lending. However, without regulation, there is a tendency of banks towards overexposure in terms of lending risk. In a financial system of complete laissez-faire, one may then observe cycles of boom (with "too much lending") and bust (when banks have difficulty attracting deposits, because potential depositors fear their loss). This is, in a sense, similar to the bush-fire cycle or the Lotka–Volterra cycle. Such laissez-faire banking might show stable long-run mean values of the bank equity ratio of bank loans but with great intertemporal variance.

In practice, the government intervenes, for example, by providing government guarantees for bank deposits. However, thereby bank competition is likely to lead to an additional overextension in terms of risk-bearing bank loans and thus again to the boom-bust cycle: the reason being that the risk of the bank loans is partly borne by the taxpayer. Therefore, Admati and Hellwig argue for the need of a government regulation concerning sufficient bank equity exposure to risky bank loans. As they show, contrary to a general belief, such regulation for substantially higher equity exposure of banks do not raise the social cost of capital. The parallel of the Admati–Hellwig proposal in the forest case would be forest management to ensure that bush fires become unlikely.

The general point I want to make is this: the fact that complex systems like large forests or interdependent financial systems are prone to exhibit up-down cycles does not contradict the near-decomposability theory developed by Herbert Simon. His argument is an evolutionary one: and for any kind of evolution, up-down cycles are quite typical.

Private Property and Compossibility

In a market economy, the institution of private property is a lead example of near-decomposability. In the following, I describe the production system of the economy. Human cooperation occurs in two different modes: the vertical and the horizontal.

The vertical mode may also be called the subordination mode. The horizontal mode may also be called the coordination mode or the exchange mode. In the capitalist market economy both modes are present. Markets are the phenomena of the horizontal mode. Firms are the institutions of the vertical mode. Human cooperation and interaction is much closer within any given firm than between firms. We may therefore consider firms subsystems of a larger system, according to the principle of near-decomposability. However, the economy at large is divided up into different markets, again according to the principle of near-decomposability. In anti-trust proceedings, the concept of the "relevant market" mirrors this de-composition of the economy at large into subsystems, which we call "markets". The interaction between employees in different competing firms is much more intensive (perhaps "antagonistic") than the average interaction intensity between employees working in two non-competing firms. We then already have three layers of systems: 1) the economy at large, 2) the set of subsystems called markets, 3) within any given market the set of sub-subsystems called firms.

Here I refrain from a near-decomposability description of the total economy, including the private consumption subsystem and including the subsystem of the government. The point I want to make is the function of private property in the production system of the economy. Ever since Ronald Coase's 1937 paper, "Nature of the Firm", economists have explained the existence of firms by means of the concept of transaction costs. People do not exclusively rely on the horizontal mode of cooperation because such a hypothetical system could only be maintained by incurring very high transaction costs. Within certain limits the same production results can be achieved by partly also using the vertical mode, which characterizes the organization of firms. And this with much lower transaction costs and therefore with less effort.

The owner of the firm (or the group of owners) is at the top of the firm hierarchy. He/she tells the firm's employees what is to be done. Private property of firms then is the institution by which the vertical mode of subordination can be embedded in the economic production system. And it turns out, as Coase 1937 explains, that this dual use of the horizontal and vertical mode of cooperation is a particularly successful way of producing the goods required by the consumers. Note, however, that in an economy characterized by competition, the horizontal mode of cooperation is dominant: for any particular firm the vertical mode within the firm only can survive if the firm obeys the laws of the market. A firm under competitive pressure disappears if it does not adapt to its market.

However, as we discussed already in the preceding chapter, in most cases we do not see "perfect competition" but "monopolistic competition". This means that it is not so easy for the owner of the firm to read the "commands of the market". And indeed, attempted innovation by any one competitor can be seen in analogy to a mutation in the gene pool of a living organism. If that mutation or innovation is successful, it may change the "rules of the game" in that market. So, any given firm owner has to make nontrivial decisions almost permanently. In that respect, we see him/her as a person with some entrepreneurial freedom.

This means that we can view this market also under the aspect of compossibility of freedom. As we discussed at length in Book IV, we opt for pragmatic compossibility precisely because we are in a world of competitive markets, and, as a society, we aim at competitive markets. We now can add to this by pointing to the important function of private property for a high degree of pragmatic compossibility. Under a competitive regime, the business decisions taken by the owner of a firm tend to be within the range of pragmatic compossibility. A change in the firm's pricing policy or product policy is intended to be to the owner's advantage, and this advantage tends to be greater than the negative of the side effects of this decision for his/her competitors and customers. I say, "it tends to be greater", for it is of course possible to construct counterexamples. However, if society "believes" in competition in product markets, then people essentially accept the idea that firm decisions taken under competitive pressure are appropriate for the benefit of people at large. This means: for lack of superior institutional alternatives, such competition-controlled decisions are pragmatically compossible with the decision freedom of all other people in this society.

Private property of firms and of assets like real estate enable society to distribute responsibilities for those assets among many different agents. There are then boundaries, borderlines between separate asset collections. These borderlines minimize interference from one such asset collection to other asset collections. In this way, many agents can be included in the collective task of optimizing the composition and the use of assets in the economy at large. For a sufficiently small asset collection, a single owner can effectively optimize its composition and its productive use. This precisely because of the borderline between his assets and the other assets in the economy. Moreover, within a competitive environment, the owner, by striving after his/her own wellbeing, has the incentive to organize the firm's operation for the benefit of society at large.

I repeat this economics textbook wisdom here to provide it as a lead example for Simon's principle of near-decomposability. For me, his insight makes Herbert Simon the "Adam Smith" of the twentieth century. The "invisible hand" (i. e. evolution) creates complex – and welfare-enhancing – social systems by means of the principle of near-decomposability. Splitting up ownership of the economy's assets into many distinct hands with corresponding in-between borderlines generates the nearly decomposable complex system of the highly productive social division of labor. The point for the general topic of this book, liberty, is the high degree of pragmatic compossibility of individual actions – generated by the borderlines between the assets owned by different owners. Even with a very high degree of action interdependence (including the division of labor), private property of most of the means of production together with pervasive competition on the markets generates the compossibility of the citizens' economic freedom in the production system of the economy.

We may quote from the history of thought to show that this insight into the advantage of private property has been there for a long time. In the "Summa

Theologica", Aquinas 1268, we read: "As everybody pays more attention to that which belongs to him private property brings about a better use of resources for the common good" (as quoted by Vaubel 2020).

Democracy

The competitive private ownership production system needs the State. The function of the three branches of government, the legislative, the executive and the judicial branches, is to generate a framework of law giving, law enforcement and independent law interpretation for its citizens.

What about the State itself? Democracy? Dictatorship? It is obvious that democracy provides much more political freedom than does any form of dictatorship. Can we give the same answer for freedom in the economic sphere? There is the theoretical possibility of a stable dictatorship with a free market economy. Indeed, there are a few historical attempts of this, like the Pinochet dictatorship in Chile half a century ago.

Ever since 24 February 2022, the world is in a new format of the cold or even not-so-cold war between democracy and totalitarianism. Gone are the perspectives, prevailing 30 years ago, of an "end of history" due to the worldwide victory of democracy, Fukuyama 1989. It is the war between the primacy of the horizontal mode of human cooperation and the primacy of the vertical mode of human cooperation. Any society is well advised to use both modes of cooperation. However, one of the two modes of cooperation characterizes the way to implement the roles the two modes are to play in society. In a democracy with a rule of law, the horizontal mode prevails in politics (elections, government by majority vote, rule of law) and in economic affairs (competition in markets). The vertical mode of cooperation by private property is used to implement near-decomposability; however, its legitimacy derives from the fact that this private property has to prove its social value under competitive conditions, that is, under a horizontal mode of interaction.

In a totalitarian dictatorship, it is the vertical mode of cooperation (i.e. "subordination") which determines where to use subordination and where to use horizontal cooperation. This means in particular that a dictatorship does not allow truly private property. To keep his "private property", an "oligarch" has to prove his loyalty to the dictator. However, to a certain extent, the dictator can use the advantages of a competitive price system in order to enhance the efficiency of the economy. As economists, we frequently use the theoretical figure of the "benevolent" dictator. However, the real-world dictator always wants to provide for his own security against attempts to replace him. Therefore, he cannot afford that other people be secure in their ownership of assets. The ensuing insecurity of private property in a dictatorship induces their owners to take decisions which from the social efficiency point of view are inferior to decisions taken under the rule of law with secure private property in a competitive environment. The typical long-termism of the private property owner with secure property rights does not exist in a totalitarian dictatorship. Here the private property owner is characterized by a system-induced short-termism.

This efficiency-inferiority of dictatorship relative to a democratic market economy does not mean that democracy wins in the new cold war. It is not at all self-evident that democracies generate the will to sustain a sufficiently strong countervailing military power against the totalitarian dictatorship. Such security against aggression by maintaining sufficient military power is an example of the economists' concept of "public goods".

Public Goods

Within our framework of "Freedom and Adaptive Preferences", substantial government action belongs to the causal mode and not to the freedom mode of legitimation. Some government action, including its budgetary consequences, is required for the implementation of a system of freedom within the range of pragmatic compossibility. In particular, private property and the rule of law require the Leviathan principle of the government monopoly for the use of physical force. Adam Smith's "invisible hand" builds on the Hobbesian Leviathan. 1776 is 125 years after 1651, the year of publication of "Leviathan" by Hobbes.

How does a democratic society decide about the provision of public goods? Using the Lindahl–Samuelson (1954) approach, economics provides an answer for the optimum level of a public good: for fixed preferences. In a world of adaptive preferences, we should observe that voters have a strong tendency to stay where they are. Their preferences for public goods are in fact very much formed by the level of public goods inherited from the past. Citizens think in the causal mode about the impact of the public goods on their own wellbeing. It is therefore the case that people evaluate this impact very much by their past experience. As we know, budgets for public goods show a high degree of inertia.

These facts may provide problems in situations of rapid change in the societal environment. The Putin-led aggression by Russia in the Ukraine is an example. Suddenly the need for much greater military defense expenses arises. It is then not clear that the democratic world society is willing to live up to this challenge. Many people, perhaps a majority, may cling to former beliefs concerning the usefulness or uselessness of additional defense expenses. After all, the provision of other public goods may suffer from budgetary shifts towards large increments in defense expenses. People may find so many excuses for refusing this expansion of defense expenses.

This is to the advantage of an aggressive totalitarian dictator. He can hide his aggressive intentions for a long time – and then, exploiting the ensuing military weakness of democratic societies, suddenly transgress borders to overwhelm the resistance in a neighboring democratic country. The economic inferiority of totalitarian dictatorships does not preclude the possibility that they should prevail over the democratic world – by the use of physical force. Democracies must be on their watch.

References

Admati, Anat and Hellwig, Martin, 2013, The Bankers' New Clothes – What's Wrong with Banking and What to Do About It, Princeton, NJ, Princeton University Press, 398 pages.

Aquinas, Thomas, 1268, Summa Theologica, Vol. 2, London, Eyre and Spottiswoode, 2006.

Coase, Ronald, 1937, The Nature of the Firm, Economica, 4 (16), 386–405.

Fukuyama, Francis, 1989, The End of History, The National Interest, 16, 3–18.

Hobbes, Thomas, 1651, Leviathan or the Matter, London, Forme & Power of a Common-Wealth Ecclesiasticall and Civill.

Samuelson, Paul A., 1954, The Pure Theory of Public Expenditure, Review of Economics and Statistics, 36, 387–389.

Simon, Herbert, 1962, The Architecture of Complexity, Proceedings of the American Philosophical Society, 106 (6), 467–482.

Smith, Adam, 1776, Inquiry into the Nature and Causes of the Wealth of Nations, 2 volumes, London, W. Strahan and T. Cadell.

Vaubel, Roland, 2020, Die Begründung von Freiheit, ORDO, 70, 373–385.

27

TWO GENERALIZED MEDIA OF EXCHANGE

Karl Popper vs Erich Fromm

Money is a generalized medium of exchange that allows cooperation between two persons at a substantially lower transaction cost than would have to be borne in a barter economy. Here I want to explain that there are two different generalized media of exchange which complement each other; however, there is also substantial antagonism between the two. My analysis has a basis: the universal presence of adaptive preferences.

Adaptive preferences also apply to interpersonal sympathies and antipathies. The child obtains love and help from his/her mother. The mother's sympathy for her own offspring is a universal phenomenon – and not restricted to the human species. We can take it as a given. In the child, it implants love and respect for his/her mother. Out of this grows the general phenomenon of reciprocity: sympathy of person A for person B tends to generate reciprocal sympathy of person B for person A. And, like a mirror image, antipathy of person A against person B tends to generate antipathy of person B against person A.

As a rule, adaptive sympathy and antipathy preferences generate a great sympathy inertia and a great antipathy inertia. This is the root of the family as the most important micro-organization of any society. Parents hope for their children and for the children of their children to live a happy life. They arrange their own affairs very much for the benefit of their offspring. The family is society's main source of long-term planning, of a strong provision for the future.

In particular, this also implies that parents educate their children for fitness in the many forms of competition in the social world at large. Apart from useful skills like reading, writing and arithmetic, such education also is designed to motivate their children for "long-termism", to sacrifice present pleasures against incremental benefits in the future. A large part of experimental economics and psychology concerns itself with this trade-off between immediate and deferred satisfaction of

DOI: 10.4324/9781032726410-32

wants. This literature, in implicit or explicit form, presupposes that more "long-termism" is to the benefit of the subject. Compare, for example, Heckman et al. 2013

Parents differ by their ability and their motivation to educate their children. As the children enter the competitive world outside of their family, their chances of success are unequally distributed. This is on top of their genetically determined ability differences. Inequality is an unavoidable consequence of parental care for their children. Inequality is an unavoidable result of family-based long-termism.

As we discussed in the preceding chapter, democracy and the rule of law are the prerequisite for a productive, competitive private property economy. Democracy is deeply rooted in the ideal of "equality". "One person – one vote". This ideal of equality itself derives from the intra-family dynamics, in particular the competition among siblings for parental love and care. Parental altruism generates "long-termism". However, unequal parental treatment of children generates unequal outcomes for them when grown up. Survival chances of the genes of the favored children are much better than are those of the children who received below family average love and care. "Envy", the resistance against being treated worse than others, is therefore firmly imbedded in the genes of the human race. The consequence for parental education of their offspring is an "equal-treatment norm" – to avoid or minimize a highly destructive "war among siblings".

The needs and wants of the children depend on their gender, their position in the sibling order, their inborn talents, their age, their appearance. Treating different children equally well requires from their parents many comparisons of apples with pears. This has important consequences for the other generalized means of exchange.

Money allows the instantaneous exchange of things between two persons: A provides some physical good or some service for B, and B pays for it in money form at the same time. Moreover, the two objects exchanged at the same time also have the same money value. This last statement sounds like a tautology. However, under competitive conditions it is more than that: ideally, prices formed by competition represent the scarce resources used up for the production of the goods. The money paid for the good represents the same amount of scarce resources as the good itself: Hayek 1945. This exchange of two objects of equal value is a particular form of reciprocity.

What about reciprocity outside of the money world? Reciprocity in the family, reciprocity among friends, among colleagues working in the same organization? Typically, the "give and take" within such reciprocal relation is not instantaneous. Person A may help person B in some way one day, whereas person B provides some service to person A at some other day. We then stipulate another generalized medium exchange: it is "Time". By the fact that such reciprocal relation between two (or more than two) persons is stable (due to adaptive preferences), it can become much richer and much more productive than it could be with the additional requirement that the "give" and the "take" have to be instantaneous. Stretching the non-monetary exchange over time makes such trust relationships substantially richer – and it makes “Time” another generalized medium of exchange, in addition to the well-known generalized medium of exchange: “Money”.

If you look closer, you see that the medium “Money” is embedded in the medium “Time”. For a money system to work properly, the seller of the good or service must have “trust” in the money he/she receives in exchange. He/she must expect to be able to buy goods and/or services for this money in the future. In this sense, the medium “Money” already relies on the medium “Time”. It is “embedded” in “Time”.

Historically, the generalized medium of exchange “Time” is of course much older than the generalized medium of exchange “Money”. “Stone Age Economics” (Sahlins 1972) describes an economy without a money veil. The economic facts were open to the naked eye. People in the Stone Age lived in small hunter-gatherer groups; trust, parental care, personal reciprocity held the group together. “Time” was the exclusive generalized medium of exchange.

There is a fundamental difference between the two generalized media of exchange. “Money” relies on *value quantification*. As a generalized medium of exchange, “Time” abhors value quantification; “Time” imposes a *value quantification taboo*. There is no need to explain the value quantification requirement for transactions involving money payment. The taboo against value quantification for activities connected to the generalized medium of exchange “Time” results from the “apple-and-pears-comparison-problem”. For the market system using the “Money” medium of exchange, economists understand the solution for this “apple-and-pears-comparison-problem” by means of the prices for apples and pears. For the trust system outside the market, using the “Time” system of exchange this solution is not available. Here the answer is the value quantification taboo: you are not allowed to quantify the worth of your “give” and of your “take”. Thereby “give” and “take” are considered somehow “equal” in merit even though they are not weighed, counted or measured in some other way. Of course, if items are equal in kind (only apples of the same quality and size) this valuation taboo breaks down – and there will be protests from those members of the community who received less than others. Generally, if the valuation taboo prevails, anyone protesting against a given arrangement has the burden of proof of not being treated fairly. Without an agreed valuation procedure and hence with a valuation taboo this burden of proof is a difficult task. This then tends to stabilize the prevailing setup. Nevertheless, very, very unjust distribution arrangements can be challenged in a community, as long as it is reasonably democratic in its structure.

Small communities with “Time” as the generalized medium of exchange typically assign “roles” to their members. It is then everybody’s task to perform his/her role in a satisfactory way. For the cohesion of the community, the different roles of its different members must be reasonably comparable in terms of the burden of playing the role. And it is important for the coherence that each member feel appreciated for a good performance of his/her role. We can easily understand that the stability of this community would be heavily upset if the provisions of the different members would be measured by some valuation scheme and it would turn out that the provisions are highly unequal without some generally agreed justification of inequality. One such justification could be age: adults are required to provide more than small children do. Apart from these justifications, a valuation taboo is the best answer to legitimize the prevailing status quo.

Altruism is a concept frequently used for the intra-family interaction but also for other small groups of friends. As we discussed, altruism of the mother for her children is deeply rooted in the genes of the human species, as it is generally among mammals and birds. Beyond the motherly love for her children, the appearance of altruistic behavior may represent true altruism, but it also may be motivated by the corresponding expectation of return by other members of the small group: "give" may be motivated by the expectation of future "take". For our analysis, we are not obliged to distinguish between sincere altruism and other motives of "altruistic" behavior. I only bring it up at this point because I want to make sure that we well understand the function which is played by the societal "division of labor" between seemingly or sincere altruistic behavior and the egoistical behavior, which generally is associated with the attitudes of agents under the regime of the "Money" form of generalized means of exchange.

First of all: almost every citizen is partly a member of interaction groups that use the "Money" form of means of exchange and is partly a member of interaction groups that use the "Time" form of means of exchange. If, according to a widespread belief, the "Time" form is associated with primarily altruistic behavior, whereas the "Money" form is associated with primarily egoistical behavior, then almost everybody is split between a membership in the class of altruists and a membership in the class of egoists. Altruism or egoism then is not an alternative between two classes of personalities. It is an alternative between two forms of human interaction, where both forms play an important role for the functioning of society at large.

Returning to the main theme of my book, "freedom", we then can connect our preceding analysis to Karl Popper's concept of the "Open Society". In the first volume of this two-volume work Popper criticizes Plato's "collectivism", as developed in particular in his *Republic*. There, as Popper describes it, Plato identifies "collectivism" (Popper's way to describe Plato's position) with altruism and "individualism" (Popper's way to describe the Athenian democracy in Plato's time) with egoism. Popper insists that this Platonian identification is wrong – and that one should distinguish between the two oppositions of "collectivism vs individualism" and "egoism vs altruism". His "Open Society" and my concept of "freedom" or "liberty" are individualistic and anti-collectivistic. However, the society, as we understand it in the tradition of the enlightenment, individualistic as it is, is full of egoistic behavior and is full of altruistic behavior. As I indicated, the "Money" form of medium of exchange is strongly associated with egoistic behavior; indeed, under the pressure of competition, egoistic ("profit maximizing") behavior is the

"Moses and the prophets" (Marx 1867, p. 580) of capitalism. On the other hand, as already discussed, the "Time" form of generalized medium of exchange is associated with (sincere or pretended) altruism. Altruism and egoism fulfil their specific functions within a well-working modern society. The same person tends to perform egoistic societal functions as well as altruistic societal functions.

As we have seen, the original altruism of the mother for her child together with reciprocity of sympathy between persons induces the family form of mutual altruism under the "Time" mode of a generalized medium of exchange. Adaptive preferences help to maintain this structure. Because of the prevailing adaptive preferences, there is also feedback from the activities of the person to his/her preferences. A person who is quite successful in the world of the "Money" form of generalized means of exchange, tends to put heavy weight on material wealth and on material well-being. A person who mainly spends his/her time within the family, with relatives and friends, emphasizes the "Time" form of exchange and thus emphasizes friendship and altruism. In a sense, we then observe two "camps" of "Money"-oriented and of "Time"-oriented citizens, despite the fact that almost every adult citizen is part of both generalized means of exchange.

The coexistence of the two generalized media of exchange "Money" and "Time" shows up in many different forms. One such form are the "LETS": the "local exchange trading systems", which by now can be found in many places. The German expression is "Tauschgemeinschaften". People involved in such a community provide services to each other, and they receive payment in the form of a LETS-specific currency. Typically, the "prices" of the different services correspond to the amount of time spent on a unit of such service. The idea is that these are fair prices, collectively agreed upon in the LETS. Members can obtain such services from others without immediately returning a service of equal value. However, the idea is that within a reasonable time span there is a balance between "give" and "take". In a highly readable book, Daniela Meier 2001 provides theory and empirical results on such LETS – including the "ideology" connected with such organizations. The latter focuses on the "Time" medium of exchange. The fact that there are "prices" in the system comes from the idea that there should be reciprocity in this community, and they should not be seen as price signals of the relative scarcities of the different services. That is why the LETS has its own idiosyncratic "currency". And there is a taboo against expressing the price of that idiosyncratic currency in terms of money. The rules are "anti-capitalistic", because the rate of interest on positive or negative currency balances is zero – and because one should not generate permanent positive or negative balances. The rules are "anti-globalist", as the services provided and consumed are supposed to be from the same town. We can interpret LETS as an attempt to widen the potential of the "Time" general medium of exchange with its altruistic connotations.

However, the fact that LETS do not adhere to the valuation taboo generates a slippery slope in the direction of the "Money" general means of exchange.

In the field of social theory or social philosophy, we find two historical lines: one that is aligned to the "Money" form of exchange and emphasizes "egoism" and competition, the other that is aligned to the "Time" form of exchange and emphasizes "altruism" and solidarity.

A note on terminology: psychologists and behavioral economists use the term "social preferences" for the observed fact that agents, to a certain extent, do behave altruistically; three examples: Murphy et al. 2011, Fehr and Charness 2023 or Steimanis and Vollan 2022. On the other hand, traditionally welfare economics has used the term "social welfare function". To avoid confusion in Book VI on cost-benefit analysis, I there use the term "collective preferences", or "collective quasi-preferences", to mean "society's" basis for deciding about projects in terms of a cost-benefit analysis.

Karl Popper's *Open Society and Its Enemies* is representative of the "Money" form of exchange (Popper 1945). Another refugee from fascist Central Europe of the same generation, Erich Fromm (1976), wrote the bestselling book *To Have or to Be*, which is representative of the "Time" form of exchange. The two authors provide a fascinating scene of conflict between "good" and "evil", only the "good" in one author's set-up is the "evil" in the other author's drama. As I reported earlier, Popper sees the "collectivism" in Plato's *Republic* as the source of modern totalitarianism and announces the Open Society, which quite obviously corresponds to the "Money" form of exchange. Erich Fromm, the psychoanalyst, sees two modes of human existence, the mode of "To Have" and the mode of "To Be". The latter is the "good" one, whereas "To Have" induces egoistical and aggressive behavior, which, given modern weapons, can be dangerous for the world at large. Fromm argues that a capitalist world induces the human character to stay in the "To Have" mode of existence. To save the world, capitalism must be relinquished and must be replaced by a large collection of small villages. The latter looks like a democratic variant of Plato's *Republic*: the philosopher-king replaced by a permanent town meeting where citizens discuss and decide everything. And, of course, no private property; indeed, if I read Fromm correctly, almost no privacy either.

We can trace the Popper position and the Fromm position back to the past. Karl Popper, a founding member of the Mt. Pèlerin Society, sees himself in the liberal tradition, which was an important part of the enlightenment movement of the 18th century. Bernard De Mandeville and then later, of course, Adam Smith emphasize the wealth creating function of egoistic behavior, the famous "invisible hand". At the same time Jeremy Bentham 1789 and others generated utilitarianism with its distinctly individualist and quantifying approach. John Stuart Mill 1859 continued this school of thought – and it merged into the subjectivist school of neoclassical economics. The measuring rod for the performance of society and, in particular, of the economy was a kind of sum of the welfare of the citizens, as measured by means of their own preferences. This tradition is individualistic and works with the assumption of agents who behave in an autonomous manner. The "Money" form of exchange enables society to generate a quasi-optimal distribution of goods among the citizens, because in market equilibrium, marginal utilities of a good are equal between different persons. The autonomy axiom of human behavior enables this theory to build a bridge between individual welfare and collective welfare – and thus between individualistic free choice and good performance of the society at large. The attractiveness of this individualistic school of course also derives from the undeniable fact that material progress was one overwhelming result for a world society which gave its citizens the freedom to invent and to innovate.

In his anthropology, Erich Fromm essentially denies the autonomy axiom of human behavior, as long as people exist in the "To Have" mode. Whereas his particular approach of distinguishing between the "To Have" mode and the "To Be" mode is highly original, he refers to earlier witnesses, in particular to Albert Schweitzer, to the early Karl Marx (1837–1848), to the medieval mystic Eckhart, to Buddhism and to other spiritual scriptures, among them Maimonides. Although not quoted in his book, we may also refer to Thomas More's *Utopia* and to Rousseau's anthropology. Fromm translated the writings of the early Marx into English and commented on them in other books (Fromm 1961). In Marx, he finds the proposition that capitalist society distorts human consciousness, and from there he justifies the proposition that you cannot let people simply decide for themselves about their conduct. It is also of interest that Fromm associates the enlightenment idea of "progress" with the "To Have" mode – and thus explicitly dissociates himself from the goal of material progress.

Whatever we think about this proposition of the "false consciousness", we have to accept the fact that throughout modern times the capitalist market system was heavily criticized, and this not only by people in poverty but also, and in particular, by writers and by other intellectuals. So we have two threads in the capitalism debate, one centered on the "Money" form of exchange, pro-market, individualistic, favoring competition, tolerating, even encouraging, egoism and insisting on quantification; the other thread centered on the "Time" form of exchange, critical of the market system, holistic, emphasizing solidarity, altruism, collective decisions and abhorring the quantitative "give and take" calculation.

Modern economics has continued the debate between the "Money" form and the "Time" form of social life. In two impressive overviews Samuel Bowles 1998 and 2016 collected and improved our understanding of this debate. On Bowles' work, see also Kranton 2019. It is one of the great privileges of democracy and of a free society that it encompasses open debate about its own foundations, something which a totalitarian system cannot afford.

The individualistic "Money" form establishes the normative guideline from the utilitarian calculus, that is, essentially from the idea of a fixed ordinal utility function or fixed preferences. Here the measuring rod of social performance are the preferences of the citizens. In Fromm's theory, citizens first have to be in the "To Be" mode, and then the permanent village meeting decides for its citizens what is to be done for their benefit. For Fromm, quoting Karl Marx, this society, which transgressed class conflict, no longer suffers from tensions between any particular private interests and the "common good". Everybody then agrees to adapt his/her own goals to the common good of the village. Altruism reigns. And people are satiated with a minimum of material consumption goods – so that there is no longer conflict between citizens about the provision of material goods.

As remarked earlier, everybody is part of the "Money" system as well as part of the "Time" system. Everybody then is partly "egoist" and partly "altruist". This dual human nature also corresponds to two modes of trust between persons. There is "specific trust" – and there is "encompassing trust". When I say "I trust my brother", it is an expression of "encompassing" trust, meaning that whatever the issue is, I trust him because he is my brother. He is part of my family; he is, together with myself, part of a "Time" community, where the "give and take" is mediated by the "Time" general medium of exchange. Or, we may express is this way: "by encompassing trust". By "altruism". By "Gemeinschaft" ("Community"), to quote Ferdinand Tönnies 1887. When I say "I trust my banker", it is an expression of "specific" trust, which tends to be limited to a specific field of transactions, like, in this example, monetary transactions. He is, like me, part of the "Money" community, where the "give and take" is mediated by the "Money" general medium of exchange. Or we may express it this way: by "specific trust", by the absence of mutual altruism, by "Gesellschaft" ("Society"), to quote Ferdinand Tönnies 1887.

Rainer Klump reminds me that the "Money"–"Time" dichotomy also corresponds to Max Weber's dichotomy between "Zweckrationalität" ("purposive rational action") and "Wertrationalität" ("value rationality"). On this, see Baurmann 2000.

It is obvious that my book on adaptive preferences belongs to the thread of the individualistic "Money" form of generalized means of exchange. Nevertheless, I want to show that the idea of non-convexity of improvement sets $A(x)$, as described in Chapter 23, mutatis mutandis, could be applied to Fromm's two modes of existence. For convenience, I reproduce the corresponding figure from Chapter 23. The difference in interpretation from that chapter is that here we talk about a kind of hypothetical "collective" movement of individual preferences. Keeping this difference in mind, we may identify the long-run equilibrium point **B** with

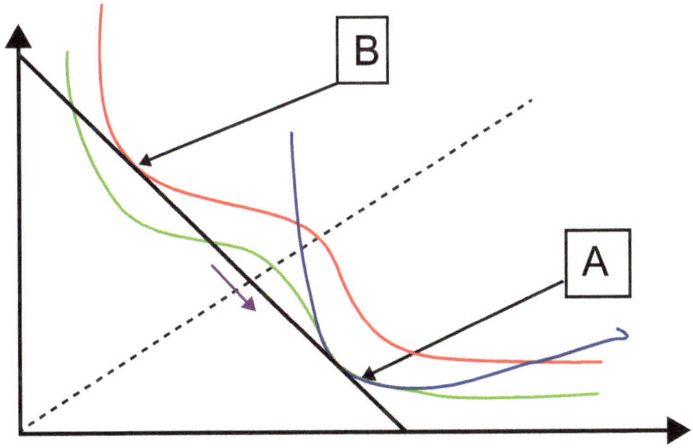

FIGURE 27.1 Path Dependence of Long-Run Demand

the "To Be" mode of existence, as proposed by Fromm, and we may identify the long run equilibrium point **A** with the "To Have" mode of existence. We may then interpret the horizontal variable x_1 as the average citizen's provision with material goods, and we may interpret the vertical variable x_2 as the average citizen's free time outside of the working time for the production of material goods. To a large portion, this "free" time in an altruistic society will be spent for unpaid services for other citizens, for example, by attending the town meeting.

From the Fromm point of view, the equilibrium **A** is a kind of collective addiction of the citizens, which keeps them in the "bad" "To Have" mode of existence. But, by our theory of adaptive preferences, we know that there exists an improvement path wandering from the "To Have" mode of existence to the "To Be" mode of existence **B**. In Chapter 23, we applied this figure to support the Akerlof–Shiller argument that there is a government role of interfering in the market economy with the purpose of preventing "phishing" activities. Correspondingly, Erich Fromm pleads for government prohibition of almost all kinds of advertising and for many other government interventions. And he sees the rising anti-consumerism movement of the sixties and seventies as an encouraging sign of a gradual change away from the "To Have" mode of existence. I leave the issue at this point.

The critical question is this: is there a potential "To Be" long-run equilibrium of free people, and is such equilibrium welfare superior to the prevailing "To Have" equilibrium? We do not know. To quote Hayek's formula, it would be a "pretense of knowledge" if we stated the superiority (or even the feasibility) of a societal "To Be" mode of human existence over the existing "To Have" mode of human existence. It would be a "pretense of knowledge" to announce like a prophet that there is out there a stable "To Be" societal equilibrium without the "alienation" of the human "To Have" mode of existence (Hayek 1974).

Remaining in the "piecemeal engineering" philosophy of Karl Popper's "Open Society", we therefore should not take Erich Fromm's anthropology and its political consequences for granted. Incrementalism has served the western world well in the past.

References

Baurmann, Michael, 2000, Der Markt der Tugend – Recht und Moral in der liberalen Gesellschaft – Eine soziologische Untersuchung, Tübingen, J.C.B. Mohr, XIX + 681 pages.

Bentham, Jeremy, 1789, An Introduction to the Principles of Morals and Legislation, in: Burns, J. H. and Hart, H. L. A. (eds), The Collected Works of Jeremy Bentham, Oxford, Oxford University Press, 1998.

Bowles, Samuel, 1998, Endogenous Preferences: The Cultural Consequences of Markets and Other Economic Institutions, Journal of Economic Literature, XXXVI, 75–111.

Bowles, Samuel, 2016, The Moral Economy: Why Good Incentives Are No Substitute for Good Intentions, New Haven, CT, Yale University Press, 288 pages.

Fehr, Ernst and Charness, Gary, 2023, Social Preferences: Fundamental Characteristics and Economic Consequences, CES-Ifo Working Paper 10488, 13 + 32 pages.

Fromm, Erich, 1961, Marx's Concept of Man, New York, Frederick Ungar Publishing, 85 pages.

Fromm, Erich, 1976, To Have or to Be? The Nature of Psyche, New York, Harper & Row, 182 pages.

Hayek, Friedrich A., 1945, The Use of Knowledge in Society, American Economic Review, 35 (4), 519–530.

Hayek, Friedrich A., 1974, The Pretense of Knowledge (Nobel Prize Lecture 1974), in: Caldwell, Bruce (ed.), The Collected Works of F.A. Hayek: The Market and Other Orders, Vol. 15, Chicago, University of Chicago Press.

Heckman, James, Pinto, Rodrigo and Savelyev, Peter, 2013, Understanding the Mechanisms Through Which an Influential Early Childhood Program Boosted Adult Outcomes, American Economic Review, 103 (6), 2052–2086.

Kranton, Rachel, 2019, The Devil Is in the Details: Implications of Samuel Bowles's *The Moral Economy* for Economics and Policy Research, Journal of Economic Literature, 57 (1), 147–160.

Marx, Karl, 1837–1848, "Die Frühschriften", ed. by Siegfried Landshut, Stuttgart, Kröner, 1953, 588 pages.

Marx, Karl, 1867, Das Kapital, Vol. 1, Hamburg, Verlag Otto Meissner, 784 pages.

Meier, Daniela, 2001, Tauschringe als besondere Bewertungssysteme in der Schattenwirtschaft – Eine theoretische und empirische Analyse, Berlin, Duncker & Humblot, 273 pages.

Mill, John Stuart, 1859, On Liberty, London, Walter Scott Publishing Company, 1903, with an Introduction by W. L. Courtney, LLD, XXVIII + 219 pages.

Murphy, Ryan O., Ackermann, Kurt A. and Handgraaf, Michel J. J., 2011, Measuring Social Value Orientation, Judgement and Decision Making, 6 (8), 771–781.

Popper, Karl, 1945, The Open Society and Its Enemies, Vol. 1 Plato, Vol. 2 Hegel and Marx, London, Routledge and Kegan Paul, 361 pages and 420 pages.

Sahlins, Marshall, 1972, Stone Age Economics, London, Routledge.

Steimanis, Ivo and Vollan, Björn, 2022, Prosociality as Response to Slow- and Fast-Onset Climate Hazards, Global Sustainability, 5, e10 [1–13].

Tönnies, Ferdinand, 1887, Gemeinschaft und Gesellschaft – Abhandlung des Communismus und des Socialismus als empirischer Kulturformen, Leipzig, Fues's Verlag (R. Reisland), XXX + 294 pages.

28

THREE LEVELS OF ECONOMIC ACTIVITY

Externalities

This Chapter 28 prepares for the last chapter of this Book V: Chapter 29 entitled "Social Market Economy". Chapter 28 is adapted from a paper which I published four decades ago, Weizsäcker 1981 (in German) and Weizsäcker 1984 (in English). The title, "Rights and Relations in Economic Theory", refers back to Böhm–Bawerk's Habilitations-Thesis, which appeared in 1881 under the title "Rechte und Verhältnisse vom Standpunkt der volkswirtschaftlichen Güterlehre". ("Whether Legal Rights and Relationships Are Economic Goods") (Böhm-Bawerk 1881). My publication arose out of the invited Böhm–Bawerk Lecture at the University of Innsbruck in 1980 and was published in German exactly 100 years after the publication of Böhm–Bawerk's book: Von Weizsäcker 1981.

Early on in this lecture, I presented a table, which now will be the main topic of this chapter. For this table, I distinguished three levels of economic activity: the consumption level, the production level and the innovation level. The lowest level of economic activity is the consumption level. It provides benefit directly. The middle level is "production": it provides benefits indirectly, as it raises the possibilities of consumption: the third level is "innovation": it provides benefits indirectly via two steps in between. It enhances the potential for production. Thereby, eventually it enhances the potential for consumption.

To encourage production, the free access to consumption goods must be prevented by means of private property institutions. To encourage innovation, intellectual property rights are introduced. They limit free access to the available production technologies.

I characterize the general concept of "competition" by "free access to . . .". As this table indicates, we can associate negative externalities with the uncompensated use of (scarce) resources. To the extent that consumption involves scarce resources, insufficient compensation for their use generates negative externalities.

DOI: 10.4324/9781032726410-33

TABLE 28.1 The Three Levels of Economic Activity

Level	*Criterion = Goal*	*Competition at Level 1*	*Competition at Level 2*	*Competition at Level 3*	*Appropriate Behavioral Norms*	*Social Control*
1 "Consumption" Given quantities of goods	"Justice" (equality)	Free access to goods. Hobbes. Negative externalities	Property in things = consumption goods by purchase	Property in things = consumption goods by purchase	Orientation to norms and tradition, conformism	Education to altruistic behavior. Compulsion
2 "Production" Production of goods with given technology	Allocative efficiency	-	Free access to available production technologies	Restrictions on imitation. Intellectual property rights	Utility and profit maximizing	Competition at level 2
3 "Innovation" Creation of new production technologies	Progress	-	-	Innovation competition, positive externalities	Search, satisficing, non-conformism	Competition at level 3, "competition as discovery process"

Free access to consumption goods only then comes without negative externalities if these goods are available in abundance. In human history, there have been many conflicts about free or limited access to goods. There is the "classic" of Hugo Grotius, *Mare Liberum* (Grotius 1609), in which the author argues for the right of every nation to use the sea for seafaring trade. Implicit in this argument of the "founder of international law" is the position that the resources of the sea were available in abundance. Today we know that free access to ocean fishing generates an inefficient "overfishing" equilibrium.

In the ideal case of production, all inputs are paid for with their equilibrium scarcity price, and every output again is paid for with its scarcity price. Thus, in this ideal case, production generates no externalities. This ideal case is associated with "competition at level 2": free access to the available production methods. It is the world of Walras–Arrow–Debreu General Equilibrium – and of Hayek's theory of the price system as an aggregator of local, dispersed knowledge (Hayek 1945).

At the level of innovation, new knowledge is generated. It is almost impossible to completely internalize the production of new knowledge. Some of this internalization takes the form of intellectual property rights (IPRs), for example, patents. However, IPRs work at the expense of competition at the level 2, that is, at the expense of free access to available production techniques. There is then a trade-off between stimulating level 3 activities and optimizing level 2 activities. It is one of the important tasks of anti-trust policy to find an optimum for this trade-off.

This trade-off between level 2 and level 3 activities implies that there is a kind of trade-off between two different kinds of liberties: the liberty to produce (level 2) and the liberty to innovate (level 3). If, due to strengthened IPRs, (potential or real) innovators obtain greater opportunities, this may be at the expense of some operators at level 2; their access to available technologies may be diminished. Our framework in this book provides an answer: as long as the optimal trade-off is not implemented, a changeover to this optimum satisfies the criterion of pragmatic compossibility. Again, there is no conflict between the liberty to compete and economic efficiency. I have taken this point up in more detail in a German language publication, Von Weizsäcker 2009.

Concerning level 3, there is an additional important point: generally, innovation generates positive externalities: for the innovator it is not possible to obtain a profit which equals his contribution to the welfare of the society. People buy his/her innovative product only at a price, so some consumer surplus remains. However, this does not mean that a further strengthening of IPRs is appropriate. There is competition among innovators. Thus, it could happen that too many resources are devoted to obtaining, say, a patent. In my book on "barriers to entry" (Von Weizsäcker 1980) I discuss this issue in some detail. Nevertheless, it remains correct to say that level 3 activity generates substantial positive externalities.

I then associate negative externalities with level 1 activities, no externalities for the ideal case of level 2 activities and positive externalities with level 3 activities. In the real world, the activity of production tends to be associated with negative as well as with positive externalities. These days we associate the process of production with damages for the climate, for example, by the emission of CO_2. On the other hand, we also associate many production activities with positive externalities: take as an example medical practice, which, as a byproduct, generates additional useful medical knowledge. A substantial fraction of the ever-increasing life expectancy of the world population is due to this learning byproduct of medical practice.

As these two examples of positive and negative externalities show, there is a difference: how to cope with them. In the meantime, the political process has adopted the idea of pricing for greenhouse gases. Nobody talks about a pricing of the learning side effect of medical practice. This difference mirrors the distinction between private and public goods. The learning side effect of medical practice is a public good. As we know from the Lindahl-Samuelson (1954) tradition in public economics, pricing of public goods is almost an impossibility. In Chapter 26, I therefore refer the provision of public goods to the "causal mode" of government activity. On the other hand, the emission of greenhouse gases – as a byproduct of consumption or production – uses a scarce resource – and it is therefore a private good. Here pricing makes sense. The setting of a price for greenhouse gases is part of the "causal mode" of government activity. However, once the price is set, the actual allocation of emission licenses by the price mechanism is part of the "freedom mode" of government activity. And the latter is consistent with the compossibility principle of freedom, because the corresponding allocation is superior to any other allocation of the same total quantity.

In this book, I refrain from an extensive discussion of climate policy. Here it is only an example for Pigou's answer to the problem of negative externalities: finding an appropriate price in order to internalize the negative externality. The politics of setting the greenhouse gas price (and the lack of knowledge about its correct value) may lead to a price which is "too low", or it may lead to a price which is "too high". As the world started with a greenhouse gas price of zero, adaptive preferences indicate that the price for a long time was set too low. However, there also exists the possibility that at some time in the future the price will be set too high. After all, the recipient of the payments for greenhouse gases is a kind of monopolist: it is the state treasury. Once the price is set and the government revenue thereby is established and spent, adaptive preferences may make it difficult to cut the price. A reason the correct Pigou price of greenhouse gases may decline in the long run are innovations induced by a high price so that we obtain greenhouse-gas–saving technical progress beyond the initial expectations.

I now want to direct the reader's attention to the last two columns of the "three-levels tableau". They have the headings "Appropriate Behavioral Norms" and "Social Control". In a "paradise" world, where people simply can eat or otherwise consume the fruits growing on the trees without any labor input, national output is simply there. No incentives are necessary to stimulate some production effort. The just distribution then is equality. People should follow the behavioral norms overcome from the past. The best way to achieve all that is education to altruism, "love thy neighbor as thyself". These norms remind us of Erich Fromm's "To Be" mode of existence, as discussed in the preceding Chapter 27. And they are inconsistent with the "freedom mode" of government action. As we have discussed, it was Karl Popper's fear that totalitarian systems would arise out of the norms designed to suppress egoism. Nevertheless, it is highly plausible that the "family values", which we discussed in the preceding Chapter 27, are indispensable for a free democratic society. Some "family conformism" or "family solidarity" is an element of stability of society, and they are indispensable for the "long-termism" of society.

In the second row of our tableau, "production", the last two columns read "utility and profit maximization" and "level 2 competition". Indeed, if the social control mechanism for the production activity is "competition", then operators are forced to behave egoistically. "Competition among altruists" is almost a contradiction in terms, unless the social game is "disappearance": the person has won who has disappeared first. Buddha's "Nirvana". The discrepancy between the "family values" and the competitive production economy is the source of the everlasting critique of capitalism. And, based on Marx, it led to the idea of a centrally planned economy, which should operate without competition as the social control mechanism. It did not work, for reasons which, I think, are well understood by "bourgeois economics". On this, see Kornai 1992. Unless we take Erich Fromm's position that material wealth and material progress is the opposite of "true progress", our modern societies must live with this tension between altruistic family values and egoistic competition values.

Competition implies decentralized decision making – and, as such, freedom. However, as discussed before, the manufacturing operator must follow the signs of the market. Therefore, the freedom is not so much his as that of his/her customer. It is level 1 which mainly commands what is to be done on level 2. "The customer is king". Obviously, the level 1–level 2 relation is more complicated than that. In Chapters 23, 24 and 25 I have discussed several issues in this respect. However, at the core of the market economy is the principle that consumers should decide what the production system does.

Concerning freedom, as opposed to conformity, level 3, "innovation", is of particular interest. I am not aware of an updating of the Kornai list of innovations made in market economies vs those made in centrally planned economies (Kornai 1971; there pp. 273–278). At the time, Kornai produced this list as an empirical "proof" of his "Anti-Equilibrium" thesis, which also gave the title of that book. For Kornai, both systems are characterized by a "system equilibrium" (my words) of the non-existence of an equilibrium between supply and demand for goods. Inherent to the capitalist economy is "pressure"; inherent to the centrally planned economy is "suction". In the latter – without market prices – "demand" for goods is always larger than "supply". The tactics or politics of everybody there is to find ways and excuses to enhance the delivery of goods to them from those "supplied" by the system. This, according to Kornai's nomenclature, is "suction". In the capitalist market economy, suppliers always try to sell more than they are able to sell – at the going price. In Kornai's nomenclature, this is "pressure". In other publications, for example, in Von Weizsäcker 2009, I give an analytical description of the typical market structure, which I call "market asymmetry": after the transaction, the buyer is "transaction saturated", whereas the seller remains "transaction hungry". I explain this typical "monopolistic competition" structure by referring back to Adam Smith: his explanation of wealth due to the division of labor. Discussing "advertising" in Chapter 25, I have a few sentences on this market asymmetry. This market asymmetry is equivalent to the "pressure" phenomenon described by Kornai.

Innovation, level 3 activity, if successful, is a way out of the pressures of level 2 competition. A better product or a better (lower cost) production method secures a price margin above average cost. This holds for a while, until competitors have caught up by imitation or by another innovation. However, this attempt to escape from level 2 competition is risky. The supplier is free to incur this risk or to refrain from it. It is this decision freedom which generates the social progress obtained from level 3 activity. The great innovator behaves in an unconventional manner. It is deviation from conformity which brings material progress for society. The Kornai tableau referred to previously is the factual proof.

In a society dominated by vertical coordination, that is, dominated by subordination, deviation from conformity is much more difficult than it is in a society, which primarily operates by means of horizontal coordination, that is, by means of cooperation. We have discussed these two modes of coordination in Chapter 26, in the subsection on private property. This explains the historical fact that a market economy within a democracy generates many more innovations than does an economy in a totalitarian system. Here, I believe, you can learn from history.

For the main topic of our book, freedom, our tableau generates the following propositions: "justice" or "equality" and some conformity are necessary ingredients in the spectrum of values of a well-functioning society. They correspond to the level 1 activities of people. "Competition" is important for well-functioning level 2 activities; "efficiency" generates the corresponding value of wealth or material well-being. Utility maximization and profit maximization go with level 2 activities. "Non-conformism" and "freedom" provide progress; they correspond to level 3 activities. It then turns out that free societies gain material advantages in the long run over totalitarian societies.

References

Böhm-Bawerk, Eugen Ritter von, 1881, Rechte und Verhältnisse vom Standpunkte der volkswirtschaftlichen Güterlehre, Innsbruck, Wagner Verlagsbuchhandlung, 153 pages.

Grotius, Hugo, De Mare Liberum, 1609.

Hayek, Friedrich A., 1945, The Use of Knowledge in Society, American Economic Review, 35 (4), 519–530.

Kornai, Janos, 1971, Anti-Equilibrium – On Economic Systems Theory and the Tasks of Research, Amsterdam, North-Holland Publishing Company, 402 pages.
Kornai, Janos, 1992, The Socialist System – The Political Economy of Communism, Princeton, NJ, Princeton University Press, 672 pages.
Samuelson, Paul A., 1954, The Pure Theory of Public Expenditure, Review of Economics and Statistics, 36, 387–389.
Von Weizsäcker, Carl Christian, 1980, Barriers to Entry. A Theoretical Treatment. Lecture Notes Economics and Mathematical Systems Nr. 185, Heidelberg, Springer, 220 pages.
Von Weizsäcker, Carl Christian, 1981, Rechte und Verhältnisse in der modernen Wirtschaftslehre, Kyklos, Bd., 34 (3), S. 345–376. English Translation: Rights and Relations in Modern Economic Theory, The Journal of Economic Behaviour and Organization, 1984, 133–157.
Von Weizsäcker, Carl Christian, 2009, Asymmetrie der Märkte und Wettbewerbsfreiheit, in: Vanberg, V.J. (ed.), Evolution und freiheitlicher Wettbewerb, Erich Hoppmann und die aktuelle Diskussion, Untersuchungen zur Ordnungstheorie und Ordnungspolitik, Bd. 58, Tübingen, Mohr-Siebeck, pp.211–244.

29

SOCIAL MARKET ECONOMY

As we argued in Chapter 26, good performance of the competitive private property economy presupposes that the political system operates as a democracy with the rule of law. In Chapter 27, we showed that the family is the main source of long-termism in society. A democratic political system works on the principle that the voters do not have the expertise to decide directly about the measures to be taken by the political system. In elections, they vote for candidates or political parties, and one expects that the elected politicians have enough expertise to make good decisions. How can voters evaluate the performance of politicians? Not being experts, they look at the present state of the country as they perceive it. "It's the economy, stupid". This voting behavior forces the politicians to "short-termism". When they are in power, they attempt to obtain good performance of the economy for the time of the coming election. Further down in this chapter I analyze the consequences of such behavior for the theme of public debt.

This induced short-termism of politicians is well understood among experts in politics. Many voters understand it as well. There exist many proposals how to cope with this short-termism. Quite a few constitutions contain provisions aiming to curtail politicians' short-termism. We should note that politicians' short-termism is just one example of the general short-termism in principal-agent relations. The principal hires an agent for a certain time. Typically, the agent is the expert and the principal is not as well informed about the relevant issues as is the expert. Typically, the expert is interested in renewing the contract with the principal. In choosing his/her problem-solving strategy, the expert therefore aims at providing good results before his/her current contract with the principal ends. Thereby he/she hopes to improve the chance for renewing the contract. This is the short-termism of the agent in a principal-agent relation. Depending on the details of the issues involved in this relation, certain remedies may be available to alleviate the problem

DOI: 10.4324/9781032726410-34

of the short-termism. But the basic phenomenon of principal-agent induced short termism remains. I published a more detailed analysis on this topic in German (Von Weizsäcker 1994).

This observation reinforces my statement in Chapter 27 that in a society, the main source of long-termism is the family, in particular the care of parents for their children and – indirectly – for their grandchildren. But the altruism in the family is the basis of the "Time" form of exchange, which, as I derived in Chapter 27, is also the source of egalitarianism.

The political system of democracy and the market system of private property then have to compromise between the efficiency advantages of private property and the voting majority's request for equality. In this book, I do not go into the details of such compromise. Every economist (in Fromm's "To Have" mode) will agree that perfect equality of income cannot be the solution, because such a state of affairs would revoke any material incentive to produce in an efficient manner. It appears that some form of progressive income taxation is part of a reasonable compromise. Based on the path-breaking theory of optimal income taxation by Mirrlees 1971 there exists a substantial literature on the theory and practicality of the optimal income tax.

In the spirit of Karl Popper's "piecemeal engineering" and based on the idea of adaptive preferences, we can state the hypothesis that the reference point for any proposal for tax reform are the prevailing tax laws. One reason for this principle is that policy makers have to be well informed about the potential consequences of any change in the tax laws. These consequences are difficult to forecast when the change in the tax schedule is quite large. A change in the tax laws is a special case for the "project" theory of change and progress with adaptive preferences. This is the general topic of Book VI.

Here I mention a phenomenon that I like to call the paradox of long-termism. It came into being through the 20th century as a result of a long time of prosperity and growth after the Second World War. Together with my co-author, I devoted a book to explain this paradox of long termism (Von Weizsäcker and Krämer 2021). In a nutshell, the proposition is the following: because of the high life expectancy of the world population and the present high standard of living in the OECD countries plus China, the propensity to save is substantially higher than the propensity to invest. We express this in terms of a modernized "Austrian" capital theory: the "waiting period" in the private household sector is much higher than the "period of production" in the production sector, and this is so even at a real rate of interest of zero. The main reason the period of production cannot catch up to the waiting period is the same as the cause of the long waiting period: technical progress. The secular rise of the waiting period is due to the secular rise in life expectancy, which is due to the steady rise in technical, scientific and medical knowledge: in the last 50 years, the average pension period of the OECD + China world has doubled. For this reason, the "waiting period" also has risen by about 100 percent. The "waiting period" is the average time delay between the earnings and the consumption of a person. This means that the wealth–annual consumption ratio also has doubled. On the other hand, the steady flow of technical improvements generates a steady rate of obsolescence of existing capital equipment: this means that at a certain value (of roughly four years) of the period of production labor and land productivity have reached their maximum, so that there the marginal productivity of the period of production has reached the value zero. Beyond roughly four years, more "roundaboutness" is counterproductive. From there on, additional obsolescence outweighs additional GDP per worker. This is the reason that the capital–annual consumption ratio has remained constant over a period of more than a century.

Niehans, Feldstein, Homburg and others have pointed to the fact that the value of land should converge to "infinity", as the real rate of interest approaches zero. If this result holds up to reality, then the equilibrium real rate of interest remains positive; indeed, following Homburg 1991, it would have to remain above the long-run rate of growth of the economy. However, as we show extensively in our book, substantial uninsurable risks of owning land invalidate this proposition. In this context I specifically want to refer to Arnott and Stiglitz 1979. There the authors show that a high taxation of urban land rents is Kaldor–Hicks–Scitovsky superior in comparison to other sources of taxation for the same total government revenue combined with a low land rent taxation.

Our book contains an extensive empirical analysis for the OECD world and for the People's Republic of China. It corroborates our theory, which I here called the paradox of long-termism. Our theory overlaps with the hypothesis of "secular stagnation", which originally was announced by Alvin Hansen 1939 but was recently further developed by Larry Summers 2014.

The paradox of long-termism consists of the fact that the government has to go into debt to compensate for the gap between the private waiting period and the private period of production: in this sense, concerning public debt, the government has to invoke some "artificial" short-termism in order to allow its citizens to implement the "waiting period" they prefer. Almost 50% of private net wealth is held in the form of net government debt. Most of this net government debt is "implicit" public debt in the form of future payment obligations to social security pensioners, future pensions to government employees and future health care payments to social security–covered pensioners. Our way of accounting for the government corresponds to the accounting procedures of private life insurance companies and private health insurance companies – except that the governments in the OECD area and China, with very few exceptions, do not hold collateral pools against these future payment obligations. And they could not hold such an enormous collateral pool, because there would be no demand for all this capital.

We should emphasize that this paradox of long-termism is a modern phenomenon. When Böhm-Bawerk 1889 published his great book on capital theory, he could indeed explain the positive real rate of interest by his analysis that there are insufficient private savings to enable society a period of production which would exhaust all labor productivity advantages of a greater period of production, of greater "roundaboutness". In this sense, Böhm-Bawerk was right in explaining the positive real rate of interest as a price signal for the scarcity of capital.

Here, in the present book, I am interested in describing a society with a maximum of freedom, taking account of the constraints which derive from pragmatic compossibility of individual rights. Following Alfred Müller–Armack 1947, I call the economic-political part of this society the "Social Market Economy". The three most important differences to a complete "laissez-faire economy" are the following: 1) the social market economy has a well-developed social security system; 2) there is a progressive tax system, in particular with a progressive income tax; 3) the government intervenes in markets on behalf of citizens who lack sufficient autonomy of behavior.

We have discussed the third item – lacking autonomy – in Chapters 23, 24 and 25. In this chapter, I first discuss item 1 and then item 2.

Modern social security systems started in the late 19th century, and – in one form or another – they are now reality in every OECD country. Their expansion is due not least to their popularity among voters. Social security in a large part is responsible for the steady growth of life expectancy in most advanced economies. With the social security system, everybody has access to treatment in the health system. In addition, a large majority of citizens and voters obtains old age pensions.

There is positive feedback of causation between life expectancy and the size of the social security system. As described, the latter causes rising life expectancy. On the other hand, the thereby rising population share of pensioners has an impact on the ballots in general elections. No party can afford to offer the citizens a substantial reduction in social security benefits. So far, in most advanced economies the social security system did not overburden the financial resources of the government. However, there are signs that the expansion of the social security system partly came at the expense of other public goods. In particular, defense expenditures may not have caught up with the rising threat of totalitarianism.

Although some government debt may be called for, as described, there are limits to government debt: too much government debt generates real interest rates at levels which make it impossible for the government to borrow in the world capital market. Generally, then, a wise government will take account of the undeniable fact that too large a social security system will hamper the provision of needed public goods. Here I do not go into more detail. This book is not a detailed treatise on public finance.

However, the progressive income tax requires some more detailed attention – in particular because it provides additional justification for our freedom criterion of pragmatic compossibility. In discussing the progressive income tax, I follow the general "philosophy" of the optimal income tax literature, which builds on Mirrlees 1971. However, I connect it with the insight of another Scotsman: Adam Smith 1776. Every reader of my book knows the opening sentence of the *Wealth of Nations*: "The greatest improvement in the productive powers of labour, and the greater part of the skill, dexterity, and judgement with which it is anywhere directed, or applied, seem to have been the effects of the division of labour." Let us accept this proposition. We then should also recognize that modern tax systems mainly impose taxes on the division of labor. Quantitatively, the two most important taxes are the income tax and the value added tax. Both of them impose on the value added of any given part of a system, which combines the production of goods with selling them on a market. This means that this system operates in a "division of labor mode". Production and consumption of goods within the same household are exempt from the taxation by means of the income tax or the value added tax. There are good reasons why the modern tax system has this structure. But it is clear that the allocative distortions going with this tax system mainly are distortions at the expense of the efficiency advantages derived from the division of labor. In pointing this out, I do not deviate from the optimal tax theory, as developed in recent decades. The models used in that literature are all simplified descriptions of a system in the "division of labor mode".

Following the Kaldor–Hicks–Scitovsky tradition, I now look at some changes in the operation of the economic system. An example may be the introduction of free trade. Another example may be construction of an additional piece of infrastructure, like a new bridge across a river. A further example could be a Schumpeterian innovation, like the introduction of a new product in the market. From the Kaldor–Hicks–Scitovsky tradition, including the Stolper–Samuelson 1941 paper, we accept the proposition that such a change of operation raises national income in terms of the "old" price system, as well as in terms of the "new" price system. It is therefore a change that corresponds to the freedom principle of pragmatic compossibility.

However, such a change is not a Pareto improvement. Nevertheless, as I will show now, the rules of the social market economy approve this change. The reasoning has three layers. In the first layer, I replace the idea of "Pareto improvement" by the idea of "Suppes improvement". The second layer is a "law of large numbers" or, as I call it: "generalized compensation". In the third layer, I take account of the progressive income tax.

What about adaptive preferences? In the three-layer exposition that follows, adaptive preferences are in the background. However, Book VI is devoted to the particular issues arising out of the fact that preferences are not fixed but adaptive.

The First Layer: Replacing Pareto Improvement by "Suppes Improvement"

In Book II, Chapter 12, I discussed the Atkinson–Mirrlees social welfare function. It takes account of income distribution; however, an improvement by the standard of the Atkinson–Mirrlees social welfare function need not be a Pareto improvement. The Atkinson–Mirrlees improvement can cause losses for some citizens. If one cares about income distribution one can apply a weakened Pareto improvement. Rather than look at every citizen, we could divide people into groups according to their income: we can form income percentiles of citizens. We then can ask the question: does a potential change of the economy improve the income of each income percentile? In a paper published half a century ago, Suppes 1966 provided a formalism taking account of this idea. We may then call a "Suppes improvement" an improvement that happens to all income percentiles. A Suppes improvement may involve losses for some citizens and thus is not necessarily a Pareto improvement. Of course, the other way round: a Pareto improvement is also a Suppes improvement: if every person is better off, then each income percentile is better off.

As a first step towards a reasonable social welfare evaluation, I then propose that we use the criterion of Suppes improvement rather than Pareto improvement.

The Second Layer: Generalized Compensation

We should be aware that our criterion of pragmatic compossibility is quite general. It applies to many decisions of distinct "projects" for the deviation from the default option of "non-decision", that is, from the status quo. Is there another decision principle available for comparison with pragmatic compossibility? Is it a regime of Pareto improvement? This would mean that for each "project", government or its agencies would have to develop a scheme of compensation for the losers in that project, at the proportionate expense of the winners. If such compensation is to be expected, there is a strong incentive for people to report too high levels of project-induced losses and too low levels of project-induced gains. Therefore, a project which in reality was pragmatically compossible would appear to generate a loss in net social product – and thus would be a "false-negative". All this is well known among economists. I may add from the perspective of adaptive preferences that the preference conservatism reinforces the danger of "false-negative" if we compare the ex-ante preferences with the ex-post preferences induced by the project. The conclusion is: the criterion of Pareto improvement would hamper material progress substantially.

We then, instead could use the Suppes improvement as a criterion. If some individualized compensation would still be required to let the change be Suppes compatible, the same incentives to under-report gains and to over-report losses still apply. If the legislator decides against any compensation for the change, it would still be difficult to show that the change would improve the lot of all income percentiles.

Another alternative criterion for project evaluation could be an Atkinson–Mirrlees social welfare function, which we already discussed in Book II, that is, in the book on the classroom model of adaptive preferences. Atkinson and Mirrlees have formalized society's "preferences" for equality by means of a welfare function of the following form

$$W^*(Y) = \sum_{i=1}^{m} W(Y^i)$$

Y^i = real annual income of citizen i, $\boldsymbol{Y} = Y^1, Y^2, \ldots\ldots. Y^m$ the corresponding real income vector, and W a concave function, rising with Y^i.

We then would have to compare the pragmatic compossibility regime of the criterion

$$\widehat{W}(\boldsymbol{Y}) = \sum_{i=1}^{m} Y^i$$

with the regime that each project is evaluated according to the Atkinson–Mirrlees welfare function. The main difference between the two regimes is that the $W^*(\boldsymbol{Y})$ regime requires knowledge of the distributive effects of the project, whereas the pragmatic compossibility regime $\widehat{W}(\boldsymbol{Y})$ does not require such knowledge. Again, we can predict that any survey of expected real income changes from the project will be downward biased due to the preference conservatism of adaptive preferences. As an example, we may take any project of technical progress which induces job losses. Protests against such projects can be expected from the people, who fear for their jobs. Consumers who would benefit from lower prices of the output produced by means of the new technology will be insufficiently aware of these future benefits. So the social conflict between winners and losers of the project tends to provide a bias against the project. Generally, an Atkinson–Mirrlees test applied to every project provides a hurdle for attempts to overcome the status quo of the economy. We therefore can expect that the $W^*(\boldsymbol{Y})$ regime involves substantially fewer outbreaks from the status quo than the pragmatic compossibility regime $\widehat{W}(\boldsymbol{Y})$.

In a market economy with competition among producing firms we expect spontaneous changes from the status quo to enhance social product. Then prices involved in a project represent the input of scarce resources. The input value then is the opportunity cost of the project in terms of scarce resources. The output value represents the addition of utility for the citizens, as evaluated by market prices. Because such a project depends on the expectation that the output value exceeds the input value, the project enhances social product.

A closer look finds the following modifications of this statement. First, people are risk averse. Second, there is the problem of the winner's curse. The summed risk borne by the citizens is much larger than the macroeconomic risk. This means that a net gain in terms of expected value from a potential project may not be enough for the implementation of the project. A "risk premium" is required in addition. A project undertaken anyway a fortiori has a higher expected output value than expected input value. On the other hand, there is a bias in the expectations of the entrepreneur. He/she may be overly optimistic. This is the "winner's curse" problem. Generally, it is very likely that the risk aversion effect exceeds the winner's curse effect. The proposition then is realistic that on average of undertaken projects the market value of their output exceeds the market value of their inputs.

Now I first assume that on average of all projects undertaken there is no income distribution bias. There may be projects which favor rich citizens. There may be other projects which mainly benefit low-income citizens. A project taken at random out of all implemented projects then, by assumption, has an expected net benefit distribution across different income groups such that the relative income distribution does not change. Then we can apply a "law of large numbers". A single project with a positive net gain may hurt people at the lower end of the income schedule. But with many projects, all of them with a positive net gain for the economy at large, and, in the average, with no distribution bias, the sum of net gains will be positive for all income percentiles. To put the same thing in different words: Take a particular income percentile. The expected value of the net gain of a randomly chosen new project is positive for that income percentile because of the assumption that there is no distribution bias among new projects. We then can apply the law of large numbers to the sequence of gains of new projects for this percentile. We then can conclude that the probability that the sum of all project gains for this income percentile is positive converges to 100 %, as the number of new projects becomes larger and larger.

We then can form the income difference between an Atkinson–Mirrlees $W^*(Y)$ regime and the pragmatic compossibility $\widehat{W}(Y)$ regime. We apply the "law of large numbers" idea to those projects which are only implemented under the $\widehat{W}(Y)$ regime. If these "$\widehat{W}(Y)$ minus $W^*(Y)$" projects still have no distribution bias, then by the "law of large numbers" we obtain the following graphical description of the cumulative income distribution for the two regimes.

I call this result the *law of generalized compensation*. For reasons well known among economists, specific compensation for each project would lead to stagnation – and therefore is not advisable. However, due to distribution neutrality, in the aggregate of all new projects – each with a net social gain – each income percentile benefits from the dynamics of new projects in the market economy. In this sense every income percentile is compensated in the long run for any possible net losses in the short run.

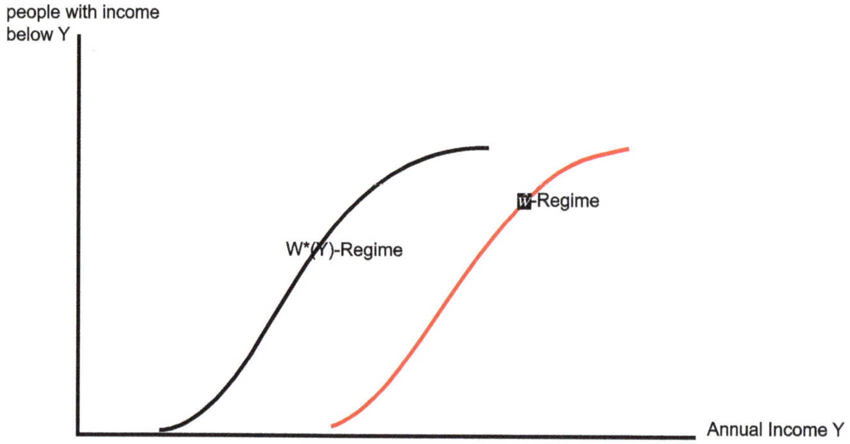

FIGURE 29.1 Cumulative Income Distribution in Two Regimes

The question is: is the assumption realistic that "$\widehat{W}(Y)$ minus $W^*(Y)$" projects still have no distribution bias? Could it be that the Atkinson–Mirrlees $W^*(Y)$ regime can successfully select so many projects which favor gains for small income percentiles over gains for large income percentiles that the remaining "$\widehat{W}(Y)$ minus $W^*(Y)$" projects show a bias for large income percentiles? In that case, it would not be clear that the red cumulative income curve is fully to the right of the black cumulative income curve.

This theoretical possibility is unlikely. Society's representative, the government, simply does not have enough foresight to anticipate what kind of projects in the $\widehat{W}(Y)$ regime will come about in the future. This in particular because these $\widehat{W}(Y)$ projects build upon each other. The further in the future the end of the planning horizon of the society lies, the more difficult it is to anticipate the character of most $\widehat{W}(Y)$ projects within this period. And, as we argued in Chapter 27, the family is society's most important source of long-termism, to a large degree due to intra-family altruism, that is, parents' love of their children and grandchildren. Here, we then speak of a time horizon stretching over several decades into the future. As grandparents, we may love our grandchildren, but we know very little about all the inventions and innovations developing throughout this vast number of future years. If we have some trust in the well-functioning of a competitive market economy, and if we are aware of the lack of knowledge of detailed progress in the future, we should deny our government a distribution driven veto power against social product–enhancing projects. This denial is reinforced by the fact that government action quite generally suffers from "short-termism". One component of such "short-termism" is strong voter resistance against the introduction of more restrictive social security benefits – despite the fact that the rising trend in life expectation may require such legislation. On this, see Pierson 1996.

For reasons well understood in economics, we accept that it would be counterproductive to compensate losers in any particular social product-enhancing project. However, as we argued, to the extent that on average new social product projects are distribution neutral, we can show that an economy operating in the pragmatic compossibility mode provides a higher income for each income percentile than would an alternate regime which applies an Atkinson–Mirrlees test for each new project. The social product–enhancing property of new projects in a competitive market economy does provide compensation for any losses of a particular income percentile in any particular project, because that percentile will benefit from other new projects. The term "generalized compensation" should catch this very property of a regime of freedom under the rule of pragmatic compossibility.

I suggest another name too: *Leviathan 2.0*. Thomas Hobbes 1651 produced the theory of state monopoly of the use of physical force – under the name "Leviathan". As he describes in that book, life under "Leviathan" (and be it a dictatorship) is much superior to level 1 competition (in the table of our Chapter 28), that is, to "free" access to (scarce) goods. As Hobbes describes this form of level 1 competition:

> no place of Industry; because the fruit thereof is uncertain; and consequently no Culture of the Earth; no Navigation, nor use of the commodities that may be imported by Sea; no commodious Building; no Instruments of moving, and removing such things as require much force; no Knowledge of the face of the Earth; no account of Time; no Arts; no Letters; no Society; and which is worst of all, continuall feare, and danger of violent death; and life of man, solitary, poore, nasty, brutish, and short.

Under Leviathan each citizen then gives up his/her use of physical force against others – in exchange for the regime that every other citizen also gives up his/her use of physical force against fellow citizens.

A little more than a century later Adam Smith wrote his *Wealth of Nations*. In that book, he implicitly assumes the rule of Leviathan. He then describes, using the formula of the "invisible hand", the wealth-enhancing power of free markets not the least because the division of labor can best be organized by exchange of goods, by "barter". Formally, the pragmatic compossibility regime of free and competitive markets has a similar structure to the Hobbesian Leviathan structure. Citizens refrain from resistance against socially productive projects, even if in some of these projects they lose income – in exchange against corresponding restraints by the other citizens, thereby enabling the pragmatic compossibility regime to the benefit of all income percentiles. This formal analogy allows me to speak of "Leviathan 2.0".

Concerning implementation of Leviathan 1.0 and Leviathan 2.0, it is in both cases the government's task. In Leviathan 1.0, the government uses the police and the criminal justice system to deter citizens from breaking the rules. For the implementation of Leviathan 2.0, the government has the authority and the task to be a watchdog over competition in free markets.

This idea of Leviathan 2.0 also corresponds to the German ordo-liberal tradition, the "Freiburg School". On this approach, I refer the reader to Eucken 1940, 1952, and Böhm 1966. In my present book, I do not go into the policy details of the pragmatic compossibility regime of individual freedom.

In a recent paper, Schulz et al. 2023 present a model of "generalized compensation", which can be considered of the same philosophy as my "generalized compensation". Originally, I introduced the concept in a German-language publication ("Generalkompensation"), Von Weizsäcker 1984, but then without reference to endogenous preferences.

The Third Layer: Progressive Income Taxation

In the second layer, I have assumed that the sum of the gains of all projects in the pragmatic compossibility regime is distribution neutral. For the world as it actually works this may not be the case. For example, globalization may have favored high-income groups of advanced countries relative to the low-income groups in advanced countries. There is an intensive debate on this point. Thus, even though globalization may have helped low-income groups in emerging market countries, exports from these countries to the advanced economies have put competitive pressure on a large part of the workforce in the advanced countries. The Stolper–Samuelson 1941 paper is still relevant today.

We therefore cannot exclude the possibility that, at its lower end, the red cumulative income curve of the $\widehat{W}(Y)$ regime is to the left of the black cumulative income curve of the $W^*(Y)$ regime.

An answer to this problem is the progressive income tax, more generally an income redistribution scheme with funds flowing from rich to poor. We then are in the midst of the optimal income tax issues. The basic model of the optimal income tax literature is consistent with our pragmatic compossibility approach. In its simplest form, there is just one exogenous input factor; call it labor. Different members of the model society have different abilities, but these different kinds of labor supply are perfect substitutes for each other. There are no public goods. An income tax serves to redistribute earned income. The income tax is designed to maximize a social welfare function of the Atkinson–Mirrlees type. The optimal income tax then is a compromise between equality and efficiency. The marginal tax rate being positive, there is a gap between the marginal productivity of labor and the after-tax marginal income. In this sense, the overall allocation of resources is inefficient, but after-tax incomes are more equally distributed than before-tax incomes. In this simple model, there is no other government intervention into markets. If there were no redistribution, the simple model economy would implement the pragmatic compossibility principle: as compared to any other tax schedule, national income is maximized with a zero income tax.

The fact that a more equal distribution of a given national income enhances the value of the social welfare function makes the optimal tax schedule a progressive one. Thereby it deviates from the pragmatic compossibility criterion. However, in an enhanced sense, that is, in a political-economic sense, there is no contradiction between pragmatic compossibility and an optimal tax schedule. As we argued in Chapter 26 and again in Chapter 28, it is in a democracy with the rule of law that the productive breakaways from the status quo by market-driven inventions and innovations are higher and more frequent than in a totalitarian regime. Karl Popper's "Open Society" is a democratic society. But majority vote in a democracy pushes for some kind of redistribution towards greater equality.

The following graph connects real income per head and the Atkinson–Mirrlees social welfare function (Atkinson 1970, Mirrlees 1971). Real income per head is on the horizontal axis. A measure of inequality (in terms of the Atkinson inequality index) is on the vertical axis – with rising inequality depicted from north to south. The red curve is the "possibility frontier" in terms of the redistributive tax system. If the government refrains from redistribution by taxation, the economy has the "natural" inequality and the maximum income per head. Here the possibility curve has a vertical slope, because real income is at a maximum. On the other hand, at

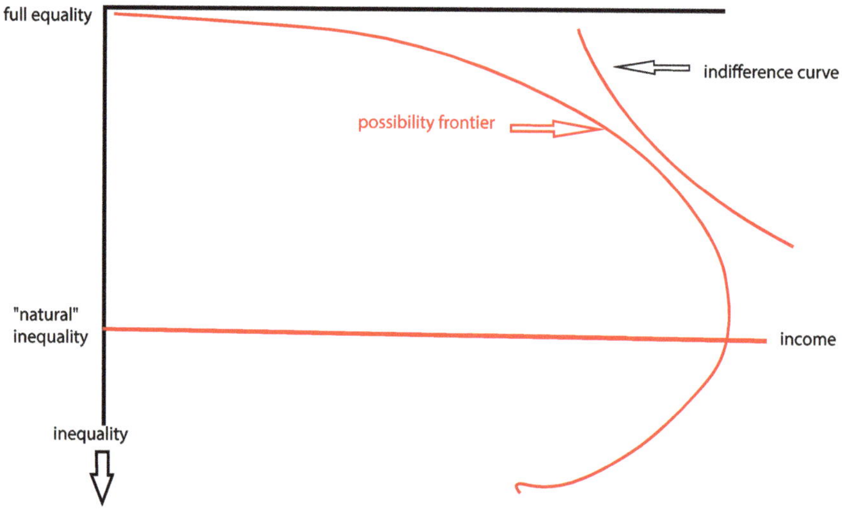

FIGURE 29.2 Optimal Redistributive Income Tax

an inequality level of zero no real income is generated, which means that here the possibility frontier has a slope of zero. Altogether, this indicates that the possibility frontier is a concave curve, which means the possibility set is convex.

Assume first that the "preferences" of society concerning income generation and income distribution are fixed. I symbolize these "preferences" by a single indifference curve in black. It is the indifference curve touching the social optimum. The optimal regime then is the point on the possibility frontier where the indifference curve through this point and the possibility frontier have the same slope. Obviously, if other things are equal, there is a preference for more equality and the tax redistribution system should be progressive. I have drawn the indifference curve as a convex curve, which corresponds to the assumption that for any income–distribution combination, the preferred combinations form a convex set. This is always the case for an Atkinson–Mirrlees social welfare function.

If the actual tax system is regressive then we are below the "natural" inequality line. Then the possibility frontier is positively sloped: a less regressive tax system would raise average income as well equality. A tradeoff between a higher average income and more equality only exists in the realm of a progressive tax system.

As I remarked earlier, voter preferences concerning the average income–equality tradeoff are formed by the actually prevailing tax system. This is the idea of adaptive preferences, here applied to political preferences. Here I refrain from discussing details of taxation politics. On those, see Bierbrauer et al. 2021. However, we can exploit the calculus of adaptive preferences to understand some of the dynamics of tax policy. I start at a point in time when taxpayers have adapted their behavior to the actual tax system, and the tax laws correspond to that behavior: we then are at the point where the possibility frontier and the indifference curve have the same slope. Now, say, due to elections, a new majority rules that represents a higher egalitarian preference. So the social indifference curve reduces its slope; the tax system becomes more progressive. Taxpayers adapt and thus the new equilibrium point is higher up and to the left of the former equilibrium point. Due to adaptive preferences, egalitarian preferences rise further, and there is a secondary shift to the northwest along the possibility frontier. In the long run, a new equilibrium occurs at some point to the northwest of the old equilibrium.

However, this is only part of the story: individual reactions of taxpayers also exhibit adaptive preferences. This means that the possibility curve also changes once the tax laws make taxes more progressive. People learn to enjoy more leisure: their tradeoff between work and leisure changes: the possibility curve between average income and equality becomes flatter. This implies: reducing inequality becomes more expensive in terms of average income. This means that for given social preferences the optimal point on the new possibility curve is to the southeast of the old point.

Granting adaptive preferences, it is then an empirical question whether changes in the tax laws shift the optimal point in the direction of more equality and less income or in the direction of more income and less equality.

The progressive tax regime in the spirit of the optimal income tax provides a further justification of pragmatic compossibility. We could ask the question: which progressive tax schedule makes sure that over the average of all Kaldor–Hicks–Scitovsky (KHS) projects the after tax net gains are distribution neutral? We could ask the same question about the set of all projects which are implemented in a $\widehat{W}$ regime but not in a W^* regime. However, perfect distribution neutrality is not necessary. If the average percentage surplus of the KHS projects is substantial, the previously discussed "law of large numbers" makes it likely that even a somewhat distribution-biased large collection of productive projects benefits every income percentile.

We conclude: progressive income taxation is a legitimate answer to any concerns that implementation of a pragmatic compossibility regime (i.e. a Kaldor–Hicks–Scitovsky regime) might have negative distribution effects.

The line of thought is this: a social system of freedom requires compossibility constraints. If one opts for pragmatic compossibility, and if one has a competitive market economy with price signals for relative scarcities of goods (Hayek 1945), then the ensuing "spontaneous order" provides material progress, because projects in the form of deviations from the status quo raise the value of the social product. Taking account of the three layers concerning distributional effects of such a regime [1) Suppes criterion, rather than Pareto criterion; 2) generalized compensation by a "law of large numbers"; 3) progressive income taxation] further corroborates the choice of pragmatic compossibility á la Kaldor–Hicks–Scitovsky as the institutional framework for a regime of liberty.

It is then also appropriate that government-led projects like building a bridge, changes of laws (including tax laws) and others should be subject to conventional cost-benefit analysis. Thereby such government projects compete with private projects on an equal footing for scarce investment resources.

In this Chapter 29, I gave a sketch of a "Social Market Economy" under the conditions of pragmatic compossibility – taking account of adaptive preferences. In Book VI, I go somewhat deeper into the technicalities of cost-benefit analysis when preferences are influenced by the projects undertaken.

References

Arnott, Richard J. and Stiglitz, Joseph E., 1979, Aggregate Land Rents, Expenditure on Public Goods, and Optimal City Size, Quarterly Journal of Economics, 93 (4), 471–500.

Atkinson, Anthony B., 1970, On the Measurement of Inequality, Journal of Economic Theory, 2 (3), 244–263.

Bierbrauer, Felix, Boyer, Pierre C. and Peichl, Andreas, 2021, Politically Feasible Reforms of Nonlinear Tax Systems, American Economic Review, 111 (1), 153–191.

Böhm, Franz, 1966, Privatrechtsgesellschaft und Marktwirtschaft, ORDO, 17, 75–151.

Böhm-Bawerk, Eugen Ritter von, 1889, Positive Theorie des Kapitales, Jena, Fischer, 489 pages.

Eucken, Walter, 1940, Die Grundlagen der Nationalökonomie, Jena, Fischer-Verlag, Xii + 300 pages.

Eucken, Walter, 1952, Grundsätze der Wirtschaftspolitik, Tübingen, Mohr-Siebeck, 398 pages.

Hansen, Alvin H., 1939, Economic Progress and Declining Population Growth, American Economic Review, 29 (1), 1–15.

Hobbes, Thomas, 1651, Leviathan or the Matter, London, Forme & Power of a Common-Wealth Ecclesiasticall and Civill.

Homburg, Stefan, 1991, Interest and Growth in an Economy with Land, Canadian Journal of Economics, 24 (2), 450–459.

Mirrlees, James A., 1971, An Exploration in the Theory of Optimum Income Taxation, Review of Economic Studies, 38 (2), 175–208.

Müller-Armack, Alfred, 1947, Wirtschaftslenkung und Marktwirtschaft, Hamburg, Kastell.

Pierson, Paul, 1996, The New Politics of the Welfare State, World Politics, 48 (2), 143–179.

Schulz, Karl, Tsyvinski, Aleh and Werquim, Nicolas, 2023, Generalized Compensating Principle, Theoretical Economics, 18, 1665–1710.

Smith, Adam, 1776, Inquiry into the Nature and Causes of the Wealth of Nations, 2 volumes, London, W. Strahan and T. Cadell.

Stolper, Wolfgang F. and Samuelson, Paul A., 1941, Protection and Real Wages, Review of Economic Studies, 9 (1), 58–73.

Summers, Lawrence H., 2014, US Economic Prospects: Secular Stagnation, Hysteresis, and the Zero Lower Bound, Business Economics, 49, 65–73.

Suppes, Patrick, 1966, Some Formal Models of Grading Principles, Synthese, 16, 284–306.

Von Weizsäcker, Carl Christian, 1984, Was leistet die Property Rights Theorie für aktuelle wirtschaftspolitische Fragen? in: Neumann, Manfred (ed.), Ansprüche, Eigentums- und Verfügungsrechte, Berlin, Duncker und Humblot, pp.123–152.

Von Weizsäcker, Carl Christian, 1994, Zeitpräferenz und Delegation, Zeitschrift für Wirtschaftspolitik, 43 (2), 121–139.

Von Weizsäcker, Carl Christian and Krämer, Hagen, 2021, Saving and Investment in the 21st Century – The Great Divergence, Cham, Springer, XXII + 344 pages, Open Access.

BOOK VI

Partial Equlibrium Welfare Economics for a Free Society With Adaptive Preferences

30
INTRODUCTION

In the preceding Books II, III, IV and V, I provide an understanding of the connection between the concept of freedom and the concept of adaptive preferences. Books II and III are devoted to the proof of Theorems 1 and 2: they show the equivalence between the assumption of adaptive preferences and the idea that the concept of "progress" remains reasonable under "normative individualism" even if the measuring rod of progress (preferences) is no longer assumed to be fixed. In other words: "normative individualism" would be in deep water if it turned out that preferences were not adaptive. This would mean that our individualistic concept of freedom would have to be abandoned.

In Books IV and V, I justify the assumption of adaptive preferences, and I draw consequences from this assumption. There exist strong evolutionary reasons why actual human behavior reflects adaptive preferences. I introduce the idea of pragmatic compossibility of citizens' rights as a rule of law framework for the implementation of individual freedom. I show that pragmatic compossibility only can work if preferences are adaptive. We need a government as a law-giver for the protection of individual liberty, that is, for the implementation of pragmatic compossibility. I introduce the distinction between government action in the "freedom mode" and government action in the "causal mode". The freedom mode should be the rule, but the causal mode is needed, for example, for the production of public goods and for the protection of people who lack a state of autonomy in their behavior. An example of the latter is the behavior of small children; another one is the behavior of people in an unfortunate state of addiction.

The philosophical background of my theory is Karl Popper's idea of the "Open Society" and his proposal of "piecemeal engineering". However, I also show that adaptive preferences are a requirement to make "piecemeal engineering" a consistent concept. By contrasting the two eminent philosophers Karl Popper and Erich

DOI: 10.4324/9781032726410-36

Fromm, I connect the historical flow of freedom ideas through the last three centuries with the parallel historical flow of intellectual critique of capitalism. Based on the preceding argument I devote the last chapter of Book V to a discussion of the "Social Market Economy".

In this last Book VI, I take a different perspective on the concept of adaptive preferences. Here I concentrate on cost-benefit analysis. Using Herbert Simon's theory of near-decomposability of complex systems, one can justify partial equilibrium analysis for practical policy advice (1962). However, the fact that preferences are adaptive and not constant has an impact on the way we justify partial equilibrium cost benefit analysis. In the Books II, III, IV and V, the main analytical tool was the connection between adaptive preferences and the acyclicity of improvement sequences. Here in Book VI the analytical tool is the "ex ante–ex post" comparison for any project of breaking away from the status quo. Apart from doing conventional cost-benefit analysis, this analytical tool also allows me to conclude that a democratic society needs the market economy. This in particular because democracy otherwise would generate stagnation. Then democracy would lose the "cold war" with totalitarian regimes. I conclude that there exists a normative "co-evolution of democracy and the market economy". On this in more detail, see my German language Hayek-Lecture at the University of Freiburg, von Weizsäcker 2014.

References

Simon, Herbert, 1962, The Architecture of Complexity, Proceedings of the American Philosophical Society, 106 (6), 467–482.

Von Weizsäcker, Carl Christian, 2014, Die normative Ko-Evolution von Marktwirtschaft und Demokratie, ORDO, 65, 13–43 (Hayek-Lecture at University of Freiburg).

31

COST-BENEFIT ANALYSIS WITH ADAPTIVE PREFERENCES, PART 1

A Simple Example

I begin with a simple example. Consider a product innovation or the construction of a new bridge across a river. Traditionally, cost-benefit analysis proceeded by estimating the benefit from the new product by means of the integral under the (compensated) demand curve for the new product. The cost is then the monetary cost of providing the new product. This procedure is correct under the assumption that there are no strong side effects on the relative prices of other goods. Compare Boardman et al. 2018. Can we carry over this cost-benefit analysis to the case of adaptive preferences? For this simple example, I make the same simplifying assumptions made in the traditional procedure. In particular, I assume that relative prices of other goods approximately remain the same. This assumption is correct if the market for the product is a subsystem of the economy in the sense of Herbert Simon's "near-decomposability" theory: Simon 1962. This "Simon Test" also applies to the traditional cost-benefit analysis.

The test of whether cost-benefit analysis remains valid under adaptive preferences is the following. The decision to go ahead with the project is taken with "ex-ante preferences", that is, with preferences as they prevail before the decision to go ahead with the project. Can the project be justified afterwards with "ex-post preferences", that is, with preferences that have changed due to the project? If this is the case, then we say that cost-benefit analysis remains valid with the feedback from the project to the preferences that provide the measuring rod for the value of the project.

Note that this test is "one sided". If the project is accepted with ex-ante preferences, we ask whether it is also justified with ex-post preferences. We do not ask whether, if the project were rejected with ex-ante preferences, its rejection would

DOI: 10.4324/9781032726410-37

also have been justified with ex-post preferences that would have prevailed had the project been undertaken. The reason for this one-sidedness is clear: we have no way to find out precisely what the hypothetical ex-post preferences with the feedback of the project on preferences would have been when the project has not been undertaken. Nevertheless, we do know the ex-post preferences, in the case where the project is being undertaken. Thus, a "preference controlling" of the project, if it has been undertaken, is possible. I return to this one-sidedness issue in the following.

For simplicity of presentation, I concentrate on the "yes-or-no" question: should the project be implemented, or should it not? I thus ignore the following question: if there are different variants of the project, which one – if any – should be implemented?

Figure 31.1 provides the argument that, in this simplified setting, cost-benefit analysis continues to work if we go from fixed preferences to adaptive preferences. The most leftward demand curve applies for ex-ante preferences. If the project is implemented and the product generated by the project is sold at a reasonable price, there is positive demand for the product. Due to their adaptiveness, preferences change so that the demand curve for the new product shifts to the right. The blue curve is the "long-run demand curve" that accounts for the preference changes induced by a certain price of the new product. The shift of the red demand curve to the right obviously means that the consumer benefit from the product rises relative to the one expected with ex-ante preferences. Thus, ex-post preferences justify the project if ex-ante preferences did. In this sense, our one-sided test for the validity of cost-benefit analysis turns out to be positive.

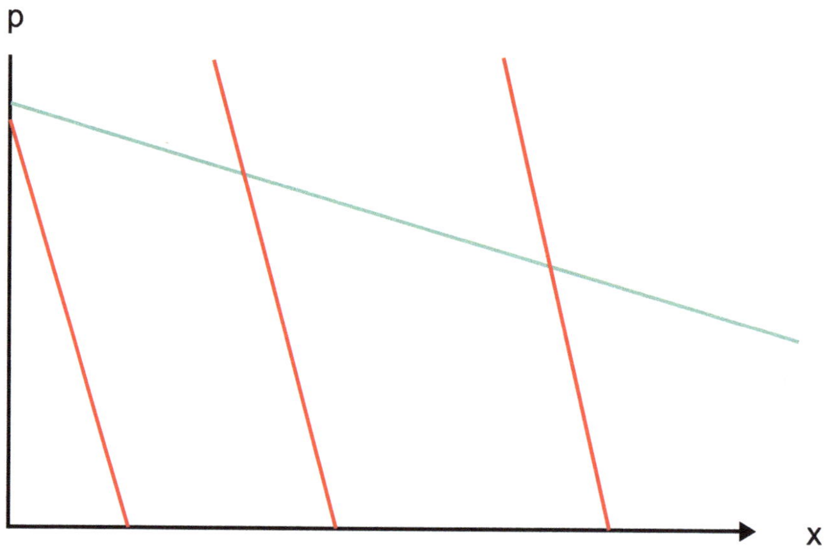

FIGURE 31.1 Dupuit's Bridge With Adaptive Preferences

I note explicitly that the validity test for cost-benefit analysis would fail if preferences were anti-adaptive, for then, the implementation of the project would induce a shift of the demand curve to the left. Thus, the expected consumer benefit of the project would be larger with ex-ante preferences than with ex-post preferences, and thus there is no guarantee that ex-post preferences justify the decision to offer the product taken under ex-ante preferences. (Without being relevant for the real world, we can state the mirror image "one-sidedness" of the cost-benefit test if preferences were anti-adaptive: if ex-ante preferences indicate a "no" to the project, then the hypothetical ex-post preferences in case the decision had been "yes" would confirm that "no" was the right decision.)

The General Case

In my thought experiment concerning the new bridge project, I have made a simplifying assumption, namely that the initial preferences are those preferences which are induced by the pre-project consumption vector. This assumption enables us to predict that adaptive preferences will shift the demand curve to the right after the bridge has been built. In the real world, as a rule, this assumption does not hold. The consumption path of the past was not always constant, and preferences did not always have time to catch up fully with the changes in the consumption baskets of the citizens. Actual ex-ante preferences, then, are a kind of (exponentially) weighted average of those preferences which are induced by the different consumption baskets of the past. (This is a mathematically correct statement in the case that the "law of motion" of preferences $\dot{q} = f(x;q)$ is a linear vector differential equation in terms of commodity baskets $z = \rho^{-1}(q)$.)

As in the simple example discussed previously, I concentrate on the case that there is a "yes or no" issue. Let $x(t)$ be the development of the "default" consumption basket through time. It is consumption of the economy in case the project is not undertaken. Let $y(t)$ be the consumption basket expected to occur if the project is undertaken. Then, $y(t)-x(t)$ is the contribution of the project from an ex-ante view. It is this expected contribution which justifies the project. We then also speak of $y(t)$ as the "project induced future ex-ante basket". Let $z(t)$ be the basket as it really develops if the project is implemented. We then also speak of $z(t)$ as the "project induced future ex-post basket". Let $q(t)$ be the preferences of the citizens through time in the "default case", which is $x(t)$. Let $r(t)$ be the preferences of citizens through time, which would come about if $y(t)$ were the consumption basket. Let $s(t)$ be the preferences of the citizens through time which actually develop if the project is undertaken.

The vectors $x(t)$, $y(t)$ and $z(t)$ are of dimension *n times m*, where n is the number of distinct commodities and m is the number of citizens in the economy. We assume that the decision about the project is made in time $t = 0$. We then describe the development of preferences by the initial condition $q(0) = r(0) = s(0)$ and by the differential equations $\dot{q} = f(x;q)$, $\dot{r} = f(y;r)$ and $\dot{s} = f(z;s)$. Moreover, we have $z(0) = y(0) = x(0)$. The vectors q, r, s are of dimension $N times m$. They represent the preferences of all citizens.

Why do I distinguish between $y(t)$ (the "project induced ex ante basket") and $z(t)$ (the "project induced ex-post basket")? I repeat: the collective decision to implement the project occurs after a comparison between $y(t)$ and $x(t)$. However, in a society of free citizens, the government may be wrong in its anticipation of actual reactions of citizens upon the implementation of the project. Therefore, $z(t)$ may occur rather than $y(t)$. And with endogenous preferences this also means that the flow of preferences $s(t)$ is different from the preference flow $r(t)$.

By traditional analysis, the project should be undertaken if $y(t)[>;q(t)]x(t)$. Here the preference relation $[.;.]$ refers to the "collective preferences" to be explained below. Frequently the decision maker is a firm that tries to make a profit out of the project – and it is the big "invisible hand" topic of traditional welfare economics under which conditions the profit orientation of firms and the welfare orientation of the impartial observer lead to the same result. To the extent that there are discrepancies in this respect in the traditional approach, these discrepancies carry over to the case of adaptive preferences. I concentrate on this question: Assume that under ex-ante preferences $q(t)$, the right decision has been taken to implement the project. Is it also the right decision under ex-post preferences?

Before I continue, I have to discuss the concept of "collective preferences". Under normative individualism, such "collective preferences" have to be anchored in individual preferences. In addition, however, some aggregation device is needed. The theory which I try to develop here is distinct from the traditional Bergson–Samuelson concept of a social welfare function. There, as discussed in detail by Samuelson (1956), the social welfare function makes different consumption baskets of the economy at large fully comparable. Bergson and later (in a generalized form) Samuelson show how one can derive such a social welfare function from the given preferences of the citizens. In the case of the Samuelson welfare function, an additional "collectivist" aggregation device is needed.

Economic policy pragmatism did not make very much use of the Bergson–Samuelson concept. What has become important in the context of practical applications like cost-benefit analysis is the Kaldor–Hicks–Scitovsky criterion of incremental real income for the population at large. My approach shares this incrementalism with Kaldor–Hicks–Scitovsky. This is also in line with Popper's philosophy of "piecemeal engineering" that he proposes for an open society, which I interpret to be closely related to the concept of a free society. In Book V, in the "social market economy chapter" (Chapter 29), I discuss and defend this criterion in more detail.

As I use the concept in this analysis, "collective preferences" refer to paths of consumption baskets $x(t)$ and $y(t)$. They then are of the form $y(t)[>;q(t)]x(t)$. By this we mean: given the path of individual preferences $q(t)$, $t \geq 0$ society prefers the consumption path $y(t)$ over the consumption path $x(t)$.

In particular, therefore, "collective preferences" need to satisfy the:

Axiom: Freedom Consistency of Collective Preferences: Let $x(t)$ and $y(t)$ be two paths through time of consumption baskets. Assume that individual rights are pragmatically compossible. Initial conditions and initial property distributions are given. Let the prevailing individual preferences be $q(t)$. Let $\hat{q}(t)$ be alternative individual preferences. Assume that under preferences $\hat{q}(t)$ and the prevailing institutions with free decisions and trading possibilities $x(t)$ would have been implemented. Assume that under the prevailing preferences $q(t)$ and the same institutional set-up and free decisions and trading possibilities the path $y(t)$ is implemented. Then $y(t)\left[>;q(t)\right]x(t)$.

The meaning of this axiom can be expressed in the following way: With the prevailing set-up of individual rights (which are pragmatically compossible), a change in preferences from $\hat{q}(t)$ to $q(t)$ generates individual behavior of citizens such that a changeover from path $x(t)$ to $y(t)$ occurs. The axiom then tells us that society (represented by government) honors the change from path $x(t)$ to $y(t)$, because it occurs due to the activities of the citizens within their compossible rights. In the case that the project in question is a government project like changing some law or constructing a bridge, government here operates in the "causal mode". However, it does so in the spirit of the "freedom mode": it decides about the proposed project, as if it were the market outcome, if that were a feasible way to decide about the project. This way of deciding about the project is also the way of the Lindahl–Samuelson proposal for decisions about public goods: Samuelson 1954.

I now introduce the concept of "quasi-induced preferences". They refer to the economy at large. Induced preferences for the individual were defined as the convergence point of preferences, if the consumption basket remains constant through time. Induced preferences are a particular single point in preference space. Quasi-induced preferences are a mapping from the non-negative part of the time axis (in continuous time) into the preference space, like $q(t)$. As we work on the individual level in the "real-world model" with the differential equation $\dot{q}=f(x;q)$, the development of preferences $q(t)$ depends on the development of the consumption basket $x(t)$. Together with the initial value of $q(0)$, it is then $x(t)$ which determines $q(t)$. We then designate $q(t)$ as "quasi-induced" by $q(0)$ and $x(t)$.

This is then the following

Definition 12: For any given path of consumption baskets $x(t)$ and any given initial value $q(0)$, let $q(t)$ be the unique solution to the differential equation $\dot{q}=f(x;q)$ which describes the dynamics of preference formation. For $t\geq 0$, we then call the preference path $q(t)$ *quasi induced* by $q(0)$ and $x(t)$.

The concept of "quasi-induced" is a mapping from the Cartesian product of the space of initial preferences and the space of consumption paths into the space of preference paths.

The concept of adaptive preferences builds on the concept of induced preferences. I now introduce the concept of "quasi-adaptiveness" of preferences, which builds on the concept of quasi-induced preferences. I apply it to collective preferences.

Definition 13: For given initial preferences $q(0)=r(0)$, let $q(t)$ be the preference path quasi-induced by the basket path $x(t)$, and let $r(t)$ be the preference path quasi-induced by the basket path $y(t)$. Collective preferences are *quasi-adaptive* if the following holds: whenever $y(t)[>;q(t)]x(t)$, then $y(t)[>;r(t)]x(t)$, and: whenever $y(t)[=;q(t)]x(t)$, then $y(t)[\geq;r(t)]x(t)$.

This means: assume society has the choice between the "default" $x(t)$ and the "project" $y(t)$ and thus decides on the basis of the preferences $q(t)$, quasi-induced by the default $x(t)$; assume further that society decides to implement the project. Then quasi-adaptive collective preferences imply that the project is also ex-post justified by the preferences $r(t)$ which are quasi-induced by the "project".

I now return to the original question: Assume $y(t)[>;q(t)]x(t)$. Can we then infer $z(t)[>;s(t)]x(t)$? As we have seen in the simple example, the answer is "yes" if preferences are adaptive and if $q(0)$ is induced by $x(0)$. We now generalize this proposition.

First I introduce another definition. For this, we observe the following. We have assumed that $q(t)$ is quasi-induced by the default $x(t)$. If the project is implemented, we expect $y(t)$. This basket path "quasi-induces" preferences $r(t)$. But $r(t)$ typically does not reproduce $y(t)$. Thus, $y(t)$ is not "self-reproducing" by means of the preferences it "quasi-induces". Eventually, by an interplay of changed preferences and changed basket paths, the economy settles down on the basket path $z(t)$ and the preference path $s(t)$. Here, this convergence is due to the fact that the actions of the citizens under preference path $s(t)$ generate $z(t)$, and the basket path $z(t)$ "quasi-induces" $s(t)$. We then see the pair $z(t)$ and $s(t)$ as a kind of dynamic equilibrium. We then introduce the following

Definition 14: For a given set of individual rights and a given initial set of preferences $s(0)$, let the preference path $s(t)$ and the basket path $z(t)$ be such that by the actions of citizens within their rights the preferences $s(t)$ generate the basket path $z(t)$ and such that $s(t)$ is quasi-induced by $z(t)$. Then the pair $z(t)$ and $s(t)$ is called an *equilibrium pair of preferences and baskets*. We also call $z(t)$ a *self-reproducing path of baskets*, and we also call $s(t)$ *a self-reproducing path of preferences*.

Applied to our three basket paths $x(t)$, $y(t)$ and $z(t)$ and the corresponding quasi-induced preference paths $q(t)$, $r(t)$ and $s(t)$, we know by construction that $z(t)$ and $s(t)$ are an equilibrium pair of preferences and baskets. We can assume that the "default" pair $x(t)$ and $q(t)$ are an equilibrium pair of preferences and baskets, whereas $y(t)$ and $r(t)$ are not necessarily an equilibrium pair: $r(t)$ is quasi-induced by $y(t)$, but $r(t)$ generally does not generate $y(t)$. If it were otherwise, then the transition from $y(t)$ to $z(t)$ would not take place, or, to put it differently, $z(t)$ and $y(t)$ would coincide.

It is the very idea of adaptive preferences and of quasi-adaptive preferences that decisions today are taken with a view of a future in mind which corresponds to the actual preferences. Thus, $y(t)$ is what the decision maker expects to occur if the project is implemented, and it is therefore the hypothetical result of the project subject to preferences $q(t)$. But then $y(t)$ induces different preferences $r(t)$, so that therefore the result of the project generally is distinct from $y(t)$.

We may put this logic also in the following terms. The path $y(t)$ corresponds to the *intended consequences* of the "project". The difference $z(t)-y(t)$ then are the *unintended consequences* of the "project". However, in a free society with compossible rights, these unintended consequences are legitimate, because they are the result of the free interplay of the activities and of the preferences of the citizens.

In the case that the project is implemented by government decision, we can say: for the transformation from $x(t)$ to $y(t)$, the government operates in the "causal mode". The transformation from $y(t)$ to $z(t)$ occurs and the government lets it occur, because here the government is in the "freedom mode".

I introduce what I call the:

Quasi-Improvement Axiom: Assume that society has the choice between 1) remaining in the "default" $x(t)$ with initial preferences $q(0)$ and preferences $q(t)$ quasi-induced by $x(t)$ and 2) a "project" $y(t)$ such that $y(t)[>;q(t)]x(t)$ and $y(t)[>;r(t)]x(t)$. Let the pair $z(t)$ and $y(t)$ be the equilibrium pair of preferences and baskets which arises out of the implementation of "project" $y(t)$ by means of the interaction of citizens in a system of rights that corresponds to the principle of pragmatic compossibility. Then, society chooses to implement the first "project" $y(t)$ irrespective of whether a direct move from the default $x(t)$ to $z(t)$ would have been accepted or rejected. That is: society acts in such a way that $z(t)$ is "revealed preferred" over $x(t)$. We then can write $z(t)[>,q(t)]x(t)$.

The Quasi-Improvement Axiom puts in other words the distinction between the causal mode and the freedom mode of government action. I call it the Quasi-Improvement Axiom because, on the collective level, it corresponds to the "Improvement Axiom" introduced in Book II for the individual level.

We can derive

Theorem 3: Assumption 1: The society is characterized by pragmatically compossible rights. Assumption 2: The axiom of freedom consistency of social preferences prevails. Assumption 3: The quasi-improvement axiom holds. Assumption

4: Collective preferences are quasi-adaptive. Consider a project leading from allocation $x(t)$ to expected allocation $y(t)$, and for the preferences $q(t)$ which are quasi-induced by $x(t)$ we have $y(t)[>;q(t)]x(t)$. Let $z(t)$ and $s(t)$ be the equilibrium pair of baskets and preferences resulting from implementation of the project. Then we have $z(t)[>;s(t)]x(t)$.

Proof: Assumption 4 of quasi-adaptiveness tautologically leads to an ex-post justification of an ex-ante "yes" decision for $y(t)$ by the preferences $r(t)$, quasi-induced by $y(t)$. The change from $y(t)$ and $r(t)$ to $z(t)$ and $s(t)$ is simply due to actions of citizens within the realm of their rights and ensuing changes in preferences. Thus, by the axiom of freedom consistency of social preferences, we obtain $z(t)[>;r(t)]y(t)$. Then, by the quasi-improvement axiom, we also obtain $z(t)[>;q(t)]x(t)$. Moreover, then again by quasi-adaptiveness, we also obtain $z(t)[>;s(t)]x(t)$. QED.

The proof of the theorem is really quite straightforward. The "difficult" part of the theory is not the math; it is a true understanding of the concepts introduced previously. Therefore, I need to explain a little more what I am doing. I discuss the four assumptions of Theorem 3. Assumptions 1, 2 and 3 derive from the idea of a society of free citizens. In addition, there is Assumption 4: quasi-adaptiveness. I discuss it in Chapter 32. There I provide a plausibility argument that it can be derived from individually adaptive preferences. Here I discuss the other three assumptions.

As I have discussed at length in Book IV, Chapters 18 and 19, and again in Book V, Chapter 29, freedom in a society rests on the prevalence of pragmatically compossible rights of citizens. This freedom implies that the consumption basket of society changes according to changes in the preferences of the citizens. This then implies the axiom that the basket result of this change in preferences is collectively preferred to the earlier basket. This is what Assumptions 1 and 2 of Theorem 3 mean. If collective preferences are a mirror of individual preferences within the framework of a free society, then collective preferences cannot deny that the result of the free interaction of its citizens is preferred over the initial allocation together with the initial preferences. Then the quasi-improvement axiom (Assumption 3) is also implied. For, if society adheres to the principles of freedom within the framework of compossible rights, then collective preference for a change away from the "default" must imply collective preference for any further changes in the basket, which are a consequence of the free reaction of people upon the initial change implemented by the government. Thus, any collective preference for a specific change by means of a "project" implies the general collective preference for any further changes implemented by the citizens within their compossible rights.

This consideration cuts both ways. On the one hand, it enables society to liberate itself from the strong adherence to the status quo, which itself is a consequence of what I have earlier called "preference conservatism" and which is the same as adaptivity of preferences. This liberation takes the form of small deviations from the default, which may be considered all right even with strong preference conservatism. The ensuing changes in preferences may then lead to further changes and thus to an improvement sequence of considerable length. On the other hand, decision makers in society may anticipate further changes as a consequence of the initial change, and they may anticipate that these changes are not of the kind they consider a good thing for society. Thus, they may resist the primary change not because they dislike it as such but because they fear consecutive further changes, which they dislike. But this latter effect of a "backward dislike of a project due to its further consequences" would, of course, contradict the freedom consistency of collective preferences in a society with fully compossible rights of citizens. Nevertheless, it is an important consideration for the "real-world societies" of imperfectly compossible rights. More on this below.

In whichever way the quasi-improvement axiom works in practice, it is unavoidable within a society that adheres to the principles of freedom. We may put it another way. Collective preferences consistent with individual freedom within the range of compossibility of rights not only refer to eventual material outcomes of government decisions but also to the *form* in which any change takes place. The decision to implement some project A may be motivated by the expected material outcome. It belongs to the "causal mode" of government action. But further changes as a consequence of the reaction of free citizens on the implementation of project A are then "preferred" by society over the non-implementation of project A, simply because they take the form of the interaction of free citizens – independent of the material outcome. This is the "freedom mode" of government action. It means that my theory of freedom and wealth generation is not a purely consequentialist theory like utilitarianism. In my theory, we have a consequentialist component in that the primary results of any "project" away from the default are evaluated by their benefit to the citizens. But, the secondary and further results of the project implementation – which are due to the interaction of free citizens and their preferences – are "collectively preferred" over the default irrespective of their material content. This is in contradiction to consequentialism.

This is in line with a "philosophy" that acknowledges that we cannot know the future. Thus, it would be futile if "society", that is, politics, were to try to "plan" the future of society globally. As a society, we may have a certain picture of future developments, essentially by extrapolation of observed trends. The "default" may be anticipated to a certain extent, and proposals for projects may have a chance to obtain majority support if they react on unsatisfactory aspects of the anticipated "default" path. Not much more can be expected in terms of manipulating the future. Change, this is the message, then comes mainly from the actions of citizens themselves and the interaction between the actions (baskets) and preferences. The acknowledgement of this structure of change by "society" means "ratification" of unforeseen consequences of any government project and thus acceptance of the quasi-improvement axiom – within the framework of pragmatic compossibility.

We need to add that there exists the possibility that the new self-enforcing paths $z(t)$ and $s(t)$ no longer fulfil the condition of pragmatic compossibility: preferences change from $q(t)$ via $r(t)$ to $s(t)$, and, as described with the example of car traffic in Book IV, Chapters 18 and 19, this change of behavior of citizens requires new laws to maintain pragmatic compossibility. But such behavior cannot be predicted, and thus the mere possibility that compossibility may be violated due to changed preferences is not a legitimate excuse to forestall the project which has the effect to change the basket path from $x(t)$ to $z(t)$. If, ex-post, it turns out that the path $z(t)$ violates compossibility, then one can implement another project to rectify the situation and thereby to return to compossibility.

Why is Theorem 3 important for welfare economics? In a nutshell: *only under the predictions of Theorem 3 can society successfully and sustainably escape from the status quo, that is, from the default option.* I explain this now.

First, it is important to understand that decisions taken on behalf of society are always formal decisions, typically involving more than one person. This means any such decision does not happen by default. It is an explicit decision. If the decision is not taken, the default prevails. As we have already seen in the case of individual decisions, the default option has a very large chance of being "chosen". This is even more so in "collective decisions". For here, substantial "transaction costs" of decision making arise. If there is resistance against a project even from a minority of persons involved in the decision, quite substantial delays are likely to arise. Negotiations about possible compromise solutions may become necessary. Negotiations to form a coalition may also become necessary. Issues of legality, conformity with laws or with the constitution of the country arise frequently. Feasibility studies may be required and so on. All this is on top of the individual preference conservatism, which is a characteristic of individual adaptive preferences.

As an example take law-making. Unless a new law is passed, the present law on the books prevails. The politics of changing a law is a complicated, time-consuming process. In a given year, only a minute proportion of laws is changed. There is a tremendous "law inertia".

In this context, it is also relevant to observe the following. Even if the prediction of Theorem 3 applies, there is a strong conservative bias in social decision making. Those projects which are being implemented will be justified by ex-post preferences. But, on the other hand, there may exist many potential projects which, if implemented, would be justified ex-post but which will not be implemented with the ex-ante preferences. We have four categories: 1)"yes" ex-ante, "yes" ex-post; 2) "yes" ex-ante, "no" ex-post; 3)"no" ex-ante, "yes" ex-post; 4) "no" ex-ante, "no" ex-post. Category 1 is clear: the projects will be implemented. If Theorem 3 applies, Category 2 is empty. Category 3 will not be implemented. Category 4 will not and should not be implemented. The conservative bias, then, is the fact that Category 3 will not be implemented, despite the fact that ex-post their implementation would be justified.

Assume now that the prediction of Theorem 3 is not valid. Category 2 would then not be empty. Take the extreme case of anti-adaptive preferences. It would then be very likely that an approved project later on would not be justified ex-post. People would frequently regret earlier decisions to deviate from the default option. We would expect society to be very reluctant to deviate from the default if experience shows that in many cases ex-post evaluation makes society regret the "project". In anticipation of regret, society would become very conservative indeed. And this would make a progressive society impossible. In particular, the legitimacy of decentralized decision-making would be undermined. However, as already remarked, decentralized decision-making is the most important institutional pre-requisite of frequent deviations from the status quo.

To be sure, even with Theorem 3, the real world experiences many cases of regret about "projects". This is due to error in evaluation, that is, due to uncertainty. The risk of error is, in any case, a large burden for potential projects that break away from the status quo. A person who is a decision maker must justify his/her decision. With few exceptions, justification is not required for "non-decision", that is, for not taking on a "project" and thus for the default decision. But the decision to undertake a project, in particular a project with initial investments, has to be justified before others. Thus, uncertainty and the risk of error in undertaking a project generate a justification bias towards the default and against projects. If Theorem 3 were not valid, this bias would be re-enforced, decentralized decision-making would lose legitimacy and society would be stagnant.

In a sense, the fact that society is not stagnant in the western world is a kind of "proof" of Theorem 3 and of adaptive preferences.

References

Boardman, E. Anthony, Greenberg, David H., Vining, Aidan R. and Weimer, David L., 2018, Cost-Benefit Analysis – Concepts and Practice, 5th edition, Cambridge, Cambridge University Press, 604 pages.

Samuelson, Paul A., 1954, The Pure Theory of Public Expenditure, Review of Economics and Statistics, 36, 387–389.

Samuelson, Paul A., 1956, Social Indifference Curves, Quarterly Journal of Economics, 70 (1), 1–22.

Simon, Herbert, 1962, The Architecture of Complexity, Proceedings of the American Philosophical Society, 106 (6), 467–482.

32

COST-BENEFIT-ANALYSIS WITH ADAPTIVE PREFERENCES, PART 2

I still have to justify Assumption 4 of Theorem 3. Why can we be rather confident that collective preferences are quasi-adaptive if we can assume that individual preferences are adaptive?

For any given project, we can divide the default consumption basket $x(t)$ and the project consumption basket $y(t)$ into three parts a, b and c. Some components of the two baskets are in category a; some components are in category b, and the remaining components are in category c. Category a consists of those goods whose production and consumption is intended to rise by the project. Thus, for the vector which only includes goods from category a, we may write $y_a(t) > x_a(t)$. Category b consists of those goods whose production and consumption is intended or expected to decline by the project. So here we can write $y_b(t) < x_b(t)$. An example of a project may be the introduction of a new product into the market. Demand for the new product and for products which are its complements is higher than it would be if the product were not introduced. The new product and its complements then form group a. Then, there are goods which are substitutes for the new product. Demand for them may go down due to the new competition. Thus, when the combustion-engine-driven car was introduced, the demand for horse-drawn carriages declined. These horse-drawn carriages then belong to group b when we talk about the introduction of the automobile as "the project".

Group c is all other goods. They are only indirectly affected by the new project. In a partial equilibrium cost-benefit analysis, they only enter indirectly by the costs incurred through the project. Thus, $y_c(t) - x_c(t)$ does not enter directly into the calculation of the decision maker. Rather, they are the outgrowth of the fact that, due to some initial investment for the project, income disposable for consumption goes down and thus the market value of the vector $y_c(t)$ may be lower than the market value of the vector $x_c(t)$ for a time interval containing small (positive) t-values.

DOI: 10.4324/9781032726410-38

We may then interpret the vector $y_c(t)$ under preferences $q(t)$ not so much as being specified in goods quantities but rather as the result of consumer utility maximizing under a budget constraint, where the "project" focused on $y_a(t)$ and $y_b(t)$ only defines the remaining budget for the vector $y_c(t)$. Seen in this light, the budget for the vector $y_c(t)$ remains the same after preferences have moved from $q(t)$ to $r(t)$. A change in the comparative valuation of $x(t)$ and $y(t)$ due to a change in preferences from $q(t)$ to $r(t)$ can then only come from $x_a(t)$, $x_b(t)$, $y_a(t)$ and $y_b(t)$. This analytic procedure of course presupposes "near-decomposability", as introduced by Herbert Simon 1962 and as discussed in Book V, Chapter 26.

I now introduce the assumption that individual preferences are adaptive. Then, we know that those goods in group a gain in esteem, relative to the earlier preferences, and those goods in group b lose in esteem, relative to the earlier preferences. But this means that the partial move from $x_a(t)$, $x_b(t)$ to $y_a(t), y_b(t)$ obtains even more approval with preferences $r(t)$ than with preferences $q(t)$, because the y-vector provides more of those goods which now are in higher esteem and provides less of those goods which now are in lower esteem. This then tells us that if $y(t)[>;q(t)]x(t)$ then $y(t)[>;r(t)]x(t)$. Thus, collective preferences are quasi-adaptive.

Note that our way to neutralize the goods in group c is precisely the same as the one applied in traditional cost-benefit analysis. There, group c also consists of those goods whose quantities change due to the costs incurred by the project. Indeed, our simple example of the bridge in the preceding chapter also operates in the same way. Of course, the background is "near-decomposability".

Again: if individual preferences were anti-adaptive, then group a would obtain lower esteem with preferences $r(t)$ than with preferences $q(t)$, whereas group b would obtain higher esteem with preferences $r(t)$ than with preferences $q(t)$. And this would mean that the esteem of $y(t)$ relative to $x(t)$ would go down as preferences move from $q(t)$ to $r(t)$. There would then be no guarantee that, with ex-post preferences, the project would still be preferred over the default.

Moreover, with anti-adaptive preferences, the cyclicity problem looms. As Theorem 1 tells us, cyclicity of improvement sequences is impossible with adaptive preferences, and, as Theorem 2 tells us, cyclicity of improvement sequences is a possibility whenever preferences are not adaptive. But observation of such cyclicity of improvement sequences further undermines the belief that deviations from the default are productive, even if proposed projects from the ex-ante point of view look favorable.

As we have seen, the Assumptions 1, 2 and 3 of Theorem 3 are justified by the assumption that we look at a free society with pragmatically compossible rights. Assumption 4 is supported by the observation that citizens' preferences are adaptive. So we can rely on Theorem 3. I have also given reasons why the predictions of Theorem 3 are important ingredients of a society that is able to pull itself away from the "default", from stagnation. Theorem 3 justifies decentralized decision making on the basis of partial equilibrium analysis. Of course, as in traditional economics, the appropriate "design" of institutions remains a big task. We have to find the institutional details that implement the "invisible hand" of conformity between the private goals of the agents and the promotion of the welfare of the other citizens.

The important consequence of Theorem 3 for a theory of decentralized decision making is that it provides conformity between ex-ante benefits and ex-post benefits of any "project" that is designed to break away from the "default". The preference changes induced by the project are such that the project itself will be justified ex-post, if it was seen as beneficial ex-ante. If this were not the case, welfare economics could not really "ratify" such a project.

As I remarked earlier, there remains a conservative bias. There is no converse theorem to Theorem 3 which would say: if a project is justified ex-post, it is also justified ex-ante and therefore implemented. Such a converse theorem only would exist if preferences were anti-adaptive. But then Theorem 3 would be invalid. The beautiful world of fixed preferences is not ours. Only in that world would we have (error and uncertainty aside) a perfect coincidence between ex-ante and ex-post justification of projects.

But from the point of view of welfare economics, of course, it is much better that ex-ante justification imply ex-post justification than vice versa. For god has created a world in which we first decide to act before we act. Thus, ex-ante evaluation is the basis for decisions. Ex-post evaluations take place anyway, and they are important for the learning process how to organize our society. The conformity between positive ex-ante evaluations and positive ex-post evaluations is an essential ingredient of a society that has the power to break away from the default option.

In my analysis, I have only looked at "yes-or-no" decisions. But this does not mean that the theory only applies to a very special case. Indeed, if there are different variants of a project, then eventually, before the "yes-or-no" decision is taken, one finds out the optimal variant of the project (as evaluated with ex-ante preferences) and then compares this optimal variant with the default to come to a "yes-or-no" decision. In this book, I do not go into the issues that arise from the politics of preparing a "yes-or-no" decision. Of course, the "optimal" variant eventually proposed is the result of a complicated interplay of "strategic" behavior of different players. With few exceptions, it is not the optimum from an ex-post point of view, even if we disregard induced preference changes.

It is, of course, very likely that the optimal "size" of the project from an ex-ante perspective is smaller than the optimal "size" from an ex-post point of view. If preferences induced by the project give a higher esteem for the goods coming out of the project, then, with these ex-post preferences, the optimum size would have been larger than the actual size optimized with respect to the ex-ante preferences. This "size" effect is an example of the one-sidedness of project decisions, which we have discussed before, that is, a remaining status-quo bias, even with Theorem 3.

In the preceding and in this chapter, I have discussed a single "project" $y(t)$ which was compared with the "default" $x(t)$. This procedure is all right for the general theory, despite the fact that many "projects" are being considered and implemented at the same time. Indeed, since any given project may have a very long life – such as a bridge to be built and to be used – very many projects overlap timewise. The procedure is all right if we understand that for the particular project under consideration, the "default" $x(t)$ comprises all other "projects" underway or even to be expected to be underway in the future. It would therefore be a misunderstanding if one considered $x(t)$ the picture of a stagnant economy. This is definitely not the case if we are in an economy of decentralized decision making, justified by the ex-post evaluation of any project that got the go-ahead due to the ex-ante evaluation.

Nevertheless, the position taken previously, namely that without the conditions of Theorem 3 we are likely to be in a stagnant economy, is correct. For without the conditions of Theorem 3, not only is the project under consideration unlikely to be implemented. Rather, any project deviating from the default is unlikely to be implemented. And then stagnation does prevail.

Provided we can rely on Theorem 3, we then have a large number of overlapping projects. Some of these projects may compete against each other. Other projects may build upon another. However, all this is included in the comparison of $x(t)$ and $y(t)$ when we consider any particular proposed project. We may give this remark the following formula: The different status quo–deviating "projects" are players in a complicated game – and we look at a Nash equilibrium of that game. Considered in this way, one may be interested to read Brandl and Brandt 2024. In that paper, the authors show that Nash equilibrium is the only game theoretic solution concept which satisfies the three criteria of "consequentialism", "consistency" and "rationality".

References

Brandl, Florian and Brandt, Felix, 2024, An Axiomatic Characterization of Nash Equilibrium, Manuscript, University of Bonn, 34 pages.

Simon, Herbert, 1962, The Architecture of Complexity, Proceedings of the American Philosophical Society, 106 (6), 467–482.

33

PRAGMATICS OF INCOMPLETE COMPOSSIBILITY

This sketch of partial equilibrium welfare economics in a world of adaptive preferences has worked with the assumption that citizens' rights are fully compossible – in the pragmatic form of compossibility. This assumption is never fully realistic. Individual rights in a State that adheres to the principles of individual freedom and democracy are slow in being modified according to new developments in society. Social networks based on the internet have exploded in size in recent times. They are a challenge to the privacy of the citizen. We may look with considerable doubt on the proposition that these social networks and the rights associated with them are compossible according to our criterion of pragmatic compossibility. Legislation may be required to bring social networks more in line with pragmatic compossibility. Similar concerns apply to the rapid rise of artificial intelligence.

The rules that regulate the car traffic can again serve as a good example of society's attempt to obtain pragmatic compossibility of individual rights. We have discussed them before in Book IV. Through time, car traffic changes. More people may own a car and may have a driver's license. Additional roads become available. There is technical progress in cars and in the regulating potential. Wages of police officers and other regulating personnel may rise. Driving habits may change.

The rules on the books are likely to change in reaction to these structural changes of the car traffic. At any given time, they may not be optimal because there is a legislation lag in answering the changes going on in the real world of car traffic. I take an example that is related to our main topic: changing – perhaps endogenously changing – preferences. Earlier, we may assume, for the sake of argument, that the system of speed limits and sanctions against violations of speed limits has been optimally adjusted to the actual driving habits of car drivers. For reasons which may lie outside of our sub-system of car traffic, driving habits change. We may now see that some people, perhaps a minority, drive more aggressively than they

DOI: 10.4324/9781032726410-39

did in the past. Given the still-prevailing rules concerning speed limits, this change in driving habits reduces the average net benefits of car driving. Even evaluated with the new preferences of the more aggressive drivers, average net benefits of car driving have been reduced, because the incremental risk, for all drivers, of getting involved in car accidents outweighs the gain obtained by the people who now drive more aggressively.

Earlier, with the then optimal rules, the rights concerning the subsystem car traffic were pragmatically compossible. The sanctions against speeding may be seen as a "price" for speeding. This "price" discouraged speeding in those cases in which the monetary equivalent of the benefit of speeding was below this "price". Speeding then took place in cases in which the benefit for the speeder was higher than the "price" to be paid – in a probabilistic sense, of course – for speeding. And the "price" of speeding reflected the net loss to the other car drivers in terms of a higher risk of getting involved in a car accident. This means that, as long as the average frequency of speeding was not changed, a single instance of "preference change" from refraining from speeding to speeding raised total income of car drivers. Other car drivers do not incur a loss, because they obtain the "price" for speeding (assuming – to keep things simple – that the money fine paid for speeding was added to the expenditures for making a better car driving system), and the speeding car driver obtains a higher benefit from speeding than the "price" he/she pays.

And, of course, vice versa, the same holds. If the car driver sped yesterday and his preferences changed so that he does not speed today, then this again raises total income, because today his benefit from speeding is below the "price" he pays for speeding, whereas the other car drivers are neutral, because they lose the "price" for speeding, but they gain slightly more safety on the road.

Now that there is a permanent shift in the direction of more speeding, the marginal "price" for speeding may be too low. Car drivers may now consider the marginal risk from another speeder to be higher than the marginal "price" paid by the speeder. Rules may have to be changed so that the "price" for speeding is now higher than it was before. Before this rule change takes place, the principle of pragmatic compossibility is violated, because a preference change towards more speeding now reduces the summed net benefit of car drivers.

Another case of a violation of pragmatic compossibility is a market with a supplier monopoly. To the extent that this monopoly simply is there and "fell from heaven", so to speak, we know that a change in the monopolist's "preferences", such that he raises his price, causes more harm than benefit to the economy at large, including the benefit of the monopolist himself. The institutions of anti-trust have been introduced to promote competition and to challenge monopolistic behavior for this very reason. However, not every positive price-cost margin is a sign that monopoly, in this sense, prevails. The many markets characterized by "monopolistic competition" do exhibit positive price-marginal cost margins. But it would be futile for government to intervene here. Indeed, "transaction costs" of such government intervention into such a competitive market are likely to exceed the benefits of a change in allocation decisions thereby accomplished. On this point, read in Book V, Chapter 25. Also, if monopoly profits are the result of a patent due to an invention, it is likely to be counterproductive if the government tries to prevent monopoly pricing. The general conclusion is that an optimal form of competition law and its pragmatic implementation are part of a regime of freedom within the realm of compossibility. We then obtain the result that there is no conflict between a freedom-oriented and an efficiency-oriented anti-trust law.

What does an incomplete implementation of the pragmatic compossibility imply for our welfare analysis, for the result contained in Theorem 3? Here, we have to distinguish between a matter of principle and a more pragmatic view. The issue is: how to deal with the fact that a project in the first instance changes the economy from $x(t)$ to $y(t)$, but then, due to quasi-induced preference changes from $q(t)$ to $r(t)$, the basket changes – after intermediate steps – to self-reproducing $z(t)$, and preferences change – after intermediate steps – to self-reproducing $s(t)$. It could happen that "society" with preferences $q(t)$ prefers $y(t)$ over $x(t)$, but, with the same preferences $q(t)$ prefers $x(t)$ over $z(t)$.

In the case of full compossibility, we referred to the freedom consistency of collective preferences and the quasi-improvement axiom to say that collective preferences rule it out that $z(t)$ is not preferred over $x(t)$ if $y(t)[>;q(t)]x(t)$ and $y(t)[>;r(t)]x(t)$. The rule of law implies that decision makers on behalf of society have to work on the *presumption* that the law on the books satisfies compossibility. Otherwise, they undermine the legitimacy of the process of law making. The lawmaker cannot say: "I have made this law, but it is a bad law". This implies that the collective decision maker must adhere to the principle that from $y(t)[>;q(t)]x(t)$ follows $z(t)[>;q(t)]x(t)$.

But the politics of law-making is different. The democratically elected government may prefer $y(t)$ to $x(t)$ but nevertheless may prefer $x(t)$ to expected $z(t)$, which then motivates it not to change the law and to stay with $x(t)$. It is against the spirit of freedom in society, but it is likely that this attitude prevails. We may call it *implicit paternalism*. The problem is that the government always can use the rhetoric that $z(t)$ in all likelihood will violate the principle of compossibility. As an example: a frequent argument against more freedom is that it would raise the frequency of crimes. Or, more generally: vested interests may have the political power to prevent de-regulation of markets – using the argument that this liberalization is likely to lead to additional sources of negative externalities- thereby violating the principle of pragmatic compossibility. Ambuehl et al. 2021 have conducted experiments to find out under which conditions people are prone to intervene paternalistically into the decisions of other people.

Private decisions about "projects" will be discussed in the next chapter.

Reference

Ambuehl, Sandro, Bernheim, Douglas and Ockenfels, Axel, 2021, What Motivates Paternalism? An Experimental Study, American Economic Review, 111 (3), 787–830.

34

PRIVATE ANTICIPATION OF PREFERENCE CHANGE

Innovation

In Book V, Chapter 29 I developed an argument why a competitive market economy should allow any private projects that deviate from the status quo (the default), provided there exists a legal-institutional framework satisfying pragmatic compossibility. Distributional concerns should not hamper this private freedom to act, because we take account of them by the principle of "generalized compensation" and by progressive income taxation.

My theory builds on the observation that, by and large, people are poor forecasters not only of events but also of attitudes and preferences. And, a fortiori, they are poor forecasters of the interaction between events and preferences. In making up their mind about their own decisions, they have a strong tendency to work with an implicit forecast which is characterized by a maximum of extrapolation of the present status quo. From Thomas Hobbes 1841 we learn: "No man can have in his mind a conception of the future, for the future is not yet. But of our conceptions of the past, we make a future."

For my analysis in the preceding Chapter 33, this means that $q(t)$, in particular, has to be seen in a rather conservative light. Basically, in most cases, $q(t)$ can be seen as an extrapolation of present preferences into the future. This accentuates the difference between ex-ante and ex-post evaluation of any given proposed project.

But it is likely that some people in the community dare to predict that preferences change. They may "know" or they may have the intuition that preferences are adaptive, that is, that there is likely to be strong positive feedback from a new project, for example, a new product, to customers' preferences. Steve Jobs' strategy of product innovation at Apple is, of course, a prime example of anticipated changes of customer preferences once a new product is on the market.

The assumption of adaptive preferences of citizens is not only empirically valid. It serves an important function for the individual citizen because it ensures that

DOI: 10.4324/9781032726410-40

improvement sequences are acyclic and that therefore individuals can rely on a more global rationality of a series of small improvement steps. In addition, adaptive preferences also serve to ensure the conditions of Theorem 3. This ex-post justification of ex-ante decisions to undertake a project is a precondition for a society with a decentralized system of decision making, where many "projects" take place at the same time. On the other hand, adaptive preferences are a structure that we have also described as "preference conservatism". So it is – perhaps paradoxically – the case that preference conservatism is the condition for the stability of a system of decentralized decision making, which is "progressive" in the sense that it takes on many "projects" that deviate from the status quo, the default option.

I now describe an additional function of decentralized decision-making. The preference conservatism of citizens induces a very conservative decision structure on the level of the collective. Government and similar decision bodies which are run by majority voting cannot be more progressive than corresponds to the preference conservatism of society's citizens. A society that simply relies on democratic majority voting of all citizens for its decisions is therefore necessarily a stagnant society with an overwhelming power of the default alternative, that is, with an overwhelming power of the status quo.

On the other hand, a regime of decentralized decision making, such as a market economy, provides the opportunity for entrepreneurs in general, but "preference entrepreneurs" in particular, to deviate from the conservative majority. These entrepreneurs may then start a project – for example, a new product – in the expectation that after they have implemented it, ex-post preferences of the citizens are quite different from their ex-ante preferences. And thus, demand for the new product after it has been launched on the market is much higher than the average citizen would have expected beforehand with his/her ex-ante preferences. In other words: the Schumpeterian 1912 "preference entrepreneur" relies on the following: ex-ante preferences of the majority of citizens would induce them to reject the project. However, once the entrepreneur has implemented the project against the majority preferences, citizen preferences change in such a way that now they agree (by "revealed preference", i.e. by buying the new product in large quantities) that undertaking the project was a good idea.

A system of decentralized decision making is thus able to cope with the welfare aspects of induced preferences as long as these induced preferences of the citizens are adaptive. Progress in society and preference conservatism not only go together; they support each other: preference conservatism provides – via Theorems 1, 2 and 3 – the justification of a regime with many projects that break away from stagnation. And social progress by decentralization supports the political views of the citizens who support the system of decentralized decision making but also supports their general pragmatism to approve only of things they have themselves experienced. And this pragmatism is, by the "principle of extrapolation", one facet of the general structure of adaptive preferences.

As I already have argued in Book V, Chapter 28, by means of the three-level scheme, freedom in a framework of pragmatic compossibility is not only a value in itself. It also helps to promote progress, to promote breakaways from stagnation. "Preference entrepreneurs" are an important ingredient for this social function of liberty.

I borrow the title of Stephen Greenblatt's (2011) fascinating book about the rediscovery of Lucretius' *De Natura* in the early 15th century: *The Swerve*. In my treatise I transform the "static" welfare economics of fixed preferences into a "dynamic" or "evolutionary" welfare economics of adaptive preferences and thereby contribute to a better understanding of civil liberty: it culminates in the "preference swerve" performed by Schumpeterian entrepreneurs. They anticipate the behavioral changes which their innovation brings about. They thereby combine their "ego", their "egoism", with their "empathy" for their fellow citizens, who benefit from that innovation after these citizens have endogenously changed their preferences.

References

Greenblatt, Stephen, 2011, The Swerve: How the World Became Modern, New York, W. W. Norton, 356 pages.

Hobbes, Thomas, 1841, Human Nature, in: Molesworth, W. (ed.), Thomas Hobbes, English Works, 4, p. 16, (as quoted in Stone, Lawrence, The Causes of the English Revolution 1529–1642, London, Routledge and Kegan Paul, 1972, 168 Pages, p.51).

Schumpeter, Joseph A., 1912, Theorie der wirtschaftlichen Entwicklung, Leipzig, Duncker & Humblot, 548 pages.

35

CONCLUDING REMARKS

1 Rather than assuming fixed preferences, we work with a *preference system:* preferences and constraints determine the consumption basket, but there is a feedback mapping from the set of consumption baskets to the set of preferences: "induced preferences". We then ask: can we maintain the idea of "progress" based on *normative individualism* if preferences are endogenously formed? For this to be the case, *improvement sequences* of baskets (with corresponding sequences of induced preferences) ought to be *acyclic.*

2 Provided that preference systems satisfy the assumptions of continuity, nonsatiation and "extended single crossing", Theorems 1 and 2 tell us: every improvement sequence is acyclic if and only if preferences are *adaptive.* The definition of adaptive preferences: *if basket y is preferred over basket x with preferences induced by x, then basket y is also preferred over basket x with preferences induced by y*. In a slightly modified form, Theorems 1 and 2 also hold for models in which we describe time as a continuum (as one does in the natural sciences).

3 For *welfare economics with endogenous preferences*, the hypothesis of adaptive preferences replaces the weak and the strong axiom of revealed preference of welfare economics with exogenously given preferences.

4 We define a society of free people by the principle of "pragmatic compossibility" of citizens' rights. The setup corresponds to the "piecemeal engineering" idea proposed by Karl Popper in his "Open Society". Pragmatic compossibility leads to the social improvement concept by Hicks–Kaldor–Scitovsky. By Theorems 1 and 2, it is the prevalence of adaptive preferences which makes this approach of pragmatic compossibility internally consistent. Indeed, adaptive preferences must prevail to make Popper's concept of piecemeal engineering internally consistent.

DOI: 10.4324/9781032726410-41

5 Moreover, the prevalence of adaptive preferences is the precondition for a feasible freedom-oriented and hence compossibility-oriented legislation by the State. Only then can the legislature realistically predict the consequences of its lawgiving. This is so because only then can the legislator extrapolate observed past behavior of people into the future. This is the essence of an *experience-based economic policy*.

6 Quite a few results of research in behavioral economics support the hypothesis that human behavior is consistent with the property of adaptive preferences. Here I mention the "appetite-satiation cycle": random or foreseen changes in consumption constraints; inter-temporal allocation of consumption, that is, saving and dissaving; bounded rationality; information acquisition as a byproduct of consumption or by search; avoidance of cognitive dissonance; education and schooling; switching costs and the default option; the "adaptive preference lemma"; decision costs; reference-dependent preferences; loss aversion; status quo bias; endowment effect; "rational inattention"; "use it or lose it"; habit formation; uncertainty aversion; "religion"; "language acquisition"; intertemporal choice and complexity avoidance; the (partial) legitimacy of "nudging"; long-run price elasticity of demand higher than short-run price elasticity; adaptive preferences as an outcome of evolution; and imitation of others as a form of adaptive preferences. *The empirical evidence supports the hypothesis of adaptive preferences*.

7 Government in a society of free citizens acts either in the "causal mode" or in the "freedom mode". In the freedom mode, government lets citizens pursue their own goals – and it thereby "ratifies" the results of such behavior as legitimate outcomes of the interaction between free citizens. In the causal mode, the government interferes to implement improvements in terms of the criteria of pragmatic compossibility. This in particular concerns the provision of public goods.

8 Agents who lack autonomy may need the interference of the government. *Autonomy must be learned*: small children lack such autonomy – and the government should interfere in their education if their parents do not properly fulfill their roles as educators. Agents may fall into some trap of addiction – and government should interfere accordingly. In these cases of interference to protect autonomy-lacking agents, the government acts in the causal mode.

9 To understand the complexity of social life, benefitting from the division of labor, it is useful to remind ourselves of Herbert Simon's *Architecture of Complexity* (Simon 1962): for evolutionary reasons, any complex system is a composition of "subsystems", which are weakly interconnected. The system is "nearly decomposable". An economic order can best organize its production system by the private property of the means of production and by competition among firms in their markets – thereby implementing "near-decomposability".

10 To achieve maximum productivity, the system of private property must be embedded in a democratic political structure. Only thereby can the "freedom

mode of government action" be implemented. Furthermore, an authoritarian or totalitarian system leads to extreme "short-termism" of citizens, because their rulers, in order to maintain their power, cannot tolerate security of their subjects' private property.

11 Nevertheless, economic superiority of the democratic market societies does not guarantee their victory in the new "cold war" between totalitarianism and democracy: not the least due to adaptive preferences, democracies may not be sufficiently prepared to spend sufficient resources for military defense against totalitarian aggressions.

12 The "Social Market Economy" differs from a pure "laissez-faire economy" by taking specific care of the weak citizens and by some appropriate income redistribution from rich to poor via the tax system. "Optimal income taxation theory" provides analytical tools for finding the optimal compromise between efficiency and equality. So far, it is not clear how adaptive preferences change the optimal income tax schedule, as compared to the traditional assumption of fixed preferences.

13 Implementation of the Social Market Economy with a progressive income tax reinforces the case for pragmatic compossibility in the form of the Kaldor–Hicks–Scitovsky criterion. A higher real income generates additional tax revenue, which allows additional redistribution for the benefit of people with a low income.

14 Cost benefit analysis, as performed in practice, can be justified in a world of adaptive preferences. However, it does take some effort to derive this result. For: implementation of a project based on "ex-ante-preferences" of citizens generates feedback on preferences, which then become the "ex-post-preferences". What are the conditions that these ex-post-preferences also justify the implementation of the project? The answer to this question is not so easy, because here we have to work with a time flow of returns from the project and with time flows of changing preferences, all extending from time zero (the decision moment about the project) to plus infinity. It is important for a system of decentralized decision-making that, as a rule, the ex-post judgement about the project have the same result as the ex-ante judgement. Otherwise, people would shy away from projects – with the result of stagnation (and thus defeat against totalitarian aggression). Ex-post justification of implemented projects (due to ex-ante justification) is only the rule when citizens' preferences are adaptive.

15 There is a "Schumpeterian swerve" in the theory of adaptive preferences. Compare Greenblatt 2011. Entrepreneurs, as described by Schumpeter 1912, introduce innovative products into the market – in the expectation that they can "swerve" the preferences of their potential customers in favor of these products. This is a decisive property of a competitive market economy: without such swerving potential, very little innovation would occur. And then the conservatism of adaptive preferences is likely to lead into a stagnating economy.

References

Greenblatt, Stephen, 2011, The Swerve: How the World Became Modern, New York, W. W. Norton, 356 pages.

Schumpeter, Joseph A., 1912, Theorie der wirtschaftlichen Entwicklung, Leipzig, Duncker & Humblot, 548 pages.

Simon, Herbert, 1962, The Architecture of Complexity, Proceedings of the American Philosophical Society, 106 (6), 467–482.

REFERENCES

Admati, Anat and Hellwig, Martin, 2013, The Bankers' New Clothes – What's Wrong with Banking and What to Do About It, Princeton, NJ, Princeton University Press, 398 pages.

Akerlof, George A., 1970, The Market for Lemons: Quality Uncertainty and the Market Mechanism, Quarterly Journal of Economics, 84 (3), 488–500.

Akerlof, George A. and Dickens, William T., 1982, The Economic Consequences of Cognitive Dissonance, American Economic Review, 72 (3), 307–319.

Akerlof, George A. and Shiller, Robert J., 2015, Phishing for Phools: The Economics of Manipulation and Deception, Princeton, NJ, Princeton University Press, 288 pages.

Ambuehl, Sandro, Bernheim, Douglas and Ockenfels, Axel, 2021, What Motivates Paternalism? An Experimental Study, American Economic Review, 111 (3), 787–830.

Andersen, Steffen, Badarinza, Cristian, Liu, Lu, Marx, Julie and Ramadorai, Tarun, 2022, Reference Dependence in the Housing Market, American Economic Review, 112 (10), 3398–3440.

Aquinas, Thomas, 1268, Summa Theologica, Vol. 2, London, Eyre and Spottiswoode, 2006.

Arnott, Richard J. and Stiglitz, Joseph E., 1979, Aggregate Land Rents, Expenditure on Public Goods, and Optimal City Size, Quarterly Journal of Economics, 93 (4), 471–500.

Arrow, Kenneth J., 1963, Uncertainty and the Welfare Economics of Medical Care, American Economic Review, 53 (5), 941–973.

Artinger, Florian M., Gigerenzer, Gerd and Jakobs, Perke, 2022, Satisficing: Integrating Two Traditions, Journal of Economic Literature, 60 (2), 598–635.

Atkinson, Anthony B., 1970, On the Measurement of Inequality, Journal of Economic Theory, 2 (3), 244–263.

Bagwell, Kyle, 2007, The Economics of Advertising, in: Armstrong, Mark and Porter, Robert A. (eds), Handbook of Industrial Organization, Amsterdam, Elsevier, Vol. 3, pp.1701–1844.

Baillon, Aurélien, Halevy, Yoram and Chen, Li, 2022, Randomize at your Own Risk: On the Observability of Ambuigity Aversion, Econometrica, 90 (3), 1085–1107.

Bain, Joe S., 1956, Barriers to New Competition, Cambridge, MA, Harvard University Press, Xi + 329 pages.

Baurmann, Michael, 2000, Der Markt der Tugend – Recht und Moral in der liberalen Gesellschaft – Eine soziologische Untersuchung, Tübingen, J.C.B. Mohr, XIX + 681 pages.

Becker, Gary S., 1993, A Treatise on the Family, Cambridge, MA, Harvard University Press, Paperback Edition, Xii + 424 pages.
Becker, Gary S., 1996, Accounting for Tastes, Cambridge, MA, Harvard University Press, 292 pages.
Becker, Gary S. and Murphy, Kevin M., 1988, A Theory of Rational Addiction, Journal of Political Economy, 96 (4), 675–700.
Bentham, Jeremy, 1789, An Introduction to the Principles of Morals and Legislation, in: Burns, J. H. and Hart, H. L. A. (eds), The Collected Works of Jeremy Bentham, Oxford, Oxford University Press, 1998.
Bernheim, B. Douglas, Braghieri, Luca, Martinez-Marquina, Alejandro and Zukerman, David, 2021, A Theory of Chosen Preferences, American Economic Review, 111 (2), 720–754.
Bernheim, B. Douglas and Mueller-Gastell, Jonas, 2021, Optimal Default Options: The Case for (Weighted) Opt-Out Minimization, NBER Working Paper 28254.
Bierbrauer, Felix, Boyer, Pierre C. and Peichl, Andreas, 2021, Politically Feasible Reforms of Nonlinear Tax Systems, American Economic Review, 111 (1), 153–191.
Boardman, E. Anthony, Greenberg, David H., Vining, Aidan R. and Weimer, David L., 2018, Cost-Benefit Analysis – Concepts and Practice, 5th edition, Cambridge, Cambridge University Press, 604 pages.
Böhm, Franz, 1966, Privatrechtsgesellschaft und Marktwirtschaft, ORDO, 17, 75–151.
Böhm-Bawerk, Eugen Ritter von, 1881, Rechte und Verhältnisse vom Standpunkte der volkswirtschaftlichen Güterlehre, Innsbruck, Wagner Verlagsbuchhandlung, 153 pages.
Böhm-Bawerk, Eugen Ritter von, 1889, Positive Theorie des Kapitales, Jena, Fischer, 489 pages.
Bolle, Friedel, 1990, Habit Formation and Long Term Contracts, Journal of Consumer Policy, 13, 273–284.
Bowles, Samuel, 1998, Endogenous Preferences: The Cultural Consequences of Markets and Other Economic Institutions, Journal of Economic Literature, XXXVI, 75–111.
Bowles, Samuel, 2016, The Moral Economy: Why Good Incentives Are No Substitute for Good Intentions, New Haven, CT, Yale University Press, 288 pages.
Brandl, Florian and Brandt, Felix, 2024, An Axiomatic Characterization of Nash Equilibrium, Manuscript, University of Bonn, 34 pages.
Buchanan, James M., 1999–2002, The Collected Works of James Buchanan, 20 volumes, Indianapolis, IN, Liberty Fund.
Christmas, Billy, 2019, A Reformulation of the Structure of a Set of Compossible Rights, Philosophical Quarterly, 69 (275), 221–234.
Coase, Ronald, 1937, The Nature of the Firm, Economica, 4 (16), 386–405.
Coase, Ronald, 1960, The Problem of Social Cost, Journal of Law and Economics, 3, 1–44.
Constantinides, George M., 1990, Habit Formation: A Resolution of the Equity Premium Puzzle, Journal of Political Economy, 98 (3), 519–543.
Cooter, Robert D. and Gilbert, Michael D., 2022, Public Law and Economics, Oxford, Oxford University Press, 581 pages.
Darwin, Charles, 1856, Quotation in Charles Darwin, Metaphysics, Materialism, and the Evolution Mind: Early Writings of Charles Darwin, Transcribed, and Annotated by Paul H. Barrett with a Commentary by Howard E. Gruber, Chicago, IL, Chicago University Press, 1974.
David, Paul, 1985, Clio and the Economics of QWERTY, American Economic Review, 75, 332–337.
Debreu, Gerard, 1959, Theory of Value – An Axiomatic Analysis of Economic Equilibrium, New York, Yale University Press.
Diamond, Peter A., 1984, Money in Search Equilibrium, Econometrica, 52 (1), 1–20.
Duesenberry, James S., 1949, Income, Saving, and the Theory of Consumer Behavior, Cambridge, MA, Harvard University Press, 128 pages.

Dynan, Karen, 2000, Habit Formation in Consumer Preferences: Evidence from Panel Data, American Economic Review, 90 (3), 391–406.
Enke, Benjamin, Graeber, Thomas and Oprea, Ryan, 2023, Complexity and Time, CES-Ifo Working Paper 10327, 67 pages.
Eucken, Walter, 1940, Die Grundlagen der Nationalökonomie, Jena, Fischer-Verlag, Xii + 300 pages.
Eucken, Walter, 1952, Grundsätze der Wirtschaftspolitik, Tübingen, Mohr-Siebeck, 398 pages.
Farrell, Joseph and Klemperer, Paul, 2007, Coordination and Lock-In: Competition with Switching Costs and Network Effects, in: Armstrong, Mark and Porter, Robert A. (eds), Handbook of Industrial Organization, Vol. 3, Amsterdam, Elsevier, pp.1967–2072.
Fehr, Dietmar and Kübler, Dorothea, 2022, The Endowment Effect in the General Population, CES-Ifo Discussion Paper 10150, 16 pages plus Appendix.
Fehr, Ernst and Charness, Gary, 2023, Social Preferences: Fundamental Characteristics and Economic Consequences, CES-Ifo Working Paper 10488, 13 + 32 pages.
Festinger, Leon, 1957, A Theory of Cognitive Dissonance, Stanford, CA, Stanford University Press, 291 pages.
Fromm, Erich, 1961, Marx's Concept of Man, New York, Frederick Ungar Publishing, 85 pages.
Fromm, Erich, 1976, To Have or to Be? The Nature of Psyche, New York, Harper & Row, 182 pages.
Fukuyama, Francis, 1989, The End of History, The National Interest, 16, 3–18.
Gabaix, Xavier and Laibson, David, 2022, Myopia and Discounting, unpublished, 50 pages.
Gaudecker, Hans-Martin von, Wogrolly, Axel and Zimpelmann, Christian, 2022, The Distribution of Ambiguity Attitudes, CES-Ifo Working Paper 10079, 38 pages.
Gigerenzer, Gerd and Selten, Reinhard (eds), 2001, Bounded Rationality – The Adaptive Toolbox, Cambridge, MA, MIT Press, XV + 377 pages.
Greenblatt, Stephen, 2011, The Swerve: How the World Became Modern, New York, W. W. Norton, 356 pages.
Greenwalt, Bruce C. and Stiglitz, Joseph E., 1986, Externalities in Economies with Imperfect Information and Incomplete Markets, Quarterly Journal of Economics, 101 (2), 229–264.
Grotius, Hugo, De Mare Liberum, 1609.
Hall, Robert E., 1978, Stochastic Implications of the Life Cycle Permanent Income Hypothesis: Theory and Evidence, Journal of Political Economy, 86 (69), 971–987.
Hall, Robert E., 1988, Intertemporal Substitution in Consumption, Journal of Political Economy, 96 (2), 339–357.
Hansen, Alvin H., 1939, Economic Progress and Declining Population Growth, American Economic Review, 29 (1), 1–15.
Hayek, Friedrich A., 1945, The Use of Knowledge in Society, American Economic Review, 35 (4), 519–530.
Hayek, Friedrich A., 1946, The Meaning of Competition (Princeton Lecture 20 May 1946), in: Hayek, Friedrich A. (ed.), Individualism and Economic Order, Chicago, IL, Chicago University Press, 1948, pp.92–106.
Hayek, Friedrich A., 1960, The Constitution of Liberty, Chicago, IL, University of Chicago Press, 570 pages.
Hayek, Friedrich A.,1974, The Pretense of Knowledge (Nobel Prize Lecture 1974), in: Caldwell, Bruce (ed.), The Collected Works of F.A. Hayek: The Market and Other Orders, Vol. 15, Chicago, Chicago University Press.
Heckman, James, Pinto, Rodrigo and Savelyev, Peter, 2013, Understanding the Mechanisms Through Which an Influential Early Childhood Program Boosted Adult Outcomes, American Economic Review, 103 (6), 2052–2086.
Hicks, John, 1939, The Foundations of Welfare Economics, The Economic Journal, 49 (196), 696–712.

Hobbes, Thomas, 1651, Leviathan or the Matter, London, Forme & Power of a Common-Wealth Ecclesiasticall and Civill.
Hobbes, Thomas, 1841, Human Nature, in: Molesworth, W. (ed.), Thomas Hobbes, English Works, 4, p. 16, (as quoted in Stone, Lawrence, The Causes of the English Revolution 1529–1642, London, Routledge and Kegan Paul, 1972, 168 Pages, p.51).
Homburg, Stefan, 1991, Interest and Growth in an Economy with Land, Canadian Journal of Economics, 24 (2), 450–459.
Houthakker, Hendrick S. and Taylor, Lester D., 1970, Consumer Demand in the United States, Cambridge, MA, Harvard University Press.
Houthakker, Hendrick, 1950, Revealed Preference and the Utility Function, Economica, 17 (66), 159–174.
Kahneman, Daniel, 2011, Thinking, Fast and Slow, New York, Farrar, Straus and Giroud, 499 pages.
Kahneman, Daniel and Tversky, Amos, 1979, Prospect Theory: An Analysis of Decision under Risk, Econometrica, 47 (2), 263–292.
Kaldor, Nicholas, 1939, Welfare Propositions of Economics and Interpersonal Comparisons of Utility, The Economic Journal, 49 (195), 549–552.
Knight, Frank H., 1921, Risk, Uncertainty and Profit, Boston, MA and New York, Houghton Mifflin Company, 381 pages.
Koehne, Sebastian and Kuhn, Moritz, 2015, Optimal Taxation in a Habit Formation Economy, Journal of Public Economics, 122, 31–39.
Kornai, Janos, 1971, Anti-Equilibrium – On Economic Systems Theory and the Tasks of Research, Amsterdam, North-Holland Publishing Company, 402 pages.
Kornai, Janos, 1993, The Socialist System – The Political Economy of Communism, Princeton, NJ, Princeton University Press, 672 pages.
Kotschy, Rainer and Sunde, Uwe, 2023, Have Preference Become more Similar Worldwide? CES Ifo Working Paper 10735, 64 pages.
Kranton, Rachel, 2019, The Devil Is in the Details: Implications of Samuel Bowles's *The Moral Economy* for Economics and Policy Research, Journal of Economic Literature, 57 (1), 147–160.
Mackoviak, Bartosz, Matejka, Filip and Wiederholt, Mirko, 2023, Rational Inattention: A Review, Journal of Economic Literature, 61 (1), 226–273.
Mankiw, N. Gregory, 1982, Hall's Consumption Hypothesis and Durable Goods, Journal of Monetary Economics, 10 (3), 417–425.
Marshall, Alfred, 1890, Principles of Economics (1920 eighth ed.), London, Macmillan, 858 pages.
Marx, Karl, 1837–1848, "Die Frühschriften", ed. by Siegfried Landshut, Stuttgart, Kröner, 1953, 588 pages.
Marx, Karl, 1867, Das Kapital Vol. 1, Hamburg, Verlag Otto Meissner, 784 pages.
McFadden, Daniel, 1974, Conditional Logit Analysis of Qualitative Choice Behavior, in: Zarembka, Paul (ed.), Frontiers in Econometrics, New York, Academic Press, pp.105–142.
Meier, Daniela, 2001, Tauschringe als besondere Bewertungssysteme in der Schattenwirtschaft – Eine theoretische und empirische Analyse, Berlin, Duncker & Humblot, 273 pages.
Mill, John Stuart, 1859, On Liberty, London, Walter Scott Publishing Company, 1903, with an Introduction by W. L. Courtney, LLD, XXVIII + 219 pages.
Mirrlees, James A., 1971, An Exploration in the Theory of Optimum Income Taxation, Review of Economic Studies, 38 (2), 175–208.
Morewedge, Carey K. and Giblin, Colleen E., 2015, Explanation of the Endowment Effect: An Integrative Review, American Psychological Association Psych Net, 19 (6), 339–348.
Mortensen, Dale T. and Pissarides, Christopher A., 1994, Job Creation and Job Destruction in the Theory of Unemployment, Review of Economic Studies, 61, 397–415.
Müller-Armack, Alfred, 1947, Wirtschaftslenkung und Marktwirtschaft, Hamburg, Kastell.

Munro, Alistair and Sugden, Robert, 2003, On the Theory of Reference Dependent Preferences, Journal of Economic Behavior and Organization, 50 (4), 407–428.
Murphy, Ryan O., Ackermann, Kurt A. and Handgraaf, Michel J. J., 2011, Measuring Social Value Orientation, Judgement and Decision Making, 6 (8), 771–781.
Pierson, Paul, 1996, The New Politics of the Welfare State, World Politics, 48 (2), 143–179.
Popper, Karl, 1945, The Open Society and Its Enemies, Vol. 1 Plato, Vol. 2 Hegel and Marx, London, Routledge and Kegan Paul, 361 pages and 420 pages.
Popper, Karl, 1949, Towards a Rational Theory of Tradition, in: Popper, Karl (ed.), Conjectures and Refutations, London, Routledge, pp.162–182.
Rawls, John, 1971, A Theory of Justice, Cambridge, MA, Belknap Press of Harvard University Press, 521 pages.
Reck, Daniel and Seibold, Arthur, 2022, The Welfare Economics of Reference Dependence, CES-Ifo Working Paper 9999, 82 pages.
Sahlins, Marshall, 1972, Stone Age Economics, London, Routledge.
Samuelson, Paul A., 1938, A Note on the Pure Theory of Consumer's Behavior, Economica, 5, 61–71.
Samuelson, Paul A., 1954, The Pure Theory of Public Expenditure, Review of Economics and Statistics, 36, 387–389.
Samuelson, Paul A., 1956, Social Indifference Curves, Quarterly Journal of Economics, 70 (1), 1–22.
Samuelson, William and Zeckhauser, Richard, 1988, Status Quo Bias in Decision Making, Journal of Risk and Uncertainty, 1, 7–59.
Schlicht, Ekkehart, 1984, Cognitive Dissonance in Economics, in: Todt, H. (ed.), Normengeleitetes Verhalten in den Sozialwissenschaften, Berlin, Duncker & Humblot, pp.61–81.
Schmidtchen, Dieter, 2004, Recht, Eigentum und Effizienz: Zu F.A. v. Hayeks Verfassung der Freiheit, ORDO, 55, 127–151.
Schubert, Christian, 2005, A Note on the Principle of Normative Individualism, Papers on Economics and Evolution, 0517, Jena, Max-Planck-Institute on Economics, 24 pages.
Schulz, Karl, Tsyvinski, Aleh and Werquim, Nicolas, 2023, Generalized Compensating Principle, Theoretical Economics, 18, 1665–1710.
Schumpeter, Joseph A., 1912, Theorie der wirtschaftlichen Entwicklung, Leipzig, Duncker & Humblot, 548 pages.
Scitovsky, Tibor, 1941, A Note on Welfare Propositions in Economics, Review of Economic Studies, 9 (1), 77–88.
Seibold, Arthur, 2021, Reference Points for Retirement Behavior: Evidence from German Pension Discontinuity, American Economic Review, 111 (4), 1126–1165.
Selten, Reinhard, 1998, Aspiration Adaptation Theory, Journal of Mathematical Psychology, 42, 192–214.
Sen, Amartya, 1977, Rational Fools: A Critique of the Behavioral Foundations of Economic Theory, Philosophy and Public Affairs, 6, 317–344.
Sen, Amartya, 2009, The Idea of Justice, Cambridge, MA, Belknap Press of Harvard University Press, 468 pages.
Simon, Herbert, 1956, Rational Choice and the Structure of the Environment, Psychological Review, 63, 129–138.
Simon, Herbert, 1962, The Architecture of Complexity, Proceedings of the American Philosophical Society, 106 (6), 467–482.
Simon, Herbert, 1971, Designing Organizations for an Information Rich World, in: Greenberger, H. (ed.), Computers, Communications, and the Public Interest, Baltimore, MD, Johns Hopkins Press, pp.37–72.
Sims, Christopher A., 1998, Stickiness, Carnegie-Rochester Conference Series on Public Policy, 49, 317–356.
Sims, Christopher A., 2003, Implications of Rational Inattention, Journal of Monetary Economics, 50 (3), 665–690.

Smith, Adam, 1776, Inquiry into the Nature and Causes of the Wealth of Nations, 2 volumes, London, W. Strahan and T. Cadell.
Sondermann, Dieter, 1982, Revealed Preference: An Elementary Treatment, Econometrica, 50 (3), 777–779.
Spence, Michael, 1973, Job Market Signaling, Quarterly Journal of Economics, 87 (3), 355–374.
Steimanis, Ivo and Vollan, Björn, 2022, Prosociality as Response to Slow- and Fast-Onset Climate Hazards, Global Sustainability, 5, e10 [1–13].
Steiner, Hillel, 1977, The Structure of a Set of Compossible Rights, Journal of Philosophy, 74, 767–775.
Stigler, George J., 1961, The Economics of Information, Journal of Political Economy, 69, 213–225.
Stigler, George J., 1978, Wealth and Possibly Liberty, The Journal of Legal Studies, 7 (2), 213–217.
Stigler, George J. and Becker, Gary S., 1977, De Gustibus non est Disputandum, American Economic Review, 67 (2), 76–90.
Stiglitz, Joseph E., 1975, The Theory of Screening, Education and the Distribution of Income, American Economic Review, 65, 283–300.
Stolper, Wolfgang F. and Samuelson, Paul A., 1941, Protection and Real Wages, Review of Economic Studies, 9 (1), 58–73.
Summers, Lawrence H., 2014, US Economic Prospects: Secular Stagnation, Hysteresis, and the Zero Lower Bound, Business Economics, 49, 65–73.
Sunstein, Cass R., 2019, On Freedom, Princeton, NJ, Princeton University Press, 127 pages.
Suppes, Patrick, 1966, Some Formal Models of Grading Principles, Synthese, 16, 284–306.
Sutter, Matthias, Untertrifaller, Anna and Zoller, Claudia, 2022, Grit Increases Strongly in Early Childhood and Is Related to Parental Background, Scientific Reports, 12, 35–61.
Thaler, Richard H. and Sunstein, Cass R., 2008, Nudge – Improving Decisions about Health, Wealth, and Happiness, New Haven, CT, Yale University Press, 312 pages.
Tönnies, Ferdinand, 1887, Gemeinschaft und Gesellschaft – Abhandlung des Communismus und des Socialismus als empirischer Kulturformen, Leipzig, Fues's Verlag (R. Reisland), XXX + 294 pages.
Vanberg, Viktor J., 2000, Der konsensorientierte Ansatz der konstitutionellen Ökonomik, in Leipold, Hellmut und Pies, Ingo (ed.), Ordnungstheorie und Ordnungspolitik – Konzeptionen und Entwicklungsperspektiven, Stuttgart, Lucius und Lucius, pp.252–276.
Vanberg, Viktor J., 2019, Introduction: Individual Choice and Social Welfare – Theoretical Foundations of Political Economy, in: Vanberg, Viktor J. (ed.), Choice and Economic Welfare, Cheltenham, Edward Elgar, CIX + 725 pages, XIII–CIX.
Vaubel, Roland, 2020, Die Begründung von Freiheit, ORDO, 70, 373–385.
Von Weizsäcker, Carl Christian, 1971, Notes on Endogenous Change of Tastes, Journal of Economic Theory, 3 (4), 345–372.
Von Weizsäcker, Carl Christian, 1980, Barriers to Entry. A Theoretical Treatment. Lecture Notes Economics and Mathematical Systems Nr. 185, Heidelberg, Springer, 220 pages.
Von Weizsäcker, Carl Christian, 1981, Rechte und Verhältnisse in der modernen Wirtschaftslehre, Kyklos, Bd., 34 (3), S. 345–376. English Translation: Rights and Relations in Modern Economic Theory, The Journal of Economic Behaviour and Organization, 1984, 133–157.
von Weizsäcker, Carl Christian, 1984a, The Costs of Substitution, Econometrica, 52 (5), 1085–1116.
Von Weizsäcker, Carl Christian, 1984b, The Influence of Property Rights on Tastes, Journal of Institutional and Theoretical Economics, 90–95.
Von Weizsäcker, Carl Christian, 1984c, Was leistet die Property Rights Theorie für aktuelle wirtschaftspolitische Fragen?, in: Neumann, Manfred (ed.), Ansprüche, Eigentums- und Verfügungsrechte, Berlin, Duncker und Humblot, pp.123–152.

Von Weizsäcker, Carl Christian, 1994, Zeitpräferenz und Delegation, Zeitschrift für Wirtschaftspolitik, 43 (2), 121–139.
Von Weizsäcker, Carl Christian, 2002, Welfare Economics Bei Endogenen Präferenzen – Thünen-Vorlesung 2001, Perspektiven der Wirtschaftspolitik, 3 (4), 425–446.
Von Weizsäcker, Carl Christian, 2009, Asymmetrie der Märkte und Wettbewerbsfreiheit, in: Vanberg, V.J. (ed.), Evolution und freiheitlicher Wettbewerb, Erich Hoppmann und die aktuelle Diskussion, Untersuchungen zur Ordnungstheorie und Ordnungspolitik, Bd. 58, Tübingen, Mohr-Siebeck, pp.211–244.
Von Weizsäcker, Carl Christian, 2014, Die normative Ko-Evolution von Marktwirtschaft und Demokratie, ORDO, 65, 13–43 (Hayek-Lecture at University of Freiburg).
von Weizsäcker, Carl Christian, 2016, Book Review on Akerlof, George A. and Shiller, Robert J.: Phishing for Phools: The Economics of Manipulation and Deception, Journal of Economics, 118 (1), 91–96.
Von Weizsäcker, Carl Christian and Krämer, Hagen, 2021, Saving and Investment in the 21st Century – The Great Divergence, Cham, Springer, XXII + 344 pages.
Welsch, Heinz, 2005, Adaptation of Tastes to Constraints, Theory and Decision, 57, 379–395.
Wilson, Edward O., 1998, Consilience – The Unity of Knowledge, New York, Knopf, 367 pages.
Witt, Ulrich, 2001, Learning to Consume – A Theory of Wants and the Growth of Demand, Journal of Evolutionary Economics, 11, 23–36.

ANNEX FOR BOOK II

Proof of Acyclic Improvement Sequences for the Classroom Model

In the following I look at the two-commodity space, assuming commodity vectors $x > 0$, that is: both components are positive: $x_1 > 0$ and $x_2 > 0$.

I introduce the following notation

yNEx means $y_1 > x_1$ and $y_2 > x_2$
yNWx means $y_1 \le x_1$ and $y_2 \ge x_2$ and $y \ne x$
ySEx means $y_1 \ge x_1$ and $y_2 \le x_2$ and $y \ne x$
ySWx means $y_1 < x_1$ and $y_2 < x_2$

Note that the relations NE, NW, SE, SW are transitive. Moreover, for $y = x$ none of the four relations apply.

Because of non-satiation we know *yNEx* implies $y(>;q)x$ for any $q \in Q$

Because of non-satiation for any $y \ne x$ with $y(=;\rho(x))x$ we have either *ySEx* or *yNWx*.

I repeat

Definition 5: Let $I(x;q) = \{y : y(=;q)x\}$. It is the *indifference curve* going through x with preferences q.

In particular, let $I(x;\rho(x)) = \{y : y(=;\rho(x))x\}$.

Let then $L(x)$ be defined by $y \in L(x)$ iff $\exists \lambda \ge 0$ such that $y = \lambda x$

Let $L^+(x)$ be defined by $y \in L^+(x)$ iff $\exists \lambda > 1$ such that $y = \lambda x$

Let $L^{-}(x)$ be defined by $y \in L^{-}(x)$ iff $\exists \lambda < 1$ such that $y = \lambda x$

Assumption of "Single Crossing": If $I(y;\rho(y))$ is not identical with $I(x;\rho(x))$, but $y(=;\rho(x))x$, then $I(x;\rho(x)) \cap I(y;\rho(y)) = \{y\}$.

Observation 1: Assume continuity and non-satiation. Let $y(=;\rho(x))x$. Then there exists $z(=;\rho(y))y$ such that $z \in L(x)$. *Proof:* For $\lambda > 0$ sufficiently small we have $\lambda x < y$. For $\lambda > 0$ sufficiently large we have $\lambda x > y$. We define the following sequence $\lambda_0, \lambda_1, \lambda_2, \ldots$ with $\lambda_0 x(<;\rho(y))y$ and $\lambda_1 x(>;\rho(y))y$ and $\lambda_{n+1} = \dfrac{Max\{\lambda_i \in \Lambda_0(n)\} + Min\{\lambda_i \in \Lambda_1(n)\}}{2}$, where $\Lambda_0(n)$ is the subset in the sequence up to n with $\lambda_i x(<;\rho(y))(y)$ and $\Lambda_1(n)$ is the subset in the sequence up to n with $\lambda_i x(>;\rho(y))y$. This sequence converges to some point λ^* so that $\lambda^* x$ neither can be preferred over y with preferences induced by y, nor can y be preferred over $\lambda^* x$ with preferences induced by y. Due to continuity of preferences it follows that $\lambda^* x(=,\rho(y))y$. QED.

Assumption of adaptive preferences: From $y(>;\rho(x))x$ follows $y(>;\rho(y))x$.

Lemma 1: With non-satiation and adaptive preferences $\lambda^* \geq 1$. *Proof:* Assume the contrary; thus $\lambda^* < 1$. Therefore, non-satiation and continuity imply for a sufficiently small vector $\varepsilon > 0$ that $x(>;\rho(y+\varepsilon))y+\varepsilon$ and $y+\varepsilon(>;\rho(x))x$, thereby violating adaptive preferences. QED.

We define three components of $I(x;\rho(x))$: $SE(x;\rho(x)) = \{y : y \in I(x;\rho(x)\, and\ ySEx\}$ $NW(x;\rho(x)) = \{y : y \in I(x;\rho(x)\, and\ yNWx\}$
The third component is x itself.

Observation 2a: For $y \in SE(x;\rho(x))$ we have $NW(y;\rho(y))$ is weakly "above" $I(x;\rho(x))$. *Proof:* $z = \lambda^* x$ is weakly "above" $I(x;\rho(x))$ because of $\lambda^* \geq 1$. Either $z = x$ or $z \in NW(y;\rho(y))$. Because of single crossing any $z \in NW(y;\rho(y))$ lies weakly above $I(x;\rho(x))$. QED.

Observation 2b: For $y \in NW(x;\rho(x))$ we have $SE(y;\rho(y))$ is weakly "above" $I(x;\rho(x))$. Proof is analogous to Proof of Observation 2a.

Observation 2a and 2b together are Lemma II.3 in the text.
Obviously then the following holds:
Let $y \in SE(x;\rho(x))$; let $z \in NW(y;\rho(y))$. Then $z(\geq;\rho(x))x$.
Let $y \in NW(x;\rho(x))$; let $z \in SE(y;\rho(y))$. Then $z(\geq;\rho(x))(x)$.

Lemma 2: Let $x^1(>;\rho(x^0))x^0$. Let $x^2(>;\rho(x^1))x^1$. Let λ and μ be chosen to fit the equations $x^1(=;\rho(x^0))\lambda x^0$ and $\mu x^2(=;\rho(x^1))x^1$. Obviously $\lambda > 1$ and $\mu < 1$.

Let $x^1 \in SE\left(\lambda x^0;\rho\left(x^0\right)\right)$. Let $\mu x^2 \in NW\left(x^1;\rho\left(x^1\right)\right)$. Then $x^2(>;\rho\left(x^0\right))x^0$.

Proof: Because of Observation 2a we have $\mu x^2(\geq)\left(\lambda x^0;\rho\left(x^0\right)\right)$. Because of $\lambda > 1$ and $\mu < 1$ and because of non-satiation we then have $x^2(>)\left(x^0;\rho\left(x^0\right)\right)$. QED.

Theorem 1A: In the class room model adaptive preferences make improvement sequences acyclic, provided preferences are continuous, with non-satiation, and have the property of single crossing.

Proof: By induction on the number of improvement steps T. By adaptive preferences we know the proposition to be true for $T = 2$. Assume it to be true for some integer $T > 2$ and for any improvement sequences shorter than T. Consider now the improvement sequence $\left\{x^0, x^1, x^2, \ldots . x^T, x^{T+1}\right\}$ of length $T+1$. Consider now a sequence of this kind such that there exists a non-negative integer $k \leq T-1$ with $x^{k+1} > x^k$. Then, due to non-satiation and due to $x^k(>)\left(x^{k-1};\rho\left(x^{k-1}\right)\right)$ we obtain $x^{k+1}(>;\rho\left(x^{k-1}\right))x^{k-1}$. Thus, we can construct the improvement sequence $\left\{x^0, x^1, x^2, \ldots . x^{k-1}, x^{k+1}\, x^T, x^{T+1}\right\}$ of length T, which by induction assumption is acyclic.

We then look at improvement sequences such that for each integer $k \leq T$ we have either $\mu_k x^{k+1} \in SE\left(x^k;\rho\left(x^k\right)\right)$ or $\mu_k x^{k+1} \in NW\left(x^k;\rho\left(x^k\right)\right)$ and all $\mu_k < 1$. If, for each integer $k \leq T$ the relation $\mu_k x^{k+1} \in SE\left(x^k;\rho\left(x^k\right)\right)$ holds then, obviously, x^{T+1} is in the south-east of x^0; and therefore the improving sequence is acyclic. If, for each integer $k \leq T$ the relation $\mu_k x^{k+1} \in NW\left(x^k;\rho\left(x^k\right)\right)$ holds then, obviously, x^{T+1} is in the north-west of x^0; and therefore the improving sequence is acyclic.

There remains the case that for some integer $k \leq T$ we either have $\lambda x^k \in SE\left(x^{k-1};\rho\left(x^{k-1}\right)\right)$ and $\mu x^{k+1} \in NW\left(x^k;\rho\left(x^k\right)\right)$ for some $\lambda < 1$ and some $\mu < 1$; or, vice versa, $\lambda x^k \in NW\left(x^{k-1};\rho\left(x^{k-1}\right)\right)$ and $\mu x^{k+1} \in SE\left(x^k;\rho\left(x^k\right)\right)$ for some $\lambda < 1$ and some $\mu < 1$. Because of Lemma 2, we then obtain the result $x^{k+1}(>;\rho\left(x^{k-1}\right))x^{k-1}$. We then can derive an improving sequence $\left\{x^0, x^1, x^2, \ldots . x^{k-1}, x^{k+1}\, x^T, x^{T+1}\right\}$ of length T, which by induction assumption is acyclic. So, we have shown that this improvement sequence of length $T+1$ is acyclic.

As we have exhausted the set of possible characteristics of improvement sequences of length $T+1$, we have provided proof of the theorem. QED.

MATHEMATICAL ANNEX TO BOOK III

Revealed Preference Lemma of Induced Preferences

Assume the discrete time model. Assumptions I (continuity) and II (non-satiation) hold. Assume further that there exists a well-defined "long-run" demand function $x = H(p) = h(p; \rho(x))$. Let $\{x^0 = H(p^0), x^1 = H(p^1), \ldots . x^T = H(p^T)\}$ be a sequence of baskets such that each x^i is revealed preferred to x^{i-1} for $i = 1, 2, \ldots . T$. This means $p^i(x^i - x^{i-1}) \geq 0$ for $i = 1, 2, \ldots . T$. Then there exists an improving sequence beginning at x^0 and ending at x^T.

Proof: The sequence starts at x^0. For $t = 1, 2, \ldots .$ we set $z^t = h(p^1; \rho(x^{t-1}))$.

Because, by assumption, $p^1 x^0 \leq 1$ we see that z^1 is revealed preferred to x^0 under preferences $\rho(x^0)$ and thus the move from x^0 to z^1 is an improvement. Generally, by the same reasoning z^t is revealed preferred to z^{t-1} under preferences $\rho(z^{t-1})$ and thus the move from z^{t-1} to z^t is an improvement. We continue this procedure until we come close enough to $x^1 = H(p^1)$ so that a jump from z^t to x^1 is an improvement. Such finite t always exists, because for $\rho(x^1)$ the basket x^1 is revealed preferred to any basket with $p^1 z \leq 1$ which applies to all z^t. Thus, because $\rho(z^t)$ converges to $\rho(x^1)$ and because of continuity of preferences there exists t such that x^1 is revealed preferred to z^t und preferences $\rho(z^t)$.

Thus, we have constructed an improving sequence from x^0 to x^1. In an analogous way we can construct an improving sequence from x^1 to x^2, from x^2 to

x^3; . . . . . . from x^{T-1} to x^T. Combining these T improving sequences into one large improving sequence then gives us the improving sequence from x^0 to x^T. QED.

Correspondence Lemma

Assume all improvement sequences of a real-world (continuous time) preference system $\{x;q;\dot{q}\}$ are a-cyclic. Assume that there is a long-run demand function $x = h(p;\rho(x)) = H(p)$ for the corresponding discrete time model. For any basket x^0 let $A(x^0)$ be the set of baskets which can be reached from x^0 by means of an improvement sequence in the real-world model. For any basket x^0 let $\hat{A}(x^0)$ be the set of baskets which can be reached from x^0 by means of an improvement sequence in the corresponding discrete time model. Then $A(x^0) = \hat{A}(x^0)$.

Proof: First observe that both, $A(x^0)$ and $\hat{A}(x^0)$ are open sets.

Next I show $\hat{A}(x^0) \complement A(x^0)$. For any given improvement sequence $\{x^0, x^1, \ldots x^T\}$ in the discrete time model I construct an improvement sequence in the continuous time model starting at x^0 and ending in finite time at x^T. The path $x(t) = x^0$ for $t \le \varepsilon$ for some small positive ε. We then set $x(\varepsilon) = x^1$. Because $q(\varepsilon) = \rho(x^0)$ the jump to x^1 is an improvement jump. We then keep $x(t) = x^1$ for $t \ge \varepsilon$ until $q(t)$ is sufficiently close to $\rho(x^1)$ so that a further jump to x^2 is an improvement. This is always possible in finite time, because preferences are continuous in preference space and because $q(t)$ converges to $\rho(x^1)$. We then jump to x^2 which is an improvement jump. We then keep $x(t) = x^2$ until – in finite time – a jump to x^3 is an improvement jump, and so on until – in finite time – we have an improvement jump from x^{T-1} to x^T. This shows $\hat{A}(x^0) \complement A(x^0)$.

Now I show $A(x^0) \complement \hat{A}(x^0)$. Because we assume that improvement sequences in the continuous time model are a-cyclic and because of $\hat{A}(x^0) \complement A(x^0)$ we then know that improvement sequences in the discrete time model are also a-cyclic. Because of Corollary 2B we then have a continuous quasi utility function $V(x)$ such that for any pair of baskets x and y there exists an improvement path in the discrete time model from x to y, if and only if $V(y) > V(x)$. Assume now, to the contrary, that there exists y such that it can be reached from x^0 in the continuous time model, but not in the discrete time model. We then have $V(y) \le V(x^0)$. In the case $V(y) < V(x^0)$ we then know that $x^0 \in \hat{A}(y)$ and thus $x^0 \in A(y)$. But then we have found an improving sequence from x^0 to x^0 for the continuous time model, contrary to the assumption that improving sequences are a-cyclic. This excludes $V(y) < V(x^0)$. If we had $V(y) = V(x^0)$ then y would not be in the interior of $A(x^0)$ and thus $A(x^0)$would not be an open set, which contradicts the fact that $A(x^0)$ *is* an open set. Thus we have shown that for $y \in A(x^0)$ it follows $V(y) > V(x^0)$ and thus, by Corollary 2B, we have $y \in \hat{A}(x^0)$. This proves the Correspondence Lemma. QED.

DEFINITIONS, AXIOMS, THEOREMS

Definitions

Definition 1: A *preference system* $\{x;q;\dot{q}\}$ is a system consisting of a commodity space $\mathcal{X}$ containing commodity baskets x, consisting of a preference space $\mathcal{Q}$ containing preferences q, and consisting of a rule $\dot{q}(x;q)$, describing the change through time of preferences as a function of the actually prevailing commodity basket x and the actually prevailing preferences q.

Definition 2: Induced Preferences. For any given preference system $\{x;q;\dot{q}\}$ preferences $\rho(x)$ are induced by basket x, if, for x constant through time, preferences converge towards $\rho(x)$.

Definition 3: Adaptive Preferences. Assume that a preference system is characterized by a well-defined mapping $\rho(x)$ of induced preferences. The preference system $\{x;q;\dot{q}\}$ exhibits adaptive preferences if the following holds: For any two baskets x and y, if $y(>;\rho(x))x$ then $y(>;\rho(y))x$. For any two baskets x and y, if $y(=;\rho(x))x$ then $y(\geq;\rho(y))x$. In words: Preferences are adaptive, if a basket y, which is preferred over x with preferences induced by x, is, a fortiori, preferred over x with preferences induced by y.

Definition 4: Let A, B, C, . . . K be a finite set of consumption baskets, which have the following properties. For preferences induced by A the basket B is preferred over A; for preferences induced by B the basket C is preferred over B; and so on. Each basket is preferred over the preceding one with preferences induced by the preceding one. Such a sequence I call an *improvement sequence*. If, in addition, each basket is different from all other baskets in the sequence we then speak of an *improvement path*.

Definition 4 ½: (Classroom model: $n=2$). Consider a sequence of baskets $\{x^0,x^1,\ldots x^T\}$ such that $\{x^0,x^1,\ldots x^{T-1}\}$ are contained in $B(x^0)$). Moreover $x^T(>;\rho(x^{T-1}))x^{T-1}$. Such a sequence we call a *semi-improving sequence.*

Definition 5 (for classroom model): Indifference curve: Let $I(x;q)=\{y:y(=;q)x\}$. It is the indifference curve going through x with preferences q. Because of continuity and non-satiation we know the set $I(x;q)$ is a curve through the two-dimensional space $\mathfrak{X}$.

Definition 6: A preference system $\{x;q;\dot{q}\}$ may have the *property of "two-dimensional mappings of improving sequences"*. By this I mean: if $\{x^0,x^1,\ldots x^T\}$ is an improving sequence in R^n a two-dimensional mapping of $\{x^0,x^1,\ldots x^T\}$ is an improving sequence $\{x^0,z^1,z^2,\ldots\ldots z^S,x^T\}$ such that all $z^t\in R^2(x^0,x^T)$ where $R^2(x^0,x^T)$ is a two-dimensional subspace containing 0, x^0 and x^T. The number of in-between steps, S, in $R^2(x^0,x^T)$, need not coincide with the number of in-between steps of the original improving sequence.

Definition 7: (Real-world model): For a given movement $x(t)$ a point in time t is an *improvement point*, if for $q(t)$ there exists $\varepsilon>0$ such that for $t-\Delta t>t-\varepsilon$ and $\Delta t>0$ we have $U(x(t-\Delta t);q(t))<U(x(\mathrm{t});q(t))$. A point in time t is a *weakly improving point*, if for $q(t)$ there exists $\varepsilon>0$ such that for $t-\Delta t>t-\varepsilon$ and $\Delta t>0$ we have $U(x(t-\Delta t);q(t))\le U(x(\mathrm{t});q(t))$.

Definition 8: (Real-world model): A path $\{x(t);q(0);T\}$ is a *weakly improving sequence*, if $q(0)=\rho(x(0))$ and every t is a weakly improving point for $0\le t\le T$. A path $\{x(t);q(0);T\}$ is an *improving sequence*, if it is a weakly improving sequence and if $T=t_K$ is a jump point with $U(x(T);q(T))>\lim_{t\to T}U(x(t);q(T))$.

Definition 9: For a given preference system $\{x;q;\dot{q}\}$ in continuous time, we define the *corresponding* discrete time preference system $[x;q;\dot{q}]$ as that discrete time model which exhibits the same induced preference mapping $\rho(x)$.

Definition 10: In the "real-world model", for a given preference system $\{x;q;\dot{q}\}$ assume that there exists an indicator function for the corresponding discrete time model for the existence of improving sequences $V(x)$. Thus, in the corresponding discrete time model, improving sequences are acyclic. Assume the existence of a cardinal utility function $U(x;q)$ with the following properties: 1.$U(x;q)\le V(x)$ for all q; 2. $U(x;\rho(x))=V(x)$; 3. $\frac{\partial U}{\partial q}\dot{q}=\frac{\partial U}{\partial q}f(x;q)\ge 0$. Then we say that preferences are *smoothly adaptive.*

Definition 11: Granted the basic rights of every citizen, a sufficient condition for the rights of the citizens of a society to be *pragmatically compossible* is satisfied if the following holds. A change of behavior of any given citizen within the realm of his/her rights provides at least as great an advantage to this citizen as the negative of the byproduct of this change to his/her fellow citizens. Advantages and disadvantages are measured in terms of economic values with prevailing prices.

Definition 12: For any given path of consumption baskets $x(t)$ and any given initial value $q(0)$ let $q(t)$ be the unique solution to the differential equation $\dot{q} = f(x;q)$ which describes the dynamics of preference formation. We then call the preference path $q(t)$ *quasi induced* by $q(0)$ and $x(t)$.

Definition 13: For given initial preferences $q(0) = r(0)$, let $q(t)$ be the preference path quasi-induced by the basket path $x(t)$ and let $r(t)$ be the preference path quasi-induced by the basket path $y(t)$. Social preferences are *quasi-adaptive* if the following holds: whenever $y(t)[>;q(t)]x(t)$, then $y(t)[>;r(t)]x(t)$ and: whenever $y(t)[=;q(t)]x(t)$, then $y(t)[\geq;r(t)]x(t)$.

Definition 14: For a given set of individual rights and a given initial set of preferences $s(0)$, let the preference path $s(t)$ and the basket path $z(t)$ be such that by the actions of citizens within their rights the preferences $s(t)$ generate the basket path $z(t)$ and such that $s(t)$ is quasi-induced by $z(t)$.

Then the pair $z(t)$ and $s(t$ is called an *equilibrium pair of preferences and baskets.*

Axioms and Assumptions

Improvement Axiom: Given the choice between a stationary consumption path and an improvement sequence, both starting with the same basket and the same preferences induced by that basket, people prefer the improvement sequence, provided they expect that any improvement sequence is an improvement path.

Assumption 1 (for classroom model): Continuity: The space $\mathfrak{X}$ of commodity baskets consists of all strictly positive baskets $x > 0$, that is, $x = (x_1, x_2)$with $x_1 > 0$ and $x_2 > 0$. $\mathfrak{X}$ has the Euclidean metric and the usual topology. The space $\mathcal{Q}$ of preferences has a topology, so that open sets can be defined. Preferences are continuous, that is, if $y(>;q)x$ then there exist neighborhoods $N_1(x)$, $N_2(y)$, $N_3(q)$ such that for $w \in N_1, z \in N_2, r \in N_3$ we have $z(>;r)w$.

Assumption 2 (for classroom model): Non-satiation: Let x and y be two baskets in $\mathfrak{X}$. Let $y_1 > x_1$ and let $y_2 > x_2$. Then for all $q \in \mathcal{Q}$ we have $y(>;q)x$.

Assumption 3 (for classroom model): Single crossing: If the indifference curve $I(y;\rho(y))$ is not identical with the indifference curve $I(x;\rho(x))$, but $y(=;\rho(x))x$, then $I(x;\rho(x)) \cap I(y;\rho(y)) = \{y\}$.

Assumption 3e (for discrete time model $n \geq 2$): ("e" for "extended"). Assumption 3 (single crossing) for $n = 2$ applies to any two dimensional subspace of R^n defined by the origin and any two linearly independent positive baskets x and y. Moreover, the following "triangle inequality assumption of preferences" holds: Consider any three baskets x, y, z such that they form an improving sequence, that is, $y(>;\rho(x))x$ and $z(>;\rho(y))y$. Then there exists some $\hat{y}$, which is a weighted average of x and z, such that $x, \hat{y}, z$ also form an improving sequence. In other words: there exists μ with $0 < \mu < 1$ such that $x, \hat{y}, z$ form an improving sequence with $\hat{y} = \mu x + (1-\mu)z$.

Axiom: Freedom Consistency of Collective Preferences (cf. Book VI): Let $x(t)$ and $y(t)$ be two paths through time of consumption baskets. Assume that individual rights are pragmatically compossible. Initial conditions and initial property distributions are given. Let the prevailing preferences be $q(t)$. Let $\hat{q}(t)$ be alternative preferences. Assume that under preferences $\hat{q}(t)$ and the prevailing institutions with free decisions and trading possibilities $x(t)$ would have been implemented. Assume that under the prevailing preferences $q(t)$ and the same institutional set-up and free decisions and trading possibilities the path $y(t)$ is implemented. Then $y(t)[>;q(t)]x(t)$.

Quasi-Improvement Axiom (cf. Book VI): Assume that society has the choice between 1) remaining in the "default" $x(t)$ with initial preferences $q(0)$ and preferences $q(t)$ quasi-induced by $x(t)$ – and 2) a "project" $y(t)$ such that $y(t)[>;q(t)]x(t)$ and $y(t)[>;r(t)]x(t)$ with $rt)$quasi-induced by $y(t)$. Let the pair $z(t)$ and $s(t)$ be the equilibrium pair of preferences and baskets, which arises out of the implementation of "project" $y(t)$ by means of the interaction of citizens in a system of rights that corresponds to the principle of pragmatic compossibility. Then, society chooses to implement the first "project" $y(t)$ irrespective of whether a direct move from the default $x(t)$ to $z(t)$ would have been accepted or rejected. That is: society acts in such a way that $z(t)$ is "revealed preferred" over $x(t)$. We then can write $z(t)[>,q(t)]x(t)$.

Theorems

Lemma II.3 (classroom model): Under Assumptions 1, 2, and 3 and under adaptive preferences, let $y \in I(x;\rho(x))$ be to the "south-east" of x. Let $z \in I(y;\rho(y))$ be to the "north-west" of y. Assume $I(y;\rho(y))$ to be not identical to $I(x;\rho(x))$. Then $z(>;\rho(x))x$ and $z(>;\rho(z))x$. Let $y \in I(x;\rho(x))$ be to the "north-west" of x. Let $z \in I(y;\rho(y))$ be to the "south-east" of y. Then $z(>;\rho(x))x$ and $z(>;\rho(z))x$.

Theorem 1A: Within the classroom model, Assumptions 1, 2, 3 plus adaptive preferences imply that every improvement sequence is acyclic – and hence is an improvement path.

Theorem 2A: Within the classroom model, assume continuity and non-satiation of all preferences in the preference space. Assume further that all improving sequences are acyclic. Then preferences are adaptive.

Theorem 1B: In a world of n distinct goods with discrete time periods and preferences induced by the consumption basket of the preceding period, as described in Book II, Chapters II, 1 and II, 2, assume continuous preferences, non-satiation and Assumption 3e. Then adaptive preferences imply that all improving sequences are acyclic.

Theorem 2B: (Discrete time model with n distinct goods): Assume continuity and non-satiation of all preferences in the preference space. Assume further that all improving sequences are acyclic. Then preferences are adaptive.

Corollary 2B: (Discrete time model with n distinct goods): Under Assumption 1 (continuity) and Assumption 2 (non-satiation), assume further that all improving sequences are acyclic and that there exists a long-run demand function $x = h\big(p;\rho(x)\big) = H(p)$, which is independent of initial preferences $q(0)$. Then the long-run demand function satisfies the strong axiom of revealed preference. Thus, there exists an ordinal quasi-utility function $V(x)$ underlying the long-run demand function. Moreover this underlying quasi-utility function is continuous and has the following property: If and only if $V(y) > V(x)$ there exists an improving sequence starting at x with initial preferences $\rho(x)$ and ending at y. Moreover, preferences are adaptive.

Revealed Preference Lemma of Induced Preferences: If in a sequence of baskets $\{x^0, x^1, \ldots..x^T\}$ each basket (except x^0) is revealed preferred to its preceding basket under the long-run demand function, then there exists an improving sequence from x^0 to x^T.

Theorem 1C: (Discrete Time Model with $n \geq 2$.) Assumptions 1 (continuity) and 2 (non-satiation) hold. Assume further the existence of a long-run demand function $x = h\big(p;\rho(x)\big) = H(p)$. Assume adaptive preferences.

Part A: For a given preference system $[x, q, \dot{q}]$, assume that every improvement sequence has a "two-dimensional mapping". Then every improvement sequence is acyclic.

Part B: Assume that every improvement sequence of a given preference system $[x, q, \dot{q}]$ is acyclic. Then every improvement sequence of that preference system has a "two-dimensional mapping"

Correspondence Lemma: Assume all improvement sequences of a continuous time preference system $\{x; q; \dot{q}\}$ are acyclic. Assume that there is a long-run demand function $x = h\big(p;\rho(x)\big) = H(p)$ for the corresponding discrete time model. For any basket x^0, let $A\left(x^0\right)$ be the set of baskets that can be reached from x^0, by means of an improvement sequence in the continuous time model. For any basket x^0, let $\hat{A}\left(x^0\right)$ be the set of baskets that can be reached from x^0, by means of an improvement sequence in the corresponding discrete time model. Then, $A\left(x^0\right) = \hat{A}\left(x^0\right)$.

Theorem 2D: Assume the "real-world model" with a given preference system $\{x, q, \dot{q}\}$. We then assume further: 1. Preferences are continuous. 2. There exists a long-run demand function $x = h\big(p;\rho(x)\big) = H(p)$ 3. Improvement sequences are acyclic. Then there exists a continuous quasi-utility function $V(x)$ with the following properties: If and only if $V\left(x^1\right) > V\left(x^0\right)$, there exists an improving sequence beginning at x^0 and ending in finite time at x^1. Thus, preferences are adaptive.

Theorem 1D: For a real-world model preference system $\{x; q; \dot{q}\}$ assume that in the corresponding discrete time model improvement sequences are acyclic and that there exists an indicator function $V(x)$ for improving sequences of the discrete time model. Assume for the real-world model that preferences are smoothly adaptive. Then improving sequences are acyclic in the real-world model.

Theorem 3: Assumption 1: The society is characterized by pragmatically compossible rights. Assumption 2: The axiom of freedom consistency of social preferences prevails. Assumption 3: The quasi-improvement axiom holds. Assumption 4: Social preferences are quasi-adaptive. Consider a project leading from allocation $x(t)$ to expected allocation $y(t)$ and for the preferences $q(t)$ which are quasi-induced by $x(t)$ we have $y(t)[>; q(t)]x(t)$. Let $z(t)$ and $s(t)$ be the equilibrium pair of baskets and preferences resulting from implementation of the project. Then we have $z(t)[>; s(t)]x(t)$.

INDEX

Note: **Boldface** page references indicate tables. *Italic* references indicate figures.

acyclic improvement sequence 12–13, 15, 31, 35, 39, 49–50, 52–55, 58–59, 62–67, 80, 87, 96, 99, 117, 174, 194, 196, 207–209
adaptive antipathy 140–141
adaptive expectations 22
Adaptive Preference Lemma 93–96, 100, 197, 208
adaptive preferences: adaptive expectations and 22; advertising and 128–131; antipathies and 140–141; assumption of 15–16, 27, 30; behavioral economics and 197; classroom model and 21–22; consilience and 110; consumer behavior and 88; decentralized decision-making and 194; decision durables and 89; definition of 24, 214; degree of, survival value of 116–117, *116*; elasticity of substitution and 117, *117*; elasticity test for 107–110; endogenous preferences and 196; evolution and 13, 16, 101, 115–117, 132–134, 136, 173, 197; fixed preferences and 68, 116; food consumption and 85; freedom and 16, 80, 173, 197; human behavior and 15, 79, 173, 197; improvement sequences and 16; indifference curves 25, *26*; induced preferences and 180; intuitive meaning of 22; Kaldor–Hicks–Scitovsky theory and 40–42, *42*; law-making and, freedom-oriented 197; learning rationality and 10; non-convexity of 118–121; normative individualism and 3–4, 173; overview 67–68; "preference conservatism" and 79; prices-quantity interaction with 32–34; in real-world model 27; Schumpeterian swerve and 198; smoothly 64–66, *67*, 214, 218; social welfare function with 43–46; sympathies and 140–141; taxes/tax laws and 169, 198; term, usage of 56; "two-persons-in-one" and 119; welfare economics and 53, 60, 68, 105–106, 195–196; *see also* cost-benefit analysis with adaptive preferences; phenomenology of adaptive preferences
adaptive sympathy 140–141
addiction 89, 118, 120, 123, 130–131, 148, 173, 197
Admati, Anat 134
advertising 128–131
Akerlof, George A. 16, 89–90, 118–119, 148
altruism 141, 143–144, 146–147, 154, 158
ambiguity aversion 102–103
Andersen, Steffen 96
anti-adaptive preferences 80, 91, 107–108, 115–117, 130, 177, 184–185, 187–188

Anti-Equilibrium thesis 154
anti-market thinking 16
anti-trust law/proceedings 76, 135, 191–192
appetite-satiation cycle 84–86, 111, 197
Aquinas, Thomas 136–137
Archimedes 13
Arnott, Richard J. 159
Arrow, Kenneth J. 89
assumptions *see specific type*
Atkinson, Anthony B. 43, 46, 161–162, 167–168
Atkinson–Mirrlees welfare function 161, 163, 168
"Austrian" capital theory 158–159
autonomy 16, 122–124, 145–146, 160, 173, 197
axioms *see specific type*

Bagwell, Kyle 128–129
Baurmann, Michael 147
Bayesian foresight model 105
Becker, Gary S. 3, 5, 27, 56, 88–89, 102, 109
Becker-Murphy theory of rational addiction 89
behavioral economics 4, 15–16, 22, 110, 145, 197
benefits of rights, net 82–83, *82*
Bentham, Jeremy 145
Bergson–Samuelson concept 178
Bernheim, B. Douglas 105, 107
Bierbrauer, Felix 168
Boardman, E. Anthony 175
Böhm-Bawerk, Eugen Ritter von 159–160
Böhm-Bawerk's Habilitations Thesis 150
Böhm, Franz 159
Bolle, Friedel 102
boom-bust cycles 134
bounded rationality 4, 89, 197
Brandl, Florian 189
Brandt, Felix 189
Buchanan, James 13–14
budget constraints 10, 23–24, *23*, 108, 123

capital-annual consumption ratio 159
cardinal utility function 64–65, 67, 214
causal mode 16, 122–124, 131, 138, 153, 173, 179, 181, 183, 197
cause/causation 9, 22, 56, 160
Charness, Gary 145
choice individualism 14
classroom model: adaptive preferences 21–22; concept of 21; continuity 215; discrete time model and 21, 215–216; feedback from actual consumption basket to preferences 21, 25–26, *26*; improvement sequences 25–28; indifference curves 21; induced preferences 21–22; Kaldor–Hicks–Scitovsky with adaptive preferences 40–42; non-satiation 215; overview 15, 67–68; preference systems 21–24; price-quantity interaction 32–34; proof of acyclic improvement sequence for 207–209; single crossing 215; social welfare function with adaptive preferences 43–46; structure 21; Theorem 1 for 29–31; Theorem 2A for 35–39; unrealistic characteristics of 49
CO_2 emissions 153
Coase, Ronald 72, 135
cold war between democracy and totalitarianism 137–138, 174, 198
collective decisions 184
collective preferences 17, 145, 178–180, 182–183, 186–187, 192, 216
collective quasi-preferences 145, 180, 187, 215
collectivism 143, 145
common good 137, 146
comparability problem 11–14, 25
compensated demand vector 125–126
competition 11, 14, 76, 89–90, 124, 129, 134–136, 140–143, 150–155, 157, 163, 165–166, 186, 191–192, 197
competitive market economy 165, 169, 193, 198
complexity 132–133
compossibility: concept of 9–10, 71–72; freedom and 15, 71–78, 136; of freedom rights 9–10, 15; government and 192; incomplete 190–192; overview 15; private property and 134–137; strict 72–73, 75; *see also* pragmatic compossibility
conformity 124, 154–155, 185, 188
consequentialism 183, 189
consilience 110
consistency 13–14, 17, 27, 78, 179–180, 182–183, 189, 192, 216
Constantinides, George M. 102
constraints: budget 10, 23–24, *23*, 108, 123; as causation 9; compossibility criterion 9–10; concept of 9–10, 11; consumption 86–87, 108, 197; consumption basket and 196;

determinism and 7; on freedom 7, 9, 160, 169; in normative theory 9; physical 9; in positive theory 9; preferences versus 6; in preference system 11
consumer behavior 88; *see also* behavioral economics
consumer durables 87, 89
consumption: anti-adaptive preferences and 107; appetite-satiation cycle and 84–86, 197; baskets 9–11, *12*, 21, 23, *23*, 26–27, *26*, 34–36, 40–41, 46, 49, 60–61, 73–74, 84, 86–87, 89, 95, 99, 126–127, 177–179, 182, 186, 196, 215–216; budget 33; capital-annual consumption ratio 159; changes in 24; constraints 86–87, 108, 197; food 84–85, 106; goods 11–12, 15, 74, 87, 89–90, 146, 150, 152; intertemporal complementarity of 87–91, 197; leisure goods 29–30; material goods 29–30, 146; negative 74; past 25, 32–33, 53, 84, 107–108; prices 74; production cost and 128; taxes and 161; vector 24, 40, 44, 73, 119, 177; wealth-annual consumption ratio 159; wealth reduction and 99
consumption level of economic activity 150, **151**
continuity assumption 29, 35, 39, 50–51, 53–55, 58, 62, 67, 87, 196, 208, 210, 214–217
continuous time model 21, 49, 60–63, 93, 95, 105, 211; *see also* real-world model
Cooter, Robert D. 77
Corollary 2B 54–55, *56*, 59, 63–64, 217
Correspondence Lemma theorem 62–64, 211–212, 217
cost-benefit analysis with adaptive preferences: bridge project *176*, 177–185; case, general 177–185; example, simple 175–177; ex-ante preferences and 174–178, 182, 184, 187–189, 193–194, 198; ex-post preferences and 174–178, 180, 182–184, 187–189, 193–194, 198; government projects 169–170, 177–185; overview 17, 174; Theorem 3 and 186–189; validity 176–177, *176*
cyclic improvement sequences 12, 26–27, **28**, 31, 38, 107, 115, 187

Darwin, Charles 102
Darwinism 13, 102, 116–117, *116*

decentralized decision-making 13, 60, 68, 95, 154, 185, 187–189, 194, 198
Debreu, Gerard 61
deception 118–121
decision box 6
decision durables 89
decision effort 94
default options 22, 91–94, 100, 105–106, 111, 162, 184–185, 188
demand: appetite-satiation cycle and 84–85; behavior 10, 54, 74; compensated 97, 125–126, 175; consumption constraints and 86; curve 97, 126, 175–177, *176*; directional price elasticity of 108–109, 194, 197; function 97, 99, 107, 117, 125–126, 210–211, 217; intertemporal complementarity of 87, 89, 93; long-run 24–25, 32–39, *37*, 41, 54–56, 58, 62–64, 107, 111, 117, *117*, *120*, 147–148, *147*, 176, 210–211, 217; for new product 186, 194; price elasticity of 16, 55–56, 107–108, 110–111, 128–129, 197; short-run 24, 33, 54, 56, *56*, 117, *117*; supply and 154–155; vector 107, 119, 126–127
De Mandeville, Bernard 145
democracy 6–7, 14, 77, 110, 137–138, 141, 143, 146, 157–158, 167, 174, 190, 198
determinism 6–7
Diamond, Peter 90, 155
Dickens, William T. 90
dictatorship 137–138
discrete time model 21–23, 49–50, 58, 64–66, 86, 94–95, 107, 210–211, 214–216
dissaving 87–89, 111, 197
division of labor 88, 128, 136, 143, 155, 161, 166, 197
"double helix" of successful selling 128–129, 131
due process 6
Duesenberry, James S. 85
durables effect 87, 89
Dynan, Karen 102

Eckhart, Meister 146
economic activity: competition and 150–155; consumption level 150, **151**; innovation level 150, **151**, 155; production level 150, **151**, 152–154
economic order 197
economics 46, 48, 72–73, 90, 104; *see also* behavioral economics; neo-classical

economics; normative economics; positive economics; welfare economics
education 90–91, 197
egoism 143–145, 154, 195
elasticity: of prices 16, 55–56, 107–110, 127–129, 197; of substitution 32–34, 116–117, *117*; test for adaptive preferences 107–110
elections 6, 71, 157, 160, 169, 194
endogenous preferences 7, 9, 11, 13, 15, 43, 54, 89, 105, 166, 178, 190, 195–196
Enke, Benjamin 105
equality 43, 76, 141, 153, 155, 158, 162, 167–169, *168*, 198
equilibrium: addiction/non-addiction 123, 130–131; Arrow–Debreau theory 22; bad 119; for budget constraints 123; conditions for 11–12; elasticity test for adaptive preferences and 108; extrapolation 80; good 119; Kornai's perspective of 154–155; language use 123–124; long-run 147–148, *147*; market 145–146; Nash 189; non-addiction 131; non-advertising 129; overfishing 152; pair of preferences and baskets 180–182, 215–216; partial 174, 186–188, 190; phishing 118–119, 118–121; preferences and 22; progressive income tax and 169; quasi-static general theory of 13; real estate 159; stationary 23; uncertainty aversion and 102; Walras–Arrow–Debreu general 73–74, 152
equivalence theorem 58–59, 217
Eucken, Walter 166
evolution and adaptive preferences 13, 16, 101, 115–117, 132–134, 136, 173, 197
ex-ante evaluation/decisions 193–194
ex-ante preferences 17, 27, 162, 174–178, 182, 184, 187–189, 193–194, 198
exogenous preferences 3–4, 13, 22, 27, 53, 64, 95–96, 99, 196
experience-based economic policy 197
experience-based legislation 79
experience goods 90
exploitation 118–121
ex-post evaluation/decisions 193
ex-post preferences 17, 162, 174–178, 180, 182–184, 187–189, 193–194, 198
extended single crossing 50–52, 215
externalities 72–73, 150, 152–155
extrapolation principle 79–80, 111, 183, 193–194
false consciousness 146
family 140–141, 143–144, 147, 154, 157–158, 165
Farrell, Joseph 91
Fehr, Dietmar 96
Fehr, Ernst 145
Feldstein, Martin 159
Festinger, Leon 90
Fisher, Irving 105
fixed preferences 3–4, 7, 12–13, 24, 27, 32, 43, 52, 68, 84, 86–89, 98, 105, 108, 116–117, 119, 130, 146, 188, 195
food/food consumption 84–85, 106
freedom: adaptive preferences and 16, 80, 173, 197; of choice 6, 76; collective preferences and 179, 181–183, 192, 216, 218; competition and 150, 152–155, 154; compossibility and 15, 71–78, 136; concept of 6; conformity and 155; consistency of collective preferences axiom 179, 181–183, 192, 216; consistency of social preferences and 179, 181–182, 218; constraints on 7, 9, 160, 169; default options and 106; between democratic constitution and totalitarian system 14; elections and 6; entrepreneurial 135; equality and 155; fixed preferences and 13; government's "veil of ignorance" and 94; historical flow of 174; inconsistency of 78; individualism and 143; to innovate 146, 154–155; of non-participation 77–78; normative economics and 6, 56, 109; normative individualism and 4, 7; Open Society concept and 143; personal 78; political 137; positive economics and 109; pragmatic compossibility and 80–81, 83, 136, 138, 160–161, 165–166, 169, 173, 182, 190, 192, 195; preferences and 1, 5; private projects and 193; progress and 155; protecting 9, 77; public goods and 138; religious 104; right "not to cooperate" and 77–78; vested interests and 192; von Weizsäcker's theory of 77, 173–174, 183
freedom mode 16–17, 88, 122–124, 131, 138, 153–154, 173, 179, 181, 183, 197–198
free society 6, 10, 13, 16, 71–72, 75, 77, 79–80, 94, 122–123, 131, 146, 181–182, 187–188
friction function/effort 94–95, 99–100

Fromm, Erich 16, 145–146, 148, 154, 173–174
Fukuyama, Francis 137

Gabaix, Xavier 105
Gemeinschaft ("Community") 147
generalized compensation 161–166, 169, 193
Gesellschaft ("Society") 147
Giblin, Colleen E. 96232
Gilbert, Michael D. 77
government: advertising ban and 129–131, 148; banking regulations and 134; branches of 137; causal mode and 16, 122–124, 153, 197; compossibility and 192; cost-benefit analysis of projects and 169–170, 177–185; debt 159–160; democratic 137–138; dictatorship 137–138; education and 197; elections and 6, 71, 157, 160, 169, 194; freedom mode and 16, 122–124, 183, 197–198; generalized compensation and 162; improving sequences and 16; intervention 17, 105–106, 118–120, 128, 134, 148, 167, 191–192, 197; law-making 76, 173, 192; Leviathan principle and 137, 166; phishing equilibrium and 118–119, 121; planning for society and 165–166; protection of rights and 77; public goods and 138; redistribution of taxes 167–168, *168*; revenue 159–160; shelf policy regulation and 106; traffic rules and 79–80; "veil of ignorance" behavior 94; *see also specific type*
Greenblatt, Stephen 195, 198
greenhouse gases, price of 153
gross benefits 82–83
Grotius, Hugo 152

habit formation 85–86, 101–102, 107, 111
Hall, Robert E. 102
Hansen, Alvin 159
Hayek, Friedrich A. 75, 89–90, 141, 152
Heckman, James 141
Hellwig, Martin 134
Hobbes, Thomas 138, 165–166, 193
Homburg, Stefan 159
homo economicus 3–4, 54
horizontal mode of human cooperation 134–135, 137, 155
household production 56, 74
Houthakker, Hendrick S. 13, 35, 102
human behavior 5, 7, 10, 13, 15, 79–80, 106, 145–146, 173, 197
human cooperation 134–135, 137, 155
hyperbolic discounting 104–105

imitation of others 125–131, *127*
implicit paternalism 192
improvement axiom 25–27, 215
improvement path 26–27, 31, 67–68, 107–108, 123, 131, 148, 211, 213, 215
improvement point 61–62, 214
improvement sequences: acyclic 12–13, 15, 31, 35, 39, 49–50, 52–55, 58–59, 62–67, 80, 87, 96, 99, 117, 174, 194, 196; adaptive preferences and 16; advertising ban and 129–131; in classroom model 25–28; concept of 12; in continuous time model 60–63; cyclic 12, 26–27, **28**, 31, 38, 107, 115, 187; definition of 26, 213; government and 16; improvement axiom and 25–27, 215; price improvements and 35–39, *37*; price reductions and 33–34, **34**; in real-world model 60–63; two-dimensional mappings of 58, 214
income distribution 164, *164*
income effect 34, 36–38, 97
income tax 161
incomplete compossibility 190–192
incrementalism 77, 83
indicator function 38, 51, 53, 59, 63–65, 68, 214, 218
indifference curves 21, 25, 29–30, *30*, 36, 55, *67*, 108, *109*, 116–117, 119, 168–169, *168*, 207, 214–215
induced preferences: Adaptive Preference Lemma and 95; adaptive preferences and 180; classroom model and 21–22; concept of 11; consumption constraints and 86; cyclic improvement sequences and 27, *28*; decision-making and 188, 194; definition of 22, 179, 213; ex-post preferences and 188; intertemporal choice and 105; mapping and 24, 60, 62, 196, 213–214; Revealed Preference Lemma of 55–56, 210–212, 217; uncertainty aversion and 103; welfare economics and 7, 46
inequality 40–41, 46, 50–51, 54, 65, 73–74, 86–87, 98–99, 141, 143, 167–169, *168*
influences on preferences, interpersonal 16, 22; advertising 128–131; causal

mode 122–124; complexity 132–133; democracy 137–138; economic activity 150–155; evolution 115–117; freedom 122–124; imitation of others 125–131, *127*; money media of exchange 140–148; near-decomposability 132–134, *133*; non-convexity 118–121; private property 136–137; public goods 138; Social Market Economy 157–170; time media of exchange 140–148
information acquisition 89–90
innovation level of economic activity 150, **151**, 155
intellectual property rights (IPRs) 152
intertemporal choice 16, 104–105, 197
intertemporal complementarity 84–93, 119
intertemporal substitutability 84–85
"invisible hand" theory 136, 138, 145, 166, 178, 188
irrationality 105–106, 110

Kahneman, Daniel 96
Kaldor–Hicks–Scitovsky (KHS) theory 40–44, *42*, 76, 110, 159, 161, 169, 178, 198
Klemperer, Paul 91
Klump, Rainer 147
Knight, Frank 102
Koehne, Sebastian 102
Kornai, Janos 154–155
Kotschy, Rainer 128
Kranton, Rachel 146
Kübler, Dorothea 96
Kuhn, Moritz 102

labor division 88, 128, 136, 143, 155, 161, 166, 197
labour theory of value economy 74
Laibson, David 105
laissez-faire advertising 129–131
laissez-faire economy 160, 198
laissez-faire financial systems 134
laissez-faire policy recommendation 129
language use 123–124
law of large numbers 161, 164, 169; *see also* generalized compensation
law-making 76, 173, 184–185, 192, 197
"laws of motion" of preferences 4–5, 115; *see also* adaptive preferences
learning rationality 10
legitimized actions 71
leisure goods 29–30
Lemma II.3 classroom model theorem 30–31, 208–209, 216
LETS (local exchange trading systems) 144
Leviathan principle 138, 166
Libertarian Paternalism 105–106
liberty 75; *see also* freedom
life expectancy 101, 153, 158, 160
Lindahl, Erik 138
long-run demand curve 176, *176*
long-run demand function 24–25, 32–39, *37*, 41, 54–56, 58, 62–64, 107, 111, 117, *117*, *120*, 147–148, *147*, 176, 210–211, 217
long-terminism 137, 140–141, 143–144, 147, 157–159, 165
loss aversion 15, 96–99
Lotka, Alfred 134
Lotka–Volterra cycle 134

Mackoviak, Bartosz 100
Maimonides 146
manipulation 118–121
Mankiw, N. Gregory 102
market asymmetry 155
Marshall, Alfred 85–86
Marx, Karl 146, 154
material goods 29–30, 146
McFadden, Daniel 100
Meier, Daniela 144
methodological individualism 109
Mills, John Stuart 100–101, 145
Mirrlees, James A. 43, 46, 158, 160–162, 167–168
money economy 88
money as exchange medium 16, 140–147
monopolistic competition/monopoly 76, 128, 135, 138, 155, 165–166, 191–192
More, Thomas 146
Morewedge, Carey K. 96
Mortensen, Dale T. 92
Mueller-Gastell, Jonas 107
Müller-Armack, Alfred 160
Murphy, Kevin M. 102
Murphy, Ryan O. 145

Nash equilibrium 189
national income 40, 45, 76, 83, 161, 167
near-decomposability 132–134, *133*, 136, 174–175, 187
negative consumption 74
negative externalities 72, 75, 150, 152–155, 192

neoclassical economics 13–14, 68, 105, 145
Niehans, Jürg 159
non-convexity of preferences 118–121, 124, 130–131, 147
non-satiation assumption 29, 35, 196, 215
non-zero decision cost 94
normative economics 3, 5–7, 9, 25, 56, 71, 109
normative individualism: adaptive preferences and 3–4, 173; Akerlof–Shiller philosophy and 119; behavioral economics and 16; behavior change and 115; challenge of 3; collective preferences and 178–180; consumer behavior and 88; in economic theory 7; freedom and, individual 4, 7; government intervention in phishing and 120; individual choice and 88; mobility of people and 89; normative economics and 109; progress and 173, 196; welfare economics and 7, 12
nudging 16, 105–107, 111, 121, 197

Open Society concept 16, 77, 79, 83, 130, 143, 145, 148, 167, 173, 178, 196
optimal choice theory 100
optimal income taxation theory 158, 160, 167, 169, 198
ordinal utility function 9, 32, 35, 38, 53, 55, 61–62, 68, 74, 146

paradox of long-terminism 158–159
parental altruism 141
Pareto optimality/improvement 73–75, 161–162
paternalism 105, 192
pecuniary externalities 72–73
"period of production" of production sector 158–159
phenomenology of adaptive preferences: Adaptive Preference Lemma and 93–96, 100; ambiguity aversion 102–103; appetite-satiation cycle 84–86; consumption constraints 86–87; default option 91–92; education/school 90–91; elasticity test 107–110; freedom 71–78; habit formation and 101–102; information acquisition 89–90; intertemporal allocation of consumption 87–88; intertemporal choice 104–105; intertemporal complementarity 84–92; intertemporal substitutability 84–85; loss aversion 96–99; nudging and 105–107; overview 110–111; pragmatic compossibility 79–83; rational inattention and 99–101; rationality vs irrationality and 110; reference-dependent preferences 96–99; religion/religious organizations 103–104; switching costs 91–92; uncertainty aversion 102–103; "use it or lose it" concept 101–102
phishing 118–121, 130–131
physical externalities 72
piecemeal engineering 77, 83, 130, 148, 158, 173, 178, 196
Pigou's answer to negative externalities 153
Pissarides, Christopher A. 90
Plato 143, 145
Popper, Karl 16, 77, 79, 83, 104, 130, 140, 143, 145, 148, 154, 158, 167, 173, 178, 196
positive economics 5–7, 9, 56, 74, 109–110
positive externalities 78, 152–153
positive feedback loop 55–56
pragmatic compossibility: benefit of rights and, net 82–83, *82*; definition of 72, 214–215; freedom and 80–81, 83, 136, 138, 160–161, 165–166, 169, 173, 182, 190, 192, 195; gross benefits and 82–83; income criterion of 77–78; incrementalism and 83; individual rights and 77; Kaldor–Hicks–Scitovsky theory and 76; liberal form of 79–80; monopoly as violation of 191–192; overview 110–111; Pareto optimality and 73–75; phenomenology of 79–83; range of 83; rights criterion of 75–76; society of free people and 196; trade-off in ideal of freedom and 80–83, *81*, *82*; traffic rules as example of 72, 79–80, 190–191; violations of 190–192; Walras–Arrow–Debreu general equilibrium and 73–75
"preference conservatism" 79
preference entrepreneur 17, 194
preferences: changes 55–56; concept of 5–7; constraints versus 6; definition of 71; for equality 43; equilibrium and 22; freedom and 1, 5; human behavior and 5, 7; "laws of motion" of 4–5, 115; non-convexity of 118–121; in normative

economics 5–7; in positive economics 5–7; private anticipation of changes in 193–195; in research program 5, 7; self-reproducing path of 180; swerve in 195, 198; *see also* influences on preferences; *specific type*
preference systems: budget constraints and 23–24, *23*; classroom model 21–24; comparability problem 11–14; concept of 11, 22; constraints in 11; definition of 22, 213; endogenous preferences and 13; preference formation and 22; real-world model 23, 64; as replacement of fixed preferences 13; two-dimensional mappings of improving sequences in 58; welfare economics and 13; working with 196
present bias 104–105
price: elasticity 16, 55–56, 107–110, 127–129, 197; ratios 32, 41–42, 44–45, 98, 107, 125; reductions and improvement sequences 33–34, **34**; vectors 23, 36–38, 40–41, 44–45, 54, 62, 73–74, 86, 119, 125–127
price-quantity interaction 32–34
privacy/privacy rules 6, 145, 190
private property 134–138, 141, 145, 150, 155, 157–158, 197–198
production level of economic activity 150, **151**, 152–154
production/production theory 56, 74, 76, 78, 88, 110, 128, 135–136, 141, 148, 158–159, 161, 186, 197
productivity 159–160, 167, 197–198
profits 102–103
progress 12–13, 25, 43, 52, 128, 146, 153–155, 158, 162–163, 165, 169, 173, 190, 194–196
progressive income tax 16, 158, 160–161, 166–170, 193, 198
pro-market thinking 16
public goods 138

quasi-adaptive preferences 180–182, 186–187, 215, 218
quasi-improvement axiom 181–183, 192, 216, 218
quasi-indifference curves 108, *109*, 116–177
quasi-induced preference path 179, 215
quasi-induced preferences 179–182, 192, 215–216, 218
quasi-preferences 53, 55, *56*
quasi-utility function 53, 53–54, 59, 63–64, 211, 217

rational addiction 89
rational inattention 89, 99–101, 104–105
rationality 10, 105, 110, 115, 189, 194
reaction amplifier 55
reaction elasticities 127–128
real income 40
real-world model: adaptive preferences 27; Adaptive Preference Lemma 95; continuous time and 21, 60–63, 93; improvement sequences in 60–63; overview 15, 67–68; preference systems 23, 64; Theorem 1B for 49–52; Theorem 1C for 58–59; Theorem 1 for 64–68; Theorem 2B for 53–59; Theorem 2 for continuous time model 60–63
rebound effect 88
reciprocity 140–142, 144
Reck, Daniel 96
redistributive income tax, optimal 167–168, *168*
reference-dependent preferences 96–99
relevant market 129, 135
religion/religious organizations 103–104
Revealed Preference Lemma of Induced Preference theorem 55, 210–212, 217
revealed preferences 13, 35–36, 38, 54–55, 126, 181, 194, 196, 210, 216–217
risk: assumption 101, 134, 155; aversion 97, 103, 163; of error 185; premium 163
Robin Hood story and wealth equality 76
"roundaboutness" 159–160
Rousseau, Jacques 146
Russian aggression in Ukraine 138

Samuelson–Houthakker axiom 13, 55
Samuelson, Paul A. 13, 35, 138, 161, 167, 178
saving 87–89, 111, 197
Schmidtchen, Dieter 75
schooling 90–91
Schubert, Christian 3
Schulz, Karl 166
Schumpeterian entrepreneurs 17, 194, 194–195
Schumpeterian swerve 195, 198
Schumpeter, Joseph A. 198
Schumpterian innovation 103, 161
Schweitzer, Albert 146
Seibold, Arthur 96, 107

self-reproducing path of baskets 180
self-reproducing path of preferences 180
semi-improving sequence 39, 214
Sen, Amartya 27, 83
serendipity 92, 100
Shiller, Robert J. 16, 118–119, 148
short-run demand function 24, 33, 54, 56, *56*, 117, *117*
short-termism 157–158, 165, 198
Simon, Herbert 100, 132–134, 136, 174–175, 187, 197
Simon Test 175
Sims, Christopher 100
single crossing assumption 29–30, 50, 196, 208–209, 215
single peakedness 67–68
Smith, Adam 88–89, 138, 145, 160, 166
smoothly adaptive preferences 64–66, *67*, 214, 218
Social Market Economy 16–17, 150, 160–161, 170, 174, 178, 198
Social Security 160
social welfare function 43–46, 145, 161–164, 167–168, *168*, 178; *see also* welfare function
Sondermann, Dieter 55
Spence, Michael 89
Steimanis, Ivo 145
Stigler, George J. 3, 5, 56, 75, 88–89, 109, 159
Stiglitz, Joseph E. 89, 159
Stolper–Samuelson paper (1941) 167
Stolper, Wolfgang F. 161, 167
strict compossibility 72–73, 75
substitution effect 34, 36–38, 97
Summers, Larry 159
Sunde, Uwe 128
Sunstein, Cass R. 105–106
Suppes improvement 161–162
Suppes, Patrick 162
supply 78, 85, 128, 154–155, 167
survival of the fittest concept 13, 101, 116, *116*
Sutter, Matthias 123
switching costs 91–92

taxes/tax laws 158, 161, 167–169, *168*, 198
Taylor, Lester D. 102
Thaler, Richard H. 105
Theorem 1 21, 29–31, 64–68, 80, 194, 196
Theorem 1A 31, 35, 38, 46, 49, 99, 216
Theorem 1B 49–52, 59, 108–109, 216–217
Theorem 1C 58–59, 217
Theorem 1D 65, 218
Theorem 2 53, 60–63, 66, 80, 117, 194, 196
Theorem 2A 35–39, 46, 216
Theorem 2B 53–57, 217
Theorem 2D 63, 217–218
Theorem 3 17, 181–182, 186–189, 194, 218
Theory of Chosen Preferences 105
Theory of Rational Addiction 89
time: causation and 22; continuous 21, 49, 60–63, 93, 95, 105, 211; decisions at particular 93–94; discrete 21–23, 49–50, 58, 64–66, 86, 94–95, 107, 210–211, 214–216; as generalized exchange medium 16, 142–148, 158; preferences 22, 62, 101, 105, 110, 211, 214
"To Be" mode 145–146, 148, 154
"To Have" mode 145–146, 148
Tönnies, Ferdinand 147
totalitarianism 14, 137, 145, 154, 160, 198
traffic rules as example of pragmatic compossibility 72, 79–80, 190–191
transaction costs 72, 87–88, 135, 140, 184, 191
transaction hungry 128, 155
transaction saturated/satiated 128, 155
Tversky, Amos 96
two-commodity model 21, 25, 29–30, 97–98, 109, 207–209
two-dimensional mappings of improving sequences 49–50, 58–59, 66, 214, 217
two-dimensional space 29, 36, 109, 214

Ukraine, Russian aggression in 138
uncertainty aversion 102–103
"use it or lose it" concept 101–102
utility function 4, 9, 29–30, 32, 35, 38–39, 52–55, 61–68, 74, 87–88, 95–96, 98–99, 146, 214
utility individualism 14
utility theory 33

value added tax 161
Vanberg, Viktor J. 13–14, 14
"veil of ignorance" behavior 7, 27, 88, 94
vertical mode of human cooperation 134–135, 137, 155
Vollan, Björn 145
Volterra, Vito 134
von Neumann–Morgenstern utility function 96–97, 99
von Weizsäcker, Carl Christian 12, 25, 91, 150, 152, 155, 166

wage system, "false" 78
"waiting period" of private household sector 158–159
Walras–Arrow–Debreu general equilibrium 73–75, 152
wants, trade-off between immediate and deferred satisfaction of 140–141
weakly declining sequence 50–51
weakly improving point 61–62, 214
weakly improving sequence 62, 66, 214
wealth-annual consumption ratio 159
wealth creation 145
wealth equality 76
wealth reduction 99
Weber, Max 147
welfare economics: adaptive preferences and 53, 60, 68, 105–106, 195–196; endogenous preferences and 7, 196; exogenous preferences and 196; fixed preferences and 13, 195; induced preferences and 7, 46; "invisible hand" theory and 178; Kaldor–Hicks–Scitosky theory and 76; long-run demand function and 24; normative individualism and 7, 12; partial equilibrium 190; person's demand behavior and 54; post-Darwinian 13; pre-Darwinian 13; preference systems and 13; real income and 40; Theorem 1 and 15; Theorem 2 and 15; Theorem 3 and 184, 188; traditional 3–5, 73, 145, 178; *see also* social welfare function
welfare function 21, 43–46, 78
Wertrationalität ("value rationality") 147
Wilson, Edward O. 110
"Winner's curse" problem 163
Witt, Ulrich 122

yes-or-no decisions 188

Zweckrationalität ("purposive rational action") 147